Special Economic Zones

"Professor Mugano's book on Special Economic Zones (SEZs) is a wonderful piece of writing that jigsaw-fit successful SEZs to the failing SEZs by creating a ladder to success for the latter. The book shows that almost every nation has caught up the SEZ fire as evidenced by 70% of developing and transition economies in SEZ establishments. In particular, the book identifies government commitment, specialisation, development of clusters, sound infrastructure, investments and good location as major success factors to any SEZs establishment and development. Of great interest is that the author highlights that the new generation of SEZs must consider new challenges associated with modern SEZs for them to perform well as one size fits all for all economies does not provide best results. The author refers to it as "copy and paste" policies, which have been a challenge for most African countries. This book is a must read for the academia, governments, development partners and the private sector."

—Professor Leward Jeke (Ph.D.), *Nelson Mandela University, Port Elizabeth, South Africa*

"This book unpacks the discourse of the nexus between special economic zones and economic development—with particular reference to the African experience. The book shows that although the majority of African economies have failed to realise meaningful gains from SEZs, few countries such as Zambia, Ethiopia, Ghana, Mauritius and, to some extent, Nigeria witnessed significant positive impact of SEZs on investment attraction, exports, job creation and economic growth. The book shows that the success of these countries was stimulated by the participation of China in the development and mobilisation of investors into these African economies' SEZs. Most importantly, using grounded empirical evidence, this book shows that most successful zones headhunted big international investors which acted as game changers in the zone since their stature became a crowd-puller for other investors who would not have come into the zones on their own. Easy to read, Special Economic Zones and Economic Development in Africa provides the reader with a buffet of useful approaches which, taken together, constitutes an excellent, forward-looking country agenda."

—Professor Laurine Chikoko (Ph.D), *Midlands State University, Gweru, Zimbabwe*

"Special Economic Zones have been used as effective vehicles for fostering industrialisation and economic transformation. Although SEZs performed exceedingly well in East Asia, in Africa, their contribution to national goals such as attracting investments, export growth and job creation is dismal. This book provides grounded evidence why SEZs failed to stimulate industrialisation and economic transformation in Africa. Most importantly, Professor Mugano, using empirical underpinnings in the African context, argues that African economies must address infrastructure gaps; improve the business environment; mainstream SEZ policy into national development agenda; build skills and capacities of officials and institutions responsible for the implementation of SEZ; secure an anchor investor into the zone which will bait other investors, promote good governance and political will."

—Professor Albert Makochekanwa (Ph.D), *University of Zimbabwe, Harare, Zimbabwe*

"Professor Mugano's book on Special Economic Zones provides grounded evidence aimed at explaining a paradox in the performance of SEZs. This book shows that although SEZs have been successful and effective in fostering economic development in China, South Korea and Taiwan, their impact in Africa has been elusive. The book identifies acute limits in infrastructure, poor governance, a shortage of skills, a failure of governance in mainstreaming SEZ policy within the national development agenda, a difficult business environment and a lack of political will as major issues for the effective performance of SEZs in Africa. Besides the need to address these issues, the book urges developing countries to support regional and global value chains as part of the strategies aimed at enhancing competitiveness and attracting investments."

—Professor Robert Newbery (Ph.D), *Newcastle Business School, Northumbria University, Newcastle upon Tyne, UK*

Gift Mugano

Special Economic Zones

Economic Development in Africa

palgrave
macmillan

Gift Mugano
Department of Public Management and Economics
Faculty of Management Sciences
Durban University of Technology
Durban, South Africa

ISBN 978-3-030-82310-8 ISBN 978-3-030-82311-5 (eBook)
https://doi.org/10.1007/978-3-030-82311-5

This Palgrave Macmillan imprint is published by the registered company Springer Nature Switzerland AG.
The registered company address is: Gewerbestrasse 11, 6330 Cham, Switzerland

Foreword

This book note that, whilst there is no universal definition for Special Economic Zones (SEZs), there is consensus in literature that SEZs come in different names which, inter alia, include free zones, industrial parks, free trade zones, export processing zones, free points, free ports, free economic zones, and science and innovation parks (Tao et al., 2016; World Bank, 2010; Zeng, 2015a, b; UNCTAD, 2019 and Farole, 2011). In these zones, governments facilitate industrial activity through fiscal, regulatory incentives and infrastructure support (UNCTAD, 2019). As noted by the World Bank (2010) and Farole (2011), SEZs have four basic characteristics: (a) they are geographically delimited areas, usually physically secured; (b) they offer non-fiscal benefits for investors which are stationed in the zones; (c) they have separate fiscal incentives and streamlined procedures; and (d) they have a single administration.

The rationale for the establishment of SEZs is based on their broader economic benefits which inter alia include investment, jobs, exports and economic growth (UNDP, 2015; Zeng, 2015a, b; Farole, 2011). In addition, many countries have embraced SEZs as effective instruments for fostering investment and industrial transformation for several reasons.

First, SEZs can serve as a vehicle for the implementation of business reforms. SEZs are also often used as feasible options for implementing nationwide reforms, especially in countries where it is difficult to implement such nationwide reforms due to weak governance systems (UNCTAD, 2019; Cheesman, 2012; Zeng, 2010, 2012a; Farole, 2011; FIAS, 2008; Johansson & Nilsson, 1997). In countries such as Mauritius, Rwanda and Eastern Asia, SEZs have been used successfully as effective mechanisms for attracting investors, especially in areas where global ranking on the ease of doing business and competitiveness is low (Farole, 2011). Moreover, through the development of backward and forward linkages as well as skills and technology transfer resulting in human upgrading and industrial spillover, SEZs have been used to stimulate domestic economy (O'Flaherty, 2008; Johansson & Nilsson, 1997; Litwack & Qian, 1997).

Second, one of the key rationales for the establishment of SEZs is that they are relatively cheap compared to building equivalent industrial infrastructure in the whole economy (UNCTAD, 2019). Interestingly, as noted by UNCTAD (2019), upfront investment costs, even in absolute terms, can be contained in the zones. For example, capital expenditures for the development of the zones, such as basic zones offering plots of land as opposed to hyper-modern "plug-and-play" zones, are most widely used by developing countries, and are favourably cost-effective. This is particularly so because additional costs, which are in many cases outsourced to private developers, are incurred progressively as the SEZs attract investors and develop individual plots (UNCTAD, 2019). The development cost and costs of common services offered in the zones such as internet are also recovered from tenants. From a government perspective, fiscal revenue, which is foregone as a result of fiscal incentives offered to investors in the SEZs, is the main cost accruing to the government which is of less concern to policymakers (UNCTAD, 2019).

Third, SEZs have been used as a tool for responding to a competitive environment. SEZs such as EPZs have been used to attract efficiency-seeking mobile investments in a competitive environment (UNCTAD, 2019). SEZs have also remained principally part of the countries' competitive investment promotion package notwithstanding the emergence of new forms of SEZs which are linked to natural resources, aimed at domestic markets or targeting innovation capabilities (e.g., science, high-tech or green zones). In recent years, particularly in 2008 and 2009 after the global financial crisis, global FDI remained very weak, which resulted in FDI in the manufacturing sector across all developing regions being structurally lower over the last five years than in the preceding period (UNCTAD, 2019). This situation forced governments to use SEZs' investment promotion packages to compete for the subdued investments.

Given the anticipated benefits of SEZs, to date, nearly 147 economies around the world, with almost three quarters of developing economies and almost all transition economies, host SEZs. Their number has grown rapidly in recent years, and at least 500 more are in the pipeline (UNCTAD, 2019). As a result, SEZs shot to 5400 in 2019, of which more than 1000 were formed in the last five years (UNCTAD, 2019). In the coming years, it is anticipated that more than 500 SEZs will be launched (UNCTAD, 2019).

Currently, there are about 237 SEZs in 38 African countries (UNCTAD, 2019). Besides this, Africa has at least 200 single-enterprise zones (or free points). Kenya, Nigeria and Egypt have the highest number of SEZs totalling 61, 38 and 18, respectively (Zeng, 2018). Ironically, Nigeria, Egypt and South Africa, which are also the largest economies in Africa, have well-developed SEZs while the smaller countries have underdeveloped and relatively smaller SEZs (UNCTAD, 2019 and UNDP, 2015).

The primary objective of the SEZs in Sub-Saharan Africa is to boost manufacturing and exports in low-skill and labour-intensive industries such as garment and textile (UNCTAD, 2019). In recent years, especially the last ten years, a number of African countries have been targeting diverse sectors and higher value addition. Morocco, for example, has refocused some of its free zones to the automotive industry and high-tech activities (UNCTAD, 2019). Likewise, Rwanda and Senegal are transforming their SEZs to focus on a wide range of value-added activities. In Nigeria, emphasis has been placed on the need to link SEZs to natural resource endowments targeting foreign investors in downstream processing industries with a view of diversifying exports which were traditionally skewed towards unprocessed resources. To this end, Nigeria has established a number of zones focusing on oil refining.

Of interest to the readers, this book reviewed specific aspects of this regulatory framework at the national and international levels. With respect to international economic law, this book demonstrates that relevant rules contained in three bodies of international economic law—international investment agreements (IIAs), the agreements of the World Trade Organization (WTO) and regional trade agreements (RTAs)—must be taken into account in promulgating the SEZs policy and laws. This book further shows that although there is little systematic research on the impact of SEZs, available evidence suggests that the effectiveness of SEZs on investment, exports and jobs has been mixed. Case studies reveals that the impact of SEZs on FDI attraction, export performance and job creation is positive. For Example, in China, as noted by the World Bank (2017), while not crowding out domestic investment, SEZs account for over 80% of cumulative FDI, and are found to have a particularly strong effect on greenfield investments. Similarly, in Costa Rica, through the use of SEZs, the country diversified its production from garments to electronic components which resulted in the contribution of SEZs in manufacturing exports, increasing from 10% in 1990 to 55% in 2003 (Gereffi et al., 2019). In the United States, job creation averaged 7% per year since 2013 in the FTZ programme compared to 2% for the wider economy. When juxtaposing the construction and running costs, empirical evidence shows that the benefits of the SEZs, especially in boosting FDI, jobs and exports, outweigh their establishment and running costs (Mongé-Gonzalez et al., 2005; Jayanthakumaran, 2003).

At the same time, anecdotal evidence shows that some zones that did not attract the expected influx of investors, or only managed to deliver limited employment and export gains, has resulted in some investors profiting from generous fiscal incentives (Farole & Akinci, 2011). In some countries, as noted by OECD (2018), decentralised policymaking for developing zones has also led to excessive competition between provinces, and a misuse of resources and land, especially in instances where zones are only partially occupied. Moreover, in some cases, SEZs have been criticised for negative social and environmental impacts which include low environmental, health and safety standards, and exploitation of workers (ILO, 2017). International experience shows that before SEZs yield the desired impacts, they require years of nurturing with consistent support from the government (OECD, 2018).

With reference to Africa, this book provides well-grounded empirical evidence on the impact of SEZs on job creation, investment attraction, export growth and diversification. In this regard, this book shows that success of SEZs in African economies is largely elusive, and very few countries such as South Africa, Mauritius, Kenya, Madagascar and Ghana have been successful. Likewise, most zones such as those in Zimbabwe, Nigeria, Namibia, Senegal, Malawi and Mali have performed dismally due to lack of effective planning and management; lack of political will; poor location and policy inconsistency; huge infrastructure deficit and skills gaps in specific areas of zone management and operations; and poor governance (Zeng, 2012b; Auty, 2011; Farole, 2011; World Bank, 2010; Stein, 2008).

Building on experience from successful countries, the book shows that critical success factors for SEZs which can be adopted by African countries include the need to provide sound and reliable infrastructure, building linkages and pullovers, mainstreaming SEZs into national development agendas and creating an enabling business environment and political will.

In addition, drawing on experience from South Korea, China and Taiwan, the book advances some critical success factors of SEZs, and presents a three-pillared analytical framework as the magic behind successful SEZs. The core argument is that countries that have adopted a well-structured approach towards SEZs that can be aligned with the broader development strategy, be executed effectively and be evaluated continuously and changed over time are more successful in achieving SEZ-led economic transformation than others. This book underscores empirical evidence from South Korea, China and Taiwan which had strategic bureaucratic competencies in making the right choices and setting clear strategic directions, strategic bureaucratic learning to dynamically and interactively engage in adjusting the strategies when needed and strategic bureaucratic strengths to implement the strategy effectively. Together with these elements, this book shows how effective political leadership with a strong development focus energised and motivated bureaucracies in successful implementation of SEZs.

Similarly, using grounded evidence on not-so-successful countries from Latin America, Africa, Eastern and Central Europe, and Asia among others, this book raises some pertinent insights into SEZ-led development strategy that emerged from the analysis. In order to stimulate wider economic impacts of the SEZs, this book argues for the institutionalisation of the zones into policy and planning. To be specific, the SEZs' legislative and policy framework must be an integral and sustainable part of the broader development strategy of a country. However, for avoidance of doubt, institutionalisation of SEZs means that SEZs must be able to respond to the dynamic realities of the economy as opposed to just entrenching SEZ practices (Aggarwal, 2019).

The book concludes by calling for the need for new-generation SEZs which will take into account specific challenges associated with modern SEZs. In particular, this book argues that although past experience on the performance of SEZs and their remarkable impact on China, South Korea and Taiwan economies provides important lessons for African economies, the context has totally changed to the extent that African policymakers cannot just imitate strategies from these successful countries. The book further argues that modern-day SEZs have to respond to new challenges which include the need to mainstream the fourth industrial revolution (4IR), sustainable development imperatives and sustainable development goals (SDGs) (UNCTAD, 2019). Accordingly, this book argues that African economies must adopt a new generation of SEZs which will take into account lessons from the successful economies on SEZs and modern demands such as those presented by the 4IR, SDGs and globalisation. This then requires absorbing lessons learned on the design, operations and impact management of zones as economies respond to modern challenges.

Harare, Zimbabwe J. P. Mangudya

References

Aggarwal, A. (2019). SEZs and Economic Transformation: Towards a Developmental Approach. *Transnational Corporations, 26*(2): 27–47. Geneva: UNCTAD. Available at: https://unctad.org/en/publication-chapters/diaeia2019d2a2_en.pdf

Auty, R. (2011). Early Reform Zones: Catalysts for Dynamic Market Economies in Africa. In T. Farole & G. Akinci (Eds.), *Special Economic Zones: Progress, Emerging Challenges, and Future Directions*. World Bank, Washington.

Cheesman, A. (2012). *Special Economic Zones and Development: Geography and Linkages in the Indian EOU Scheme* (Working Paper No. 145). Development Planning Unit, The Bartlett, University College London.

Farole, T. (2011). *Special Economic Zones in Africa: Comparing Performance and Learning from Global Experience*. World Bank.

Farole, T., & Akinci, G. (Eds). (2011). *Special Economic Zones: Progress, Emerging Challenges, and Future Directions*. World Bank Group. Available at: https://openknowledge.worldbank.org/bitstream/handle/10986/2341/638440PUB0Exto00Box0361527B0PUBLIC0.pdf

FIAS. (2008). *Special Economic Zones: Performance, Lessons Learned, and Implications for Zone Development*. World Bank.

Gereffi, G., Frederick, S., & Bamber, P. (2019). Diverse Paths of Upgrading in High-Tech Manufacturing: Costa Rica in the Electronics and Medical Devices Global Value Chains. *Transnational Corporations, 26*(1), 1–30. United Nations Conference on Trade and Development, Geneva.

Jayanthakumaran, K. (2003). Benefit-Cost Appraisals of Export Processing Zones: A Survey of the Literature. *Development Policy Review, 21*(1), 51–56.

Johansson, H., & Nilsson, L. (1997). Export Processing Zones as Catalysts. *World Development, 25*(12), 2115–2128.

International Labour Organisation (ILO). (2017, November 21–23). *Promoting Decent Work and Protecting Fundamental Principles and Rights at Work in Export Processing Zones*. Report for Discussion at the Meeting of Experts to Promote Decent Work and Protection of Fundamental Principles and Rights at

Work for Workers in Export Processing Zones. International Labour Office, Enterprises Department, Geneva, ILO.

Litwack, J. M., & Qian, Y. (1997). Balanced of Unbalanced Development: Special Economic Zones as Catalysts for Transition. *Journal of Comparative Economics, 26*, 117–141.

Mongé-Gonzalez, R., Rosales-Tijerino, J., & Arce-Alpizar, G. (2005). Cost-Benefit Analysis of the Free Trade Zone System: The Impact of Foreign Direct Investment in Costa Rica. *OAS Trade, Growth and Competitive Studies*, Organization of American States.

OECD. (2018). *OECD Investment Policy Reviews: Cambodia 2018* (OECD Investment Policy Reviews). OECD Publishing, Paris.

O'Flaherty, D. D. (2008). *Understanding Dynamic Linkages and Technology Spill-Over from Korea's Masan Free Export Zone* (Master's Thesis). Department of Globalization and International Development, University of Ottawa.

Stein, H. (2008, July 10–11). Africa, Industrial Policy and Export Processing Zones: Lessons from Asia. *Paper Prepared for Africa Task Force Meeting*. Addis Ababa, Ethiopia.

Tao, Y., Yuan, Y., & Li, M. (2016). Chinese Special Economic Zones: Lessons for Africa. *Africa Economic Brief, 7*(6), 1–11.

UNCTAD. (2019). *World Investment Report: Special Economic Zones*. Geneva, Switzerland.

UNDP. (2015). *Comparative Study on Special Economic Zones in Africa and China*. UNDP.

World Bank. (2010). *Chinese Investments in Special Economic Zones in Africa: Progress, Challenges, and Lessons Learned*. World Bank.

Zeng, D. Z. (2010). *Building Engines for Growth and Competitiveness in China: Experience with Special Economic Zones and Industrial Clusters*. World Bank.

Zeng, D. Z. (2012a). *SEZs in Africa: Putting the Cart in Front of Horse?* World Bank.

Zeng, D. Z. (2012b). *An Overview of Six Economic Zones in Nigeria: Challenges and Opportunities* (World Bank Policy Note). World Bank.

Zeng, D. Z. (2015a). *Global Experiences with Special Economic Zones – With a Focus on China and Africa*. World Bank.

Zeng, D. Z. (2015b). *Global Experiences with Special Economic Zones: Focus on China and Africa* (World Bank Policy Research Working Paper 7240). World Bank.

Zeng, D. Z. (2018). *Special Economic Zones: Lessons from the Global Experience*. World Bank.

Acknowledgements

I wish to thank God for His grace and mercy, which helped me successfully complete this book project. This journey would not have otherwise been possible.

My greatest appreciation goes to Professor Michael Brookes (Ph.D) at the University of Southern Denmark, Slagelse, Denmark, for providing his review and editorial services to this project. This was a cumbersome task which involved, on many occasions, working around the clock in order to get it done.

I would also like to thank Mackenzie Chibambo for providing language editing services, comments, criticism and suggestions which helped shape this project.

Most importantly, let me in a special way acknowledge my family members and relatives for their love, support and endurance as I spent sleepless nights researching and writing this book. My appreciation also goes to all my friends and colleagues who took their time to read, review and critic this book, which indeed further invigorated me and the project itself.

Lastly, my appreciation should go to Dr. John Mangudya, Professor Laurine Chikoko, Professor Robert Newbery, Professor Leward Jeke and Professor Albert Makochekanwa for reviewing this book and subsequently endorsing this project. I feel indebted to them and do not take these gestures for granted.

Contents

About the Author, Editors and Reviewers

Michael Brookes is the Professor of Human Resource Management at the University of Southern Denmark, Slagelse, Denmark and Research Associate at Nelson Mandela University as well as Director of the Khanyisa Project, a non-profit partnership seeking to address employability issues in the Eastern Cape of South Africa. He holds a Ph.D in Economics, M.A in Economics and B.A (Hons) in Economics. The Khanyisa Project is a long running collaboration between himself, various universities in South Africa and Siya Sebenza, a non-profit training foundation that delivers training workshops and employer support focused upon promoting employability and they currently manage a national network encompassing 45 training centres. His research interests include employment relations, international and comparative HRM and labour economics, with the central strand connecting all aspects of this research being to explore the relationship between national institutional configurations and firm level work and employment practices. He has published widely around the theme of different national institutional frameworks leading to differing economic and societal outcomes with trade arrangements being one of those. Furthermore, he has supervised 5 doctoral students in Africa to successful completions with each of them researching different aspects of how international interactions and transnational institutions constrain the development of African nations.

Mackenzie Chibambo holds a Master's of Publishing and Creative Writing from Kingston University London; a Master's of Theology and Religious Studies from United Nations University, New Orleans, USA, and a Bachelor of Education in Languages from the University of Malawi. He has published extensively in ODL and e-learning; publishing and business models, and languages and communication. He is currently completing a PhD in Philosophy of Education at the University of Johannesburg. He has also edited scores of works ranging from journal articles, books to theses at all levels of high education across the globe.

Laurine Chikoko is distinguished scholar with well over 30 articles in peer-reviewed journals. She has over 15 years of experience in administration of research grants, consultancy work and policy advisory. Currently, she is the Executive Dean of Research and Postgraduate Studies at Midlands State University in Zimbabwe. Her key responsibilities include managing the research portfolio at the institution, ensuring ethical conduct in research, intellectual property and patent applications, research grants administration and training facilitation. She has done consultancy work for international organisations such as Hand in Hand Zimbabwe and Sweden, Association of Commonwealth Universities and the Government of Canada (RoadMAPP). She has also produced technical and policy documents for these organizations. In the context of academia, government and industry collaborations, she has made prolific and invaluable contributions to national policy formulation and reforms. She has also examined PhD students regionally and internationally. Outside the academic sphere, she is a board member of the CEO Africa Round Table and participates in programmes on economic policy issues such as those run by the Wilton Park, United Kingdom, which provides a global forum for strategic discussions. She has also been recently appointed as the Advisory Board Chair for Transforming Rural Agro-enterprises and Livelihoods Organisation (TRALO).

Leward Jeke holds a PhD in Economics and has been a university lecturer for at least eight years. He participates in commissioned research projects as well as publishing research outputs in accredited journals. He is currently employed as an Associate Professor in environmental and financial economics and econometrics in the Department of Economics at the Nelson Mandela University. He has also been contracted by several private organisations on various research projects. His works have mainly focused on international businesses, labour economics, environmental economics and financial economics. Besides the Nelson Mandela University, he has worked for the University of Fort Hare, the University of KwaZulu Natal and the University of Venda. He has also presented papers at both local and international conferences. He has chaired several parallel sessions during workshops and conferences. He was a key co-organiser of the 5th Pan African Enterprise Research Council conference held on 2–3 December 2020 organised by the Nelson Mandela University in collaboration with the University of Fort Hare. He has supervised several PhDs, Master's and Honours students. He also serves as an external examiner for PhDs, Master's and Honours research projects in eight South African universities. He is currently a member of the Research Management Committee, Ethics Committee and Internationalisation Committee among others. Other than developing various programmes in economics, he is also a member of various academic and professional bodies in the field of economics.

Albert Makochekanwa is a Professor of Economics at the University of Zimbabwe and a respected economist with over 19 years of experience. He holds a Ph.D. in Economics (University of Pretoria, South Africa), a Master of Science (MSc) in Economics (University of Zimbabwe) and an Honours in Economics (University of Zimbabwe). He has worked extensively in Zimbabwe, South Africa, Botswana and Ethiopia. He has published several journal papers and book chapters on economic issues in Africa. Before joining the University of Zimbabwe, he worked for Trades Centre (Zimbabwe), Competition and Tariff Commission (Zimbabwe), University of Pretoria (South Africa), Conningarth Economists (South Africa), Commonwealth Secretariat (Ethiopia) and USAID-Trade Hub Project (Botswana). He has provided leadership to many institutions including being (i) Monetary Policy Committee member of the Reserve Bank of Zimbabwe (RBZ), (ii) Board member of the Competition and Tariff Commission (Zimbabwe), (iii) Board member of Zimbabwe Economic Policy Analysis and Research Unit and (iv) Council Member of the Zimbabwe Ezekiel Guti University (ZEGU). Over the years, he has also been a consultant for the World Bank, Washington DC; the World Bank Institute (WBI), Washington DC; the United Nations Conference on Trade and Development Virtual Institute, Geneva; the Trade and Industrial Strategies (South Africa) and Aus-AID; the Centre for Global Development, Washington DC; the United Nations Children's Fund, Harare; the African Economic Research Consortium, Kenya; the Centre for International Governance Innovation, Canada; the Namibia Chamber of Commerce and Industry; the Underhill Capital Solutions, South Africa; the University of Mauritius; the Common Market for Eastern and

Southern Africa Secretariat, Zambia; the Oxfam; the COMESA Clearing House, Harare; the Ministry of Industry and Commerce (Zimbabwe); the Zimbabwe Anti-Corruption Commission; the Zimbabwe National Water Authority; and the Trade and Development Studies Centre, Zimbabwe, among others.

Gift Mugano is a Professor of Economics at the University of Zimbabwe's Business School. He is also a visiting Professor of Economics at Durban University of Technology and Nelson Mandela University. He is a distinguished scholar and global authority on International Trade and Finance with over 16 years of extensive experience ranging from research and publications, policy advisory, trade negotiations, lecturing, administration, leadership and consultancy work. As an academic, he successfully supervised *five Doctor of Philosophy (Ph.D) degrees* and several other postgraduate students in the field of International Trade and Finance. He has also examined seven *(7) Ph.Ds.*

Professor Mugano has published extensively in international peer-reviewed journals. He has also published two books with renowned international publishers, that is, Routledge and AOSIS, respectively: (i) *Trade Liberalisation and Economic Development in Africa;* (ii) *Perspectives on Comprehensive Internationalisation of Higher Education.* He is an external examiner at Nelson Mandela University, University of Cape Town's Graduate School of Business, Durban University of Technology and University of Namibia's Business School. He is also academic supervisor with Lund University (Sweden), National University of Science and Technology and the Zimbabwe Council for Higher Education. He has done consultancy for National Opinion Research Centre (NORC) at the University of Chicago (USA), COMESA, UKAID/DFID, British Council, NIR Sweden, Adam Smith International (UK), IMC Worldwide LTD (UK), Cardno Emerging Markets (Belgium), KPMG (UK), The Palladium Group (UK), Ecorys (UK), Germany Agency for International Cooperation (GIZ), UNFPA, USAID, International Labour Organisation (ILO), United Nations Economic Commission for Africa (UNECA), World Food Programme (WFP), Parliament of Zimbabwe, Reserve Bank of Zimbabwe, Government of Zimbabwe and the private sector. Over the years, he has represented his country at various forums on trade negotiations and investment missions abroad (Heads of State and Government Summits, Council of Ministers, Senior Officials of Trade and Technical Committees) at bilateral, regional and multilateral levels in Belgium,

Switzerland, South Africa, Swaziland, Zambia, Botswana, People's Republic of China and South Korea.

Robert Newbery is an Entrepreneurship academic and Head of the Entrepreneurship, Innovation and Strategy Department at Newcastle Business School, Northumbria University, United Kingdom. He holds a PhD in Rural Entrepreneurship, an MSc in Rural Social Science and an MBA. He is a development scholar who draws on his interdisciplinary base as an engineer, entrepreneur, academic and leader to affect real change in the world. His research focuses on entrepreneurship in developing countries' contexts. This draws upon debates in the mainstream entrepreneurship literature regarding bottom-of-the-pyramid and poverty alleviation and builds upon his extensive contacts working in Sub-Saharan Africa; this also pulls together strands in complementary fields, such as rural sociology and agriculture. His combined knowledge of entrepreneurship and rural development, with his extensive experience in Sub-Sahara Africa on entrepreneurship and rural development, is relevant for this project, given the focus on livelihood and rural development.

List of Tables

List of Boxes

PART I

Introduction

CHAPTER 1

Special Economic Zones Unpacked

1.1 Introduction

Whilst there is no universal definition for special economic zones (SEZs), there is consensus in literature that SEZs are known by different names which include free zones (FZs), industrial parks, free trade zones (FTZs), export-processing zones (EPZs), free points, free ports, free economic zones, science and innovation parks, and many others (UNCTAD, 2019; Tao et al., 2016; Zeng, 2015a, 2015b; Farole, 2011; World Bank, 2010). In these zones, governments facilitate industrial activities through fiscal and regulatory incentives, and infrastructure support (UNCTAD, 2019). As noted by Farole (2011) and the World Bank (2010), SEZs have four basic characteristics: (a) they are geographically delimited areas and physically secured, (b) they offer non-fiscal benefits for investors who are stationed in the zones, (c) they have separate fiscal incentives and streamlined procedures, and (d) they have single administration.

These various conceptions on SEZs may be used interchangeably and inconsistently. This book opts to use the term special economic zones (SEZs) as the generic term for all types of zones. This chapter discusses the context of SEZs, the rationale of SEZs and provides an overview of global SEZs.

G. Mugano, *Special Economic Zones*,
https://doi.org/10.1007/978-3-030-82311-5_1

1.2 The Context of Special Economic Zones

Prior to the twentieth century, SEZs were set up as free ports where traders were allowed to operate ships, move cargoes and re-export goods without any form of interference from local authorities (UNCTAD, 2019; Zeng, 2018; Farole, 2011). However, in the 1960s, the world witnessed the emergence of modern FZs, which were either close or adjacent to airports, seaports and/or along border corridors. With the spread of export-oriented development strategies and increased reliance on global manufacturers on offshore production particularly in Asia, the world witnessed proliferation of SEZs in the 1980s (UNCTAD, 2019).

Interestingly, the rapid growth and increase of global value chains (GVCs) and international production in the late 1990s and 2000s generated another wave of SEZs. The success of the SEZs motivated a number of developing countries across the globe to implement SEZs (UNDP, 2015).

However, some SEZs such as industrial parks, which are normally found in urban agglomerations of advanced economies, have a clearly demarcated geographical area and basic infrastructure funded by government but do not offer a regulatory regime or incentives that are distinct from the rest of the economy (UNCTAD, 2019).

Likewise, the majority of science parks, which are common in developed countries—for example, the 360 plus science parks within the European Union (EU)—are in demarcated spaces and have infrastructure support (see Box 1.1).

Box 1.1 Science and High-tech Special Economic Zones

The International Association of Science Parks and Areas of Innovation defines the objective of science parks as fostering the culture of competitiveness and innovation by knowledge-based institutions in its associated businesses. Like SEZs, science parks come under different names and in different forms. The United Nations Educational, Scientific and Cultural Organization (UNESCO) observed that, in the early 2010s, there were over 400 science parks.

The activities in high-tech zones and science parks are distinct. Science parks focus on the commercialisation of the incubation or start-ups and research while high-tech zones focus on scaled-up manufacturing in technology-intensive industries.

In 2013, evidence from the EU shows that there were 366 science and technology parks in the EU member states covering an area

(*continued*)

Box 1.1 (continued)
of approximately 28 million square metres of completed building space and hosting some 40,000 organisations that employed close to 750,000 people (European Union, 2013). For the period 2000–2012, capital investment in these parks was estimated to be approximately €11.7 billion, of which €4.8 billion was public funding. A significant share of the capital expenditure was spent on physical infrastructures such as buildings and related works.

Likewise, by the end of 2017, China set up 156 high-tech development zones (HTDZs) (Zeng, 2018). Building on the existing knowledge and industrial base, China's early HTDZs were established in the late 1990s in major cities such as the provincial capitals Beijing and Shanghai (Zeng, 2018). In order to promote the growth of HTDZs, the Chinese government offered various incentives which included access to exemption of corporate income tax for the first two years, a preferential 15% corporate income tax, quality infrastructure, tariffs exemptions on imports of high-tech equipment and special treatment for employees which included exemptions from subsidies on housing, cars, income tax exemption, etc. These measures resulted in the phenomenal growth of HTDZs such that, in 2017, the net worth of the 156 HTDZs was US$1.42 trillion, that is, 11.5% of the Chinese economy (Zeng, 2018). Interestingly, the ratio of research and development (R & D) expenditures to total production value stood at 6.5% in the zones, that is, three times the average in the national economy. The zones had a share of 46% of all patents granted to businesses in the country (UNCTAD, 2019; Zeng, 2018).
Source: UNCTAD (2019)

FZs tend to lie next to seaports, airports or border corridors, hosting mostly firms that provide warehousing, logistics and services. In most developed economies, the FZ model has remained close to this original concept. Often, such zones have adjacent industrial parks for businesses that rely on these services, and on easy access to international markets. These adjacent areas, nevertheless, do not generally fall under a distinct regulatory regime. On the other hand, in developing countries, most SEZs are meant to attract investors in diversified industrial activities, and therefore tend to provide customs, fiscal and regulatory benefits to all businesses in larger, and integrated, industrial-free zones (Zeng, 2012a, b; 2015a, b, 2018).

Evidence from the United Nations Conference for Trade and Development (UNCTAD) (2019), Zeng (2012a, 2015a), Farole (2011) and the World Bank (2010) shows that SEZs are diverse in nature ranging from free trade zones (FTZs), multi-activity zones, specialised zones and innovation-driven zones to wide-area zones and cross-border zones (see Tables 1.1 and 1.2).

To date, 147 economies around the world, with three quarters of developing economies and almost all transition economies, host SEZs. Their number has grown rapidly in recent years, and at least 500 more are in the pipeline (UNCTAD, 2019). As a result, the number of SEZs shot to 5400 in 2019, and more than 1000 of these were formed in the last five years (UNCTAD, 2019) (see Table 1.3). In the coming years, more than 500 SEZs are anticipated to be launched (UNCTAD, 2019).

The number of SEZs increased by 68.35 times between 1975 and 2018, while the number of countries with SEZs rose by 118 (see Table 1.3). The distribution of SEZs shows that developing countries, in particular Asia, which has 4046 SEZs, host the majority of the SEZs (see Table 1.4).

Ironically, China, with 2543 SEZs, hosts over 50% of global SEZs while Africa hosts 237 SEZs (UNCTAD, 2019).

1.3 The Rationale of Special Economic Zones

Although the impact of SEZs on the economy has remained mixed, many countries have implemented SEZs. In East Asia in particular, SEZs have generated broader economic benefits which include investment, jobs, exports and economic growth (UNDP, 2015; Zeng, 2015a, b; Farole, 2011). Although these economic benefits have been hard to detect in a number of countries as several SEZs operate as enclaves with limited links to local suppliers and spillovers, many countries have used these possible benefits as their rationale for implementing SEZs.

In addition to this, many countries have embraced SEZs as effective instrument for fostering investments and industrial transformation for many reasons.

First, SEZs are an easy vehicle for the implementation of business reforms. They are often used as a feasible option for implementing nation-wide reforms in countries where it is generally very difficult to implement nationwide reforms and governance (UNCTAD, 2019; Cheesman, 2012; Zeng, 2010, 2012a, 2012b; FIAS, 2008; Johansson & Nilsson, 1997). Furthermore, SEZs have been used successfully as effective mechanism for attracting investments, especially in those countries where global ranking

Table 1.1 Types of Special Economic Zones

Organising principle	*Type*	*Description*
Specialising	Logistics Hub (free trade zones)	• Commercial, warehousing and logistics services • Trade facilitation services for trans-shipping and re-exports, at airports, seaports, borders • Can be located next to or within larger industrial estates
	Multi-activity SEZs	• General industrial development, non-specialised
	Specialised SEZs	• Focused on sectors (e.g. services, resources or agro-based) • Focused on industries (e.g. automotive, electronics, garments) • Focused on global value chain (GVC) activities (e.g. business process outsourcing, call centres, R&D centres)
	Innovation-driven SEZs	• Focused on industrial upgrading and new industries (e.g. high-tech zones, biotech zones, ecozones)
Design and Governance	Wide-area zones	• Large, integrated zones, often coinciding with a subnational administrative region or built as townships with residential areas and amenities • Original purpose of the largest zones was to pilot economic reforms
	Outward foreign direct investment (OFDI)/ Official development assistance (ODA)-driven zones	• Established under a partnership between capital-exporting economies and lower-income economies
	Cross-border/regional development zones	• Established to foster regional economic cooperation and to exploit economies of scale associated with regional markets

Source: UNCTAD (2019)

on the ease of doing business and competitiveness is low (Farole, 2011). Beyond this, through the development of backward and forward linkages as well as skills and technology transfer resulting in human upgrading and industrial spillover, SEZs have been used to stimulate domestic economies (O'Flaherty, 2008; Johansson & Nilsson, 1997; Litwack & Qian, 1997).

Second, one of the key rationales for establishing SEZs is that they are perceived as being relatively cheap to establish when compared with

Table 1.2 Common types of Special Economic Zones

- **Free trade zones (FTZs):** FTZs are also known as free commercial zones, which are small, fenced-in, duty-free areas that offer a wide range of services from distribution facilities for trade, storage, warehousing, and trans-shipment to re-export operations (Tao et al., 2016). Most of the FTZs are located in ports of entry around the world. The Colón Free Zone of Panama is one of the leading FTZs in the world (Tao et al., 2016).
- **Export processing zones (EPZs):** EPZs are designated industrial sites that offer special incentives and facilities for companies manufacturing commodities for export markets. As noted by FIAS (2008), EPZs exist in two forms: traditional and hybrid. In the traditional EPZ model, the whole area within the enclave is exclusively reserved for export-oriented firms licensed under an EPZ regime. In contrast, hybrid EPZs, regardless of export orientation, are normally subdivided into a general zone that is open to all industries, while a separate EPZ area is reserved for EPZ-registered enterprises which are export-oriented (Tao et al., 2016).
- **Free ports:** because they accommodate all types of activities which include tourism, retail sales and allow people to reside on site, they encompass much larger areas than FTZs and EPZs (FIAS, 2008). Free ports also provide a much broader set of benefits and incentives. Leading examples of large-scale free ports are in China.
- **Enterprise zones:** throtugh the provision of tax incentives and financial grants, enterprise zones are used by most developed economies such as the United States, the United Kingdom, France and to some extent South Africa to revitalise distressed rural or urban areas.
- **Free economic zones (FEZs)** or **free zones (FZs)**: these are designated by trade and commerce, and are administered by various countries. Companies in the FEZs/FZs are exempted from paying taxes for a defined period. Although each individual country determines its taxation rules on the content, conditions and benefits of FZs, countries are guided by World Trade Organization (WTO) Agreement on Subsidies and Countervailing Measures (SCM).
- **Industrial parks** (also known as industrial estates or trading estates): these refer to zones which are planned and designed with a view to advance industrial development. In contrast with business parks or office parks, which accommodate offices and light industry, an industrial park carries heavy industries.
- **Bonded logistics parks:** these are defined geographical areas with international port capabilities where trade arrangements similar to those of a bonded warehouse are carried out. In these parks, without payment of duty, goods may be stored or may undergo manufacturing operations.
- **Urban Enterprise Zones (UEZs):** these are areas where enterprises operate free of restrictions and federal taxes from local, state and federal governments. In order to attract investment and private sector companies into the UEZ, countries such as the United Kingdom and the United States have used policies such as offer tax and infrastructure incentives and reduced regulations. In other countries, regions with similar economic policies are often referred to as export-processing zones, tax- and duty-free zones, and SEZs.

Source: FIAS (2008)

Table 1.3 Number of countries and Special Economic Zones

Year	*1975*	*1986*	*1995*	*1997*	*2002*	*2006*	*2014*	*2018*
No. of countries	29	47	73	93	116	130	140	147
No. of SEZs	79	176	500	845	3000	3500	4300	5400

Source: UNCTAD

Table 1.4 Number of Special Economic Zones by region in 2019

Region	Total No. of SEZs	Under Development SEZs	Additional Planned SEZs
World	**5383**	**474**	**507**
Developed Economies	**374**	**5**	**-**
Europe	105	5	-
North America	262	-	-
Developing Countries	**4772**	**451**	**502**
Asia	4046	371	419
East Asia	2645	13	-
China	2543	13	-
South – East Asia	737	167	235
South Asia	456	167	184
India	373	142	61
West Asia	208	24	-
Africa	237	51	53
Latin America and the Caribbean	**486**	**28**	**24**
Transition Economies	**237**	**18**	**5**
LDCs	173	54	140
LLDCs	146	22	37
SIDS	33	8	10

Source: UNCTAD (2019)

building equivalent industrial infrastructure in the whole economy (UNCTAD, 2019). Importantly, UNCTAD (2019) observes that upfront investment costs, even in absolute terms, can be contained within the zones. For example, capital expenditures for the development of basic zones, such as those offering plots of land as opposed to hyper-modern "plug-and-play" zones, are widely used by developing countries and are favourably cost-effective. This is particularly so because additional costs, which are in many cases outsourced to private developers, are incurred progressively as the SEZs attract investors, and develop individual plots (UNCTAD, 2019). The development cost and costs of common social amnesties such as internet services offered in these zones are recovered from tenants. From a government perspective, fiscal revenue, which is foregone as a result of fiscal incentives offered to the investors in the SEZs, is the main cost that is accrued to the government which is of less concern for policymakers (UNCTAD, 2019).

Third, SEZs have been used as tools for responding to competitive business environments. SEZs, in particular EPZs, have been used to attract efficiency-seeking mobile investments in a competitive environment (UNCTAD, 2019). SEZs have thus remained principally part of countries' competitive investment promotion package. This has been the case irrespective of the emergence of new forms of SEZs which are linked to natural resources, aimed at domestic markets or targeting innovation capabilities, for instance science, high-tech or green zones. In recent years, particularly from 2008 to 2009, after the global financial crisis, global foreign direct investment (FDI) remained very weak, which has resulted in FDI in the manufacturing sector across all developing regions being structurally lower over the last five years than in the preceding period (UNCTAD, 2019). This situation forced governments to use SEZs' investment promotion packages to compete for subdued investments. However, the importance and economic significance of SEZs, and their respective policy objectives, vary significantly among countries. In advanced economies, for example, the majority of SEZs are customs-free zones. The objective of these SEZs is to provide various regulations and rules which are aimed at reducing tariffs and the administrative burden of customs procedures as well as raising competitiveness, which is key in supporting complex cross-border supply chains (UNCTAD, 2019; Zeng, 2018).

Conversely, in developing countries, the principal objective of SEZs is basically to attract FDI with a view to build, diversify and upgrade industries (Zeng, 2018). SEZs have also been largely embraced more by economies that have traditionally struggled to attract FDI. In transition economies such as China, SEZs have been used to build market economies, and for the country's participation in foreign trade (UNCTAD, 2019; Zeng, 2018). In addition, the rationale for establishing SEZs can be explained by the SEZs development ladder and an analysis of the distribution of SEZs by type and by region (see Tables 1.5 and 1.6, respectively).

Table 1.5 shows how countries adopt SEZs which suit their stage of economic development. As argued by UNCTAD (2019) and Zeng (2015a), relatively underdeveloped economies such as African countries adopt SEZs which help them build their manufacturing base, and foster industrialisation and exports (see Table 1.6). Contrary to this, most of the advanced economies use SEZs to promote industrial upgrading, whilst in transition economies, SEZs such as technology-focused zones are most important to them (UNCTAD, 2019).

It should be understood also that the motivation for and the types of SEZs adopted by countries vary from country to country and region to region since countries are at different levels of development (see Table 1.5). Transition economies often host industry-specialised zones, while advanced emerging economies such as Asia host mainly innovation-driven zones (see Table 1.6).

The majority of SEZs found in developed economies are purely FZs specialising in facilitating trade logistics. This means 91% of the share of logistics hubs are in advanced economies (see Table 1.6). This clearly

Table 1.5 The Special Economic Zones development ladder

Region	*Zones objective*	*Prevalent zone types*
High-income economies	• Provide an efficient platform for complex cross-border supply chains • Focus on avoiding distortions in the economy	• Logistics hubs free zones only (not industrial free zones) • Innovation and new industrial revolution objectives pursued through science parks without separate regulatory framework, or though incentives not linked to zones
Upper-middle income economies	• Support transition to services economy • Attract new high-tech industries • Focus on upgrading innovation capabilities	• Technology-based zones (e.g. R&D, high-tech, biotech) • Specialised zones aimed at high value-added industries or value chain segments • Services zones (e.g. financial services)
Middle-income economies	• Support industrial upgrading • Promote GVC integration and upgrading • Focus on technology dissemination and spillovers	• Specialised zones focused on GVC-intense industries (e.g. automotive, electronics) • Services zones (e.g., business process outsourcing, call centres)
Low-income economies	• Stimulate industrial development and diversification • Offset weaknesses in investment climate • Implement or pilot business reforms in a limited area • Concentrate investment in infrastructure in a limited area • Focus on direct employment and export benefits	• Multi-activity zones • Resource-based zones aimed at attracting processing industries

Source: UNCTAD (2019)

Table 1.6 Distribution of Special Economic Zone types by region (%)

Region	*Logistics hubs*	*Multi-activity*	*Specialised*	*Innovation-driven*
World	**8**	**62**	**24**	**5**
Developed economies	91	9	1	0
Africa	1	89	10	0
Asia	2	65	26	7
China	1	93	1	6
Latin America and the Caribbean	9	77	13	1
Transition economies	3	34	59	5

Source: UNCTAD (2019)

demonstrates that the main reason for the establishment of SEZs in developed economies is to aid trade facilitation with a view to foster growth in trade. Contrary to this, in Africa, being an underdeveloped area, the main thrust of the SEZs is to attract investment to spur job creation, export diversification and economic growth. This way, the majority of the SEZs (89%) in Africa are largely multi-activity-based (see Table 1.6).

Although the foregoing discussion has provided a strong case why SEZs are established, and since the implementation of SEZs is mostly driven by political and economic considerations, without sufficiently taking into consideration the technical factors related to the economic reality of the hosting countries, evidence suggests that SEZs have had mitigated results on domestic economies (Brautigam & Xiaoyang, 2011; Farole, 2011; FIAS, 2008, Aggarwal, 2004). Insufficient linkage to development, technology transfer and human capital upgrading has been noted as the limitations of catalytic effects of SEZs on domestic economies (Aggarwal, 2004). Moreover, the effectiveness of SEZs in stimulating economies has been hampered by economic and physical isolation from the rest of the national economy as well as the concentration of FDIs in low-skill sectors (Brautigam & Xiaoyang, 2011; Farole, 2011; FIAS, 2008, Aggarwal, 2004). To make matters worse, once tax holidays grace periods have expired, Rolfe et al. (2004) argue, FDI is also likely to find better locations and abandon SEZs. In Indonesia, Korea, Malaysia and the Philippines, for example, negative effects, including foregone tax revenue, and social and environmental costs, have outweighed economic benefits deriving from FDI and export generation (Cheesman, 2012).

1.4 Overview of Global Special Economic Zones

SEZs are extensively used in various regions across the globe because of their economic significance in attracting investments, fostering jobs, trade and economic growth (UNCTAD, 2019; Zeng, 2015a; Farole, 2011; World Bank, 2010). Evidence from UNCTAD (2019), Zeng (2015a) and the World Bank (2010) also demonstrates that the highest numbers of SEZs, in descending order, are found in China, the Philippines, India, the United States, the Russian Federation, Turkey, Thailand, the Dominican Republic, Kenya and Nicaragua.

Asia

Three quarters of all SEZs in the world are hosted by Asia (UNCTAD, 2019; Farole, 2011; World Bank, 2010). Interestingly, the history and nature of the SEZs in Asia differ significantly across the region. For example, in the 1960s East and South-East Asian economies pursued SEZ programmes which were part of their export-oriented development strategies. In recent decades, especially from 2000, the East and South-East Asian economies, because their economies became more advanced, came up with transformed SEZs and brand new types of zones, which included high-tech zones and integrated wide-area zones such as amenities and residential areas (Zeng, 2018).

Contrary to this, less developed economies in East and South-East Asia have accelerated the establishment of SEZs to attract investments into labour-intensive manufacturing activities which used to be hosted by now more advanced neighbouring countries in the region (UNCTAD, 2019; Zeng, 2018).

China

China established SEZs in its four coastal cities (Shenzhen, Zhuhai, Shantou and Xiamen) as part of its economic reforms in 1978. These four coastal cities are located close to Hong Kong, Macao and Taiwan, which are gateways to international markets (UNCTAD, 2019; UNDP, 2015). In the mid-1980s, in order to fully leverage on the geographical attractiveness of the east coast on foreign investments, more SEZs were established in the cities along the east coast. Building on the success of previous SEZs, the country accelerated its expansion of SEZs in the early 1990s and 2000s (UNCTAD, 2019; Farole, 2011).

In order to promote regional development whilst responding to sluggish growth rates in the coastal regions, China shifted the geographical focus of new SEZs to the west of the country and inland (Farole, 2011). The growth of zones of various types ranging from FTZs to wide-area zones as well as specialised zones was phenomenal such that in 2018 China launched the official Zone Directory, which showcases 1991 provincial zones and five categories of 552 state-level zones, accounting for over 50% of global SEZs (UNCTAD, 2019).

Latin America and the Caribbean

Latin America has a long tradition of SEZs which were established as FTZs as early as in the nineteenth century (Zeng, 2018; Farole, 2011; World Bank, 2010). In Uruguay, FTZs were established in Colonia and Nueva Palmira in 1923. However, the majority of countries in Latin America and the Caribbean established their respective SEZs in the 1990s (Farole, 2011). The principal objective and the rationale for the establishment of the FTZs was to attract investments and promote economic growth and job creation.

To date, the region hosts around 500 SEZs with over 10,000 enterprises and a total of about 1 million people employed (UNCTAD, 2019).

Most SEZs in the region, especially the lower-income countries such as Nicaragua and Honduras which focus on labour-intensive industries such as textiles and apparel, face stiff competition from competitive firms in Asia (UNCTAD, 2019). To this end, most SEZs are being restructured to attract investments in higher value-added activities. For example, The Dominican Republic has restructured its SEZs and has placed significant emphasis on attracting new investors into more advanced manufacturing and services segments (see Box 1.2).

Box 1.2 Refocusing and Turning Around Special Economic Zones: Dominican Case Study

The Dominican Republic, which is one of the world's pioneers in SEZs, registered significant success in attracting FDI and propelling sustained economic growth especially in the1990s. For example, at its peak in 2003, SEZ enterprises accounted for 7.5% of the country's gross domestic product (GDP) (UNCTAD, 2019). The country's proximity to the American consumer market, availability of cheap labour, provision of incentives in SEZs and preferential trade agreements were major driving factors for the success of the SEZs.

(*continued*)

Box 1.2 (continued)

However, the country faced several exogenous shocks at the turn of the century: a global financial crisis, a rise in oil prices, the accession of China to the WTO, and the expiration of the Multi-Fibre Agreement with China in 2005, which was the heart of the SEZs as investors in these zones, were focusing on textiles for the Chinese market. As a result of this, the number of companies in, and exports from, SEZs declined drastically making the programme stagnant until 2010. In response, local SEZ investors lobbied for an expanded market access in the United States of America through the accession of the Dominican Republic to the Central America Free Trade Agreement (2007) and the Economic Partnership Agreement between the Caribbean and the EU (2008).

The Dominican government worked in collaboration with development agencies to develop the necessary capacities on human resources to support the upgrading of the country's production profile. Foreign manufacturers in the textiles industry, on the other hand, relocated to lower-cost economies while local enterprises invested in new technology (new types of fibres). The prior requirement was that human capital was supposed to be able to integrate vertically, and was supposed to remain competitive to guarantee low-cost producers in the country and the region.

As a result of this intervention, local investors developed diversified production and inter-industry linkages. Interestingly, some enterprises shifted production from apparel to footwear, while others ventured into new businesses altogether such as opening call centres and entered into joint ventures with Indian IT companies (Schrank, 2008). Other local firms also opened factories and SEZs in neighbouring countries such as Haiti. In addition, the National Free Zones Council, that is, the SEZ regulatory authority in the Dominican Republic, increased its efforts to attract new investors from emerging industries, including services (business process outsourcing and call centres), electrical appliances, pharmaceuticals, surgical equipment and jewellery (UNDP, 2015).

From 2010, although not yet the early 2000s levels in terms of relative contribution to GDP, total exports or output, employees and SEZ exports have increased tremendously and continue to grow. Because non-SEZ economic has also been growing, the contribution of SEZ exports to total exports and GDP has been stabilised at

(*continued*)

Box 1.2 (continued)

55% and 3.2%, respectively—lower than the past levels of 85% and 8%, respectively (UNCTAD, 2019).

Other outstanding observations are that, since 2012, the number of industrial parks has surged by a third to 73 zones in 2018. Interestingly, production in SEZs has increased and become more diversified, with exports of pharmaceuticals and medical products now constituting more than 25% of the total exports, while electronics and electrical products constitute about the same share (16%) as the traditional garment and textile industry in 2018 (UNCTAD, 2019). The United States still represents the biggest market, with the majority of companies exporting there (58%), even though that share has declined since 2000 (from 86%).

In 2017, 166,000 direct jobs and 250,000 indirect ones were created by the SEZs, of which 71% were still low-skilled workers, even though the share of technical workers has steadily grown since 2012 (UNCTAD, 2019).

Source: UNCTAD (2019)

Africa

African economies were inspired by impressive success stories of SEZs in Asian economies and adopted the SEZs as an effective instrument to deal with infrastructure and institutional weaknesses prevalent in most African economies (UNCTAD, 2019).

In particular, African countries such as Egypt, Ethiopia, Mauritius, Nigeria and Zambia were inspired by the role of SEZs in China's rapid economic growth, job creation, generation of exports revenues, technology and skills spillovers, and economic linkages (Zeng, 2010; Chen & de'Medici, 2009, Sawkut et al., 2009; Aggarwal, 2004; Johansson & Nilsson, 1997; Jones & Marjit, 1995; Wong & Chu, 1984).

Mauritius established EPZs in 1970, becoming the first African country to launch SEZs followed by Ghana, Liberia and Senegal (see Table 1.7).

Currently, 38 out of 54 countries in Africa have SEZs amounting to 237 (UNCTAD, 2019). In addition, the continent has at least 200 single-enterprise zones (free points). Kenya, Nigeria and Egypt have the highest number of SEZs totalling 61, 38 and 18, respectively (Zeng, 2018). Ironically, Nigeria, Egypt and South Africa, the three largest economies in Africa, have well-developed SEZs while the majority of smaller countries'

Table 1.7 Special Economic Zones in Africa: overview and timeline

Period	*Country*	*Agro-processing*	*Textiles*	*Apparel*	*Services*	*Mining, oil & gas*	*Other*
1970s	Liberia	X		X		X	
	Mauritius		X	X			
	Senegal	X			X		X
	Egypt			X		X	
1980s	Djibouti			X	X		X
	Togo	X		X		X	
1990s	Algeria	X					X
	Cameroon	X					X
	Ghana	X	X	X			X
	Kenya			X	X		
	Madagascar			X	X		
	Malawi		X	X	X		
	Morocco	X			X		X
	Mozambique					X	
	Namibia			X	X		X
	Nigeria		X	X	X		
	Seychelles	X	X	X			
	Tunisia			X	X	X	
	Zimbabwe	X		X		X	X
	Burundi, Cape Verde, Equatorial Guinea, Rwanda, Soudan and Uganda						
2000s	Botswana, Democratic Republic of Congo, Eritrea, Ethiopia Gabon, Gambia, Mali, Mauritania, South Africa, Tanzania and Zambia						

Source: FIAS (2008) and Zeng (2015a)

SEZs are both underdeveloped and relatively smaller (UNCTAD, 2019; UNDP, 2015).

The primary objective of the majority of SEZs in Africa, principally in Sub-Saharan Africa, is to boost manufacturing and exports in low-skilled, labour-intensive industries, mainly comprising garments and textiles (UNCTAD, 2019). In recent years, especially the last ten years, a number of African countries have been targeting diverse sectors and higher value addition. Morocco, for example, has refocused some of its FZs to automotive industry and high-tech activities (UNCTAD, 2019). Likewise, Rwanda and Senegal are transforming their SEZs to focus on a wide range of value-added activities. In some countries such as Nigeria, emphasis has shifted to linking SEZs to natural resource endowments, and, as such, foreign investors are targeted downstream processing industries with a view to diversify exports which are traditionally skewed towards unprocessed resources. Nigeria has also established a number of zones focusing on oil refining (see Box 1.3).

Box 1.3 National Resource-Based Zones: Promoting Investment in Downstream Integration

SEZs have been established around natural resources such as minerals, agriculture, fisheries, forestry and other extractive industries with a primary objective of pursuing vertical integration, value addition and beneficiation, value-added exports and broader economic transformation.

In order to promote food security and move away from subsistence farming, a number of African governments such as South Africa are developing agro-zones under the banner "agro-industrial development". In this regard, agricultural corridors such as agro-industrial parks, agro-based clusters and agro-incubators are being developed. Evidence from the UNCTAD (2019) and Zeng (2015a) shows that the size of agro-zones offers incentives such as infrastructure, customs facilitation and other supportive regulatory frameworks. For example, fiscal incentives and the size of these zones range from a few hectares in urban areas to tens of thousands across regional, national or supranational areas. In South Africa the Dube AgriZone, which is part of the Dube TradePort SEZ, is a classic example of an agro-zone. This zone has world-class infrastructure support which includes the region's largest climate-controlled, glass-covered growing area, a central packing, park-houses, laboratory and distribution centre.

In addition, in order to promote downstream value, zones based on minerals and hydrocarbons are gaining momentum in Africa, especially in Nigeria. For example, Nigeria is targeting to establish more than ten SEZs which will focus on oil and gas processing (among other activities) (UNDP, 2015). The Lagos Free Trade Zone, which is the Nigerian flagship zone, is being developed as a multi-product and logistics hub for West Africa as well as the subregion with a mandate to host petroleum and petrochemical complexes, agri-commodity and other manufacturing industries (UNDP, 2015).

Source: UNCTAD (2019)

Contrary to the traditional pattern, where national governments were solely responsible for the development of SEZs, some African countries, in particular the least developed countries (LDCs), have benefited from bilateral and multilateral assistance in capacity building and finance for the construction of the zones, especially from China (UNCTAD, 2019).

Initially, China was involved in the construction of SEZs in Africa in 1999 when it undertook to develop an industrial zone in Egypt in the Suez Canal area. Further, in 2006, as part of its 11th five-year strategic plan, China mooted to develop 50 overseas SEZs of which 7 were targeted for the African continent (UNCTAD, 2019; UNDP, 2015). Consequently, in 2016, as part of the Belt and Road Initiative, China signed an agreement with Djibouti to build an FTZ which is a ten-year project valued at US$3.5 billion which will result in the establishment of the largest FTZ in Africa measuring 4800 hectares (UNCTAD, 2019; Zeng, 2018). The SEZ, which will be a joint venture between Djibouti and China, will be managed by the Government of Djibouti as the majority shareholder and three Chinese companies, that is, the Dalian Port Authority, China Merchants Group and IZP (UNCTAD, 2019; Zeng, 2018).

In another striking example, in 2015, Turkey signed an agreement with Djibouti to develop a SEZ measuring 500 hectares. The primary objective of the zone is to promote the establishment of Turkish companies in the zone whose main role is to manufacture and export goods to the East African Community and other regional markets (UNCTAD, 2019).

From a multilateral perspective, the World Bank funded the development of Gambia's only EPZ, that is, the July 22 Business Park.

Transition Economies

Soon after abandoning planned economies, transition economies adopted SEZ regimesin the 1990s. However, the establishment of SEZs grew rapidly from the second half of the 2000s, in particular, during the 2015–2019 period. All the transition economies have established SEZs with the exception of Ukraine. The Russian Federation, which is the biggest economy within this group with over 70% of the region's GDP, hosts more than 50% of the 237 SEZs in the region. Russia has a complex network of different types of SEZs, which include free ports, innovation centres, FTZs and two wide-area zones (Kaliningrad and Magadan) (UNCTAD, 2019).

Developed Economies

Over 70% of developed economies have SEZs (UNCTAD, 2019). Most of the SEZs in advanced economies are customs-free zones. With the exception of the United States, the economic significance of the SEZs, as a share of the overall economy where they are located, is relatively limited. The United States, with 262 zones, accounts for over 70% of the zones in developed economies (UNCTAD, 2019).

The SEZs in the United States, which are also called foreign-trade zones, are largely customs-free zones. The primary objective of these SEZs is to encourage companies to carry out distribution or manufacturing operations using the US facilities, rather than elsewhere (UNCTAD, 2019; Zeng, 2015a, 2018). Most of the zones which are involved in manufacturing activities include automotive, oil refining, pharmaceutical, electronics, machinery and equipment (Zeng, 2015a, 2018).

Member states in the EU are allowed to allocate parts of the customs territory of the Union as FZs. In this regard, goods imported outside the EU will be exempted from import tariffs and other charges (UNCTAD, 2019). To this end, a number of FZs in the EU are located on the border of the Union.

Contrary to the rise of SEZs in the United States, trends of SEZs in the EU in particular have been on the decline due to what is called "exhaustion of SEZs relevance" (UNCTAD, 2019). Consequently, in 2018, Poland promulgated a law aimed at creating the "Poland Investment Zone". This new legislation provides wholesale preferential treatment of all investors in the entire territory of Poland. In the meantime, this new regime is administered by the existing SEZ authorities in their respective regions (UNCTAD, 2019). Nonetheless, in order to avoid abrupt change of law which may disrupt businesses, the current SEZs will remain in force until 2026, and will then be dissolved into the broader territories (see Box 1.4).

Box 1.4 A Phase-Out Strategy of Special Economic Zones in Poland

The SEZs in Poland were originally established for a maximum period of 20 years. However, the lifetime of the SEZs was extended from 2006 to 2026, and again in 2013. As part of the new institutional framework for the regulation of investments, in 2018, Poland promulgated a new law aimed at creating what is called the "Poland Investment Zone". This new legislation allows investors to benefit from regulatory framework and incentives associated with SEZs, as long as they meet defined criteria, in the entire territory of Poland.

The main incentives given to investors, under the existing SEZs, are corporate income tax exemptions. These incentives were offered once the thresholds on capital expenditures and job creation were met. Overall, Poland's SEZs registered significant success in attracting investment and generating employment. As noted by UNCTAD (2019), by June 2018, the cumulative investment in the 14 SEZs had reached US$35 billion while the cumulative number of jobs created had reached 448,000.

(*continued*)

Box 1.4 (continued)

However, notwithstanding their success, the SEZs were associated with a number of shortcomings. By nature, SEZs discriminated against enterprises based outside the zones. This was particularly so because the criteria used to be granted SEZ status included a defined size of investment which the majority of domestic SMEs failed to meet (UNCTAD, 2019). Furthermore, income tax exemptions were offered regardless of their location in Poland's neighbouring countries such as Czechia, Hungary and Slovakia. In this regard, the SEZ system in Poland created an uneven playing field with its neighbours which undoubtedly eroded its competitiveness for FDI as well as its exports.

To help the SMEs qualify for public support, the New Investment Support Act lowered the criteria for attaining public support. Moreover, to promote regional development and balance the economy, the new system has been designed in such a way that it awards generous support to less developed regions. Contrary to the provisions of the existing system which granted SEZ permits only to start-up enterprises, the new legislation provides public support to expanded projects (UNCTAD, 2019). In dealing with the shortcomings of the current system, the new criteria, under the new law, are not only based on quantitative measures, but also on qualitative measures such as the innovative and sustainability aspects of investments. In this regard, the new law placed less emphasis on discriminatory provisions of the previous SEZ legislation in terms of investment size and geographical location. It thus placed much emphasis on externalities which included social and environmental impacts as well as knowledge and skills generation.

Source: UNCTAD (2019)

Similarly, in line with trends in Rotterdam and Antwerp, Cyprus has just transformed its FZs to free warehouses. Evidence from UNCTAD (2019) shows that loss of FZ status does not lead to the death of the zone. It has been argued that by the time the zone loses its status, it would have reached its maturity, hence would have developed necessary survival mechanisms to sustain existing businesses while also attracting new ones. For example, Shannon, which is widely regarded as the first modern SEZ, stopped offering special concessions such as tax incentives or a regulatory framework which is different from the entire economy of Ireland. Nonetheless, using its critical mass of 170 companies and 8000 employees, Shannon continued to attract enterprises ranging from aviation and automobiles to high-tech industries, financial services, information and communications technology (ICT) and aerospace among others (UNCTAD, 2019).

1.5 Conclusion

This chapter has demonstrated that SEZs constitute FZs, industrial parks, FTZs, EPZs, free points, free ports, free economic zones, and science and innovation parks, and that these can be used interchangeably (UNCTAD, 2019; Tao et al., 2016; Zeng, 2015a, b; Farole, 2011; World Bank, 2010). The chapter also revealed that governments facilitate industrial activity through fiscal, regulatory incentives and infrastructure support to the SEZs (UNCTAD, 2019). As noted by the World Bank (2010) and Farole (2011), each SEZ has four basic characteristics: (a) it is a geographically delimited area which is physically secured; (b) it offers non-fiscal benefits for investors which are stationed within the zone; (c) it has separate fiscal incentives and streamlined procedures; and (d) it has a single administration.

The chapter further demonstrated that 147 economies around the world host SEZs. It is of interest that about three quarters of developing economies and almost all transition economies host SEZs. As of 2019, there were 5400 SEZs of which more than 1000 were formed in the last five years (UNCTAD, 2019). It is also projected that more than 500 SEZs may be founded in the coming years (UNCTAD, 2019). Importantly, China has 2543 SEZs which account for well over 50% of the global SEZs, while Africa hosts 237 SEZs (UNCTAD, 2019).

Although the impact of SEZs on economies has remained unclear, many countries have implemented SEZs. In East Asia, for example, SEZs have generated broader economic benefits such as investment, jobs, exports and economic growth (UNDP, 2015; Zeng, 2015a, b; Farole, 2011). While SEZs' economic benefits have remained undetectable in many countries because several SEZs operate as enclaves with limited links to local suppliers and limited spillovers, some countries have used these potential benefits as their rationale for implementing SEZs.

On the other hand, African economies were inspired by impressive success stories of SEZs in the Asian economies, and thus adopted them as effective instruments to deal with infrastructure and institutional weaknesses common in most African economies (UNCTAD, 2019). In particular, Egypt, Ethiopia, Mauritius, Nigeria and Zambia were all inspired by the role SEZs played towards China's rapid economic development, job creation, generation of exports revenues, technology and skills spillovers, and economic linkages (Zeng, 2010; Sawkut et al., 2009; Chen & de'Medici, 2009; Aggarwal, 2004; Johansson & Nilsson, 1997; Jones & Marjit, 1995; Wong & Chu, 1984).

The question, however, as to whether SEZs brought economic transformation and development in Africa or not will be settled in the subsequent chapters.

References

Aggarwal, A. (2004). *Export Processing Zones in India: Analysis of the Export Performance* (Working Paper No. 148). Indian Council for Research on International Economic Relations (ICRIER).

Brautigam, D., & Xiaoyang, T. (2011). African Shenzhen: China's Special Economic Zones in Africa. *Modern African Studies, 49*(1), 27–54.

Cheesman, A. (2012). *Special Economic Zones and Development: Geography and Linkages in the Indian EOU Scheme* (Working Paper No. 145). Development Planning Unit, The Bartlett, University College London.

Chen, X., & de'Medici, T. (2009). *The "Instant City" Coming of Age: China's Shenzhen Special Economic Zone in Thirty Years* (Working Paper No. 2). Centre for Urban and Global Studies at Trinity College.

Farole, T. (2011). *Special Economic Zones in Africa: Comparing Performance and Learning from Global Experience.* World Bank.

FIAS. (2008). *Special Economic Zones: Performance, Lessons Learned, and Implications for Zone Development.* World Bank.

Johansson, H., & Nilsson, L. (1997). Export Processing Zones as Catalysts. *World Development, 25*(12), 2115–2128.

Jones, R. W., & Marjit, S. (1995). Labour-Market Aspects of Enclave-Led Growth. *The Canadian Journal of Economics, 28*(0), 276–293.

Litwack, J. M., & Qian, Y. (1997). Balanced of Unbalanced Development: Special Economic Zones as Catalysts for Transition. *Journal of Comparative Economics, 26*, 117–141.

O'Flaherty, D. D. (2008). *Understanding Dynamic Linkages and Technology Spill-Over from Korea's Masan Free Export Zone* (Master's Thesis). Department of Globalization and International Development, University of Ottawa.

Rolfe, R. J., Woodward, D. P., & Kagira, B. (2004). Footloose and Tax Free: Incentive Preferences in Kenyan Export Processing Zones. *South African Journal of Economics, 72*(4), 784–807.

Sawkut, R., Vinesh, S., & Sooraj, F. (2009). The Net Contribution of the Mauritian Export Processing Zone Using Cost-Benefit Analysis. *Journal of Development Economics, 21*(3), 379–392.

Schrank, A. (2008). Export Processing Zones in the Dominican Republic: Schools or Stopgaps? *World Development, 36*(8), 1381–1397.

Tao, Y., Yuan, Y., & Li, M. (2016). Chinese Special Economic Zones: Lessons for Africa. *Africa Economic Brief, 7*(6), 1–11.

UNCTAD. (2019). *World Investment Report: Special Economic Zones.* United Nations.

UNDP. (2015). *Comparative Study on Special Economic Zones in Africa and China*. UNDP.

Wong, K., & Chu, D. K. (1984). Export Processing Zones and Special Economic Zones as Generators of Economic Development: The Asian Experience. *Geografiska Annaler, 66*(1), 1–16.

World Bank. (2010). *Chinese Investments in Special Economic Zones in Africa: Progress, Challenges, and Lessons Learned*. World Bank.

Zeng, D. Z. (2010). *Building Engines for Growth and Competitiveness in China: Experience with Special Economic Zones and Industrial Clusters.* World Bank.

Zeng, D. Z. (2012a). *SEZs in Africa: Putting the Cart in Front of a Horse?* World Bank.

Zeng, D. Z. (2012b). *An Overview of Six Economic Zones in Nigeria: Challenges and Opportunities* (World Bank Policy Note). World Bank.

Zeng, D. Z. (2015a). *Global Experiences with Special Economic Zones – With a Focus on China and Africa*. World Bank.

Zeng, D. Z. (2015b). *Global Experiences with Special Economic Zones: Focus on China and Africa* (World Bank Policy Research Working Paper 7240). World Bank.

Zeng, D. Z. (2018). *Special Economic Zones: Lessons From The Global Experience.* World Bank.

CHAPTER 2

Overview of Special Economic Zones in Africa

2.1 Introduction

The majority of African countries adopted SEZs as latecomers. Precisely, most of the SEZ programmes were implemented in the late 1990s or early 2000s as a response to preferential trade agreements such as the United States–approved Africa Growth and Opportunities Act (AGOA) and the Multi-Fibre Arrangement (MFA) (Newman & Page, 2017). According to Newman and Page (2017), many African SEZs experienced rapid growth between 2000 and 2004 because of the market access created by the preferential trade agreements. Nevertheless, the majority of the SEZs grew at a slower rate while some witnessed decline when the MFA expired in 2005. Since then, Africa has had 237 developed SEZs, 51 underdeveloped SEZs and 53 planned SEZs ((UNCTAD, 2019).

2.2 An Overview of Special Economic Zones in Africa

Based on studies by Newman and Page (2017) and Farole (2011), this section discusses various SEZs in Sub-Sahara Africa as well as the policy frameworks in place.

G. Mugano, *Special Economic Zones*,
https://doi.org/10.1007/978-3-030-82311-5_2

Special Economic Zones in Existence and Incentives Offered

Table 2.1 in Annexure 2.1 shows a comprehensive list of SEZs in various countries, respective zones and the main incentives offered. Of not in the table is that SEZs offer a wide range of different incentives to investors. The majority of countries in Sub-Sahara Africa commonly offer tax relief to SEZs as an incentive. Besides this, Newman and Page (2017) noted that Angola is the only the country in Sub-Sahara Africa which offers infrastructure and supporting services in its zones (see Annexure 2.1).

Some African countries such as Eritrea, Kenya and Zimbabwe also offer very generous tax reliefs (Newman & Page, 2017). On the contrary, the SEZs, for example in Eritrea, pay neither taxes on profits, income and dividends, nor custom duties on imports (see Annexure 2.1). The most common type of tax incentive offered by a number of countries is a zero or reduced rate of income tax or corporation for a number of years which then increases gradually thereafter (UNCTAD, 2019). Similarly, Kenya offers a tax amnesty for ten years to investors in SEZs. This later rises to 25% corporate tax for the next 10 years and thereafter. Zambia, on the other hand, offers 0% corporation tax for the first 5 years; 50% of the profits are taxed for 6–8 years, and 75% of the profits are taxed for 9–10 years (Newman & Page, 2017) (see Annexure 2.1). In Zimbabwe also, a 5-year tax holiday with a 25% rate applied thereafter, rather than the normal rate of 35%, is offered in the SEZs (Newman & Page, 2017). Unlike in Zimbabwe, Côte d'Ivoire offers an exemption on income tax for the first 5 years with a 1% income tax rate on revenue from 6 years onwards, and there is a possibility for tax rebate (Newman & Page, 2017). Likewise, SEZs in Sudan and Uganda offer tax exemptions on construction of buildings. Other than these, certain countries also do not levy taxes on imports and exports.

Conversely, SEZs in Senegal and Nigeria offer non-fiscal incentives which include flexible labour laws, and 100% ownership of firms along with 100% repatriation of profits (Newman & Page, 2017). In some countries, investors are offered long-term employment permits and visas, and flexible recruitment laws. In Senegal, for instance, the country provides one single authority for all licenses and permits as well as relaxation of laws on recruitment of foreign labour (Newman & Page, 2017). In Nigeria, investors are guaranteed that there will be no strikes or lockouts in all the 17 zones (Newman & Page, 2017).

Table 2.1 shows that African countries have undertaken an aggressive approach to establish SEZs in the last three decades. As noted in Table 2.1, Togo is among the earliest countries to establish SEZs, that is, EPZs, in

1989, which covers the food and agri-business; wood, metal and plastic engineering; clothing and textile; pharmaceuticals and other light manufacturing services (Newman & Page, 2017).

Togo followed by Zimbabwe, Nigeria, Mauritius, Cameroon, Kenya and Namibia were among the early adopters as they established a number of SEZs in the early 1990s, the majority of which have remained in operation until today (Newman & Page, 2017). However, the majority of these SEZs were established during the 2000s. Later, between 2000 and 2009, 38 zones were established in 14 countries. During the same period, Nigeria established 16 zones while Tanzania established six (Newman & Page, 2017). Nigeria further established 16 more SEZs between 2010 and 2016 (Newman & Page, 2017). It would appear that Rwanda, Sierra Leone and Uganda are the real late adopters as they established their SEZs only during the last ten years. Generally, because of the continuous interest to establish SEZs, African states have 237 SEZs which are operational now (UNCTAD, 2019).

Activities in Special Economic Zones

There is considerable variation across the zones in terms of the activities involved. Most zones accept investments from multiple sectors, and in many cases these sectors are integrated along the supply chain in some ways (Newman & Page, 2017). The Chambishi MFEZ in Zambia, for example, hosts activities which include copper smelting, manufacturing of household appliances, metal bars, electric cables, motor parts and wires among others (Newman & Page, 2017).

In addition, the majority of SEZs offer supporting services for the industry. For example, the Baluluane industrial free zone (IFZ) in Mozambique hosts both light and heavy manufacturing industries while also supporting downstream industries such as aluminium conversion and processing; packaging and labelling; and other related industries. These SEZs do not only facilitate access to input and output markets for resident firms but also for agglomeration economies and productivity spillovers along the supply chain. This particular SEZ in Mozambique offers auxiliary services such as business services, call centres, conference facilities and logistic services (Newman & Page, 2017).

Some SEZs, though, such as those in Angola, Gabon, Ghana, Nigeria, South Africa, Tanzania and Zimbabwe exclusively focus on a single activity (Newman & Page, 2017). Kenya, for example, hosts six EPZs which exclusively focus on garments manufacturing. Likewise, Tanzania's SEZs also solely focus on garments manufacturing. On the other hand, Angola, Gabon, Ghana and South Africa have SEZs that exclusively focus on oil, gas and other mineral mining. Besides, many countries have zones which focus on the agricultural sector especially in the dairy sector, livestock, agri-business and agro-processing initiatives. Nevertheless, SEZs focusing on high-end services such as biotechnology and others are uncommon. For example, the only known countries whose SEZs host high-end services include Benin, Côte d'Ivoire and South Africa's East London Development Zone and ITC.

Cooperation Between China and Africa on Special Economic Zones in Africa

Most African countries have financial constraints in key infrastructural requirements for the SEZs. But the bilateral relationship between China and Africa has proved to be an effective strategy for SEZ development in Africa. This suggests that there is a strong need for Africa to strengthen relationships with and roles of development partners so that it can help boost and develop SEZ infrastructure. In relation to this, China had pledged to share its experience in investment promotion through management of SEZs alongside African countries. This commitment was made at the 1st Ministerial Conference of the FOCAC in 2000 (FOCAC, 2000). Furthermore, at the 3rd Ministerial Conference of the FOCAC, in 2006, China's former President Hu Jintao reaffirmed China's commitment by announcing the establishment of three to five SEZs in African countries (FOCAC, 2006). Following this, China established SEZs in Egypt, Zambia, Nigeria, Mauritius and Ethiopia in early 2007. Accordingly, the following section will discuss the SEZs that China developed in these countries. This will help us build a case for similar arrangements for other African economies.

Interestingly, the selection process for the SEZ developers and managers for both state-owned and private enterprises was done through two tenders. In this process, state-owned companies took the lead for SEZ development while China's Ministry of Commerce oversaw all the tendering processes (Brautigam, 2009). Several countries such as Cabo Verde and Tanzania expressed a strong interest in hosting SEZs but their proposals were not successful because they were not feasible (Brautigam & Tang, 2011). In addition to this, part of the criteria the Chinese used during the selection processes, in the host countries, were previous Chinese FDI, market size and surplus labour (Fu, 2012). Nigeria, Egypt, Mauritius and

Zambia all had previous substantive FDI from China. Market size and surplus labour were major determining factors as in the case of Ethiopia (Zeng, 2015). Empirical evidence demonstrates that SEZs are an important vehicle for the relocation of Chinese manufacturing activity to Africa particularly in mature and labour-intensive industries such as textile, shoe manufacturing and leather goods processing (Lin & Wang, 2014; Fu, 2012). Individual Chinese enterprises have created smaller SEZs which include industrial parks and FTZs in Botswana, Nigeria, Sierra Leone, South Africa and Uganda on top of those SEZs established under the FOCAC framework (Brautigam & Tang, 2013; Brautigam, 2009).

Using these three countries as case studies alongside the studies by the United Nations Development Programme (UNDP) (2015) on the role of China in Africa's SEZs, the following section discusses the overview of existing SEZs. It also examines SEZs that are under development and those that are in their early planning stages. It ends by reviewing respective national SEZ institutional and policy frameworks. In-depth reviews of two operational SEZs, one of which was set up under the FOCAC framework, are presented. In conclusion, the chapter provides a summary of critical success factors of SEZs which include policy and institutional frameworks; political commitment and support; infrastructure development; and linkages to the local economy. Likewise, in order to draw lessons for other African countries, challenges faced during SEZ development and operation are also discussed.

China's Role in Special Economic Zones in Africa: Case Studies
This section provides an overview of how Nigeria, Ethiopia and Zambia have utilised SEZs. Empirical evidence reveals that, amongst these countries, the performance of SEZs has varied enormously. For example, Nigeria established the first SEZ in 1992 and as of today it has 14 SEZs. Zambia and Ethiopia, on the other hand, only started utilising SEZs between 2006 and 2007, and each has two and four operational SEZs respectively (Zeng, 2015). The type and focus of SEZs in these countries stretch from trade zones in Nigeria, a copper mine in Zambia to an industrial park for textiles in Ethiopia and large-scale manufacturing (Zeng, 2015). The size spans a few hundred to a few thousand hectares, with investments ranging from US$15 million to US$1.4 billion (UNDP, 2015).

Ethiopia

Ethiopia's development is guided by its Growth and Transformation Plan (GTP) 2010/11–2014/15 whose main agenda was to build an economy with modern and productive agricultural and industrial sectors to eradicate poverty (UNDP, 2015). The SEZs were identified by the GTP as one of the means for industrialisation. In this regard, it includes provisions on the establishment of SEZs for the medium- and large-scale manufacturing industries such as those dealing with leather and leather products, textile and garment, cement, sugar, chemicals, metal and engineering, pharmaceuticals and agro-processing products (UNDP, 2015). The GTP was also accompanied by policy matrix (GTP/PM) regarding the targeted number of companies in the SEZs per year. This way, two operational SEZs, the Bole Lemi Industrial Zone and the Eastern Industrial Zone, are being used to achieve these goals.

In February 2014, the Ministry of Finance and Economic Development reserved land for SEZs measuring 3537 hectares in Dire Dawa, Hawassa and Kombolcha municipal authorities of Ethiopia (UNDP, 2015). Currently, seven SEZs are being developed on these plots (UNDP, 2015). To show political will, Ethiopia's Prime Minister, Hailemariam Dessalegn, participated in the groundbreaking ceremony on 16 April 2015 to celebrate the launch of Ethiopia–China Dong Guan International Light Industry SEZ (UNDP, 2015). Likewise, the Ministry of Industry (MOI) has entered into SEZ development agreements with private investors from China, Turkey and the World Bank with a view to promote the establishment of SEZs. To this end, the World Bank has assisted the Ethiopian government with both technical and financial support for the expansion of the Bole Lemi Industrial Zone and the establishment of the Kilinto Industrial Zone (UNDP, 2015). As part of the technical assistance, the World Bank is providing support aimed at enhancing linkages between companies within and without the SEZs, and strengthening the regulatory and institutional frameworks for SEZ development (World Bank, 2014). Moreover, Chinese partners are providing FDI and training, technical support on SEZ development, and management and SEZ infrastructure financing (UNDP, 2015).

From a policy perspective, the Ethiopian government, through the Investment Proclamation, propagated regulations and outlined provisions for the development and management of the SEZs (UNDP, 2015). The definition of all SEZs has been provided in the proclamation, and it clearly states that the development of SEZs shall be undertaken by the federal government or, where deemed necessary, by joint investment of the government and private sector. From an institutional perspective, Ethiopia has established the Ethiopian Industrial Zones Development Corporation

(EIZDC) whose main mandate is to administer and supervise SEZs with the exception of the privately run ones such as the Turkish Sendafa Industrial Zone and the Chinese Eastern Industrial Zone. Furthermore, to secure foreign aid and credits from banks, the EIZDC was established as a state-owned corporation (Addis Fortune, 2012). Besides, Ethiopia developed the Proclamation on Industrial Parks in April 2015 having recognised the need for a more comprehensive and effective legal, regulatory and operational framework for SEZs (UNDP, 2015). The latest proclamation includes provisions that aim to ensure coordination between SEZs and the local economy, skills development, job creation and how to ensure environmental protection (UNDP, 2015). In addition, to promote access to international markets and develop technological capacity, the zone developer is also required to create links between companies in the industrial parks and local manufacturing companies. Similarly, to ensure skills and knowledge transfer, both developers and companies are also required to replace expatriate personnel with Ethiopian workers (UNDP, 2015).

Bole Lemi Industrial Zone

This SEZ is located about 10 kilometres south-east of Addis Ababa centre and has direct access to the Addis Ababa International Airport and the Addis Ababa–Djibouti Port highway, which is Ethiopia's main import and export corridor. The Bole Lemi Industrial Zone is also Ethiopia's first government-run SEZ which covers 156 hectares of land (UNDP, 2015). To date, 12 international textile and garment-producing and shoe companies have invested in the zone, five of which are in production and have created about 3000 jobs (UNDP, 2015).

As noted by the UNCTAD (2019) as well as the UNDP (2015), the zone's second development phase, which is anticipated to double the original size to 344 hectares once completed, is in progress. To finance this expansion, Ethiopia has secured a US$250 million grant from the World Bank on top of its own resources totalling US$113 million (UNDP, 2015).

Furthermore, through the collaboration between the EIZDC and its Chinese counterparts together with Ethiopian embassies, the Prime Minister's Office and the Ethiopian Investment Commission (EIC), Ethiopia has successfully attracted several international investors. Some of these investors include Nitton Apparels Manufacturing and George Shoes Group from China, Vestis Garment and Ashiton Apparel from India, Shintis Garment from South Korea, and Jay Garment from Sri Lanka among others (UNDP, 2015).

Besides this, to facilitate coordination between SEZ companies and local suppliers of goods and services as well as the local labour market, the EIZDC has established collaborative relationships with technical vocational education and training (TVET) institutions and industry associations (UNDP, 2015). However, the new TVET institutions are still in their early stages and hence not mature enough to respond adequately to the labour needs of the SEZs. Even then, this initiative is good enough to be emulated by other African economies.

Eastern Industrial Zone

The Eastern Industrial Zone (EIZ) is located 35 kilometres south-east of Addis Ababa in the town of Dukem, Oromia Regional State. The EIZ is one of the first six Chinese SEZs to be established in Africa under the FOCAC framework (UNDP, 2015). Dukem is situated on the Addis Ababa–Djibouti Port railway line, and it was provided with its own railway station and the Addis Ababa–Djibouti highway in 2016 upon completion of the SEZ (UNDP, 2015). Importantly, the Djibouti Port handles most of Ethiopia's overseas trade, and is located just about 730 km east of the zone.

The EIZ is entirely owned and managed by the Jiangsu Qiyuan Group (JQG), a private Chinese investor (Brautigam & Tang, 2011). The JQG has 12 subsidiaries in China, 2 in the United States and 5 in Ethiopia. Interestingly, all five subsidiaries in Ethiopia have heavily invested in the EIZ (UNDP, 2015).

Initially, the JQG invested US$146 million to run the zone which was expected to cover 500 hectares. It was assumed that within five years, it would attract over 80 Chinese companies which would then create well over 20,000 jobs for local workers (Brautigam & Tang, 2011; Geda & Meskel, 2009). However, because of financial constraints, the zone was scaled down to 200 hectares with an investment of US$101 million (World Bank, 2011). The Zhongshun Cement Company, one of the JQG subsidiaries operating in Ethiopia, in 2010, was the first company to begin its operations in the EIZ. Later on, 26 other companies which included producers of construction materials, shoes, steel products; packaging materials and garments; as well as companies focusing on leather processing and automobile assembly established themselves in the zone (UNDP, 2015). The zone has since attracted over US$205 million investment from 27 Chinese companies, and created about 4500 jobs (UNDP, 2015).

One of the key success factors for EIZ is that both Ethiopia and China demonstrated solid political will right from the beginning. The Ethiopian PM and senior government representatives frequently visited the zone although the Ethiopian government is not a shareholder in the EIZ. Likewise, China has steadily supported the zone through its overseas trade, and economic cooperation zones programme. For example, Beijing gave the developers US$ 294 million in long-term loans, and US$ 44 million in grants. China also covered up to 30% of the costs of feasibility studies and site visits to plan and negotiate with the zone's host government. It also covered legal and insurance fees on land use; rebates on the interest on loans from Chinese banks as well as paying up to 50% of moving expenses (UNDP, 2015). In addition, through the provision of technical assistance on the design of the zone, the Zhangjiagang municipal authority also supported the Qiyuan Group (Brautigam & Tang, 2011).

Besides, to allow for smooth management of the zone, as noted by the World Bank (2011), a Memorandum of Understanding (MoU) signed by the Qiyuan Group and Ethiopian Government has held the JQG responsible for the EIZ planning, development, management and promotion, including securing adequate financing. Additionally, in the MoU Ethiopia commits to provide land on a concessional basis to cover 30% of infrastructure cost and create a one-stop shop that will facilitate business operations. These essentials include customs clearances, coordination and support in the delivery of services by placing MOI officials in the office of the Qiyuan Group, and administering investment incentives for qualifying export-oriented investments (World Bank, 2011). The Qiyuan Group, on the other hand, was tasked with the development of infrastructure, such as power transmission lines, water supply and waste water treatment to and from the EIZ with a 30% reimbursement of the costs by the Ethiopian Government, which is different from the common practices wherein host governments are responsible for infrastructure development for the SEZs (World Bank, 2011).

Although the zone faced a number of challenges such as infrastructure deficits and limited raw materials, since the Qiyuan Group took over the situation significantly improved with time as the zone could eventually source 80% of its raw materials from the local market (UNDP, 2015).

Regarding job creation, most of the workers were sourced in a transparent manner within the neighbouring communities through advertisements in local newspapers and job offers displayed on a screen at the main entrance of the SEZ (UNDP, 2015). Arguably, there were skills and knowledge that were transferred to the workers through technical and managerial trainings. These workers were mostly sent to China for three to four months training programmes; hence working in the zone is generally regarded as an opportunity for obtaining skills and income (UNDP, 2015). Accordingly, Huajian Group emerged as the largest employer with well over 3800 direct jobs. The company has produced 3.8 million pairs of shoes which were exported to the EU and the United States (UNDP, 2015).

Nigeria

Nigeria, with a population of 178.5 million and a GDP of US$565 billion, is the biggest economy in Africa, and is the biggest producer and exporter of oil and gas in Africa (UNDP, 2015). Nigeria is also accelerating its industrialisation process through the establishment of SEZs to absorb its growing workforce. The primary objectives of the SEZ programme in Nigeria is to attract local and foreign direct investment as it targets Nigerian and West African consumer markets, as well as US and European markets through preferential trade agreements (UNDP, 2015). This way, in order to reduce bureaucratic tendencies, the Nigerian Federal Government, states and local authorities were allowed to use their policy autonomy to initiate industrialisation processes in their respective jurisdictions.

The implementation of FZs in Nigeria is coordinated by the Nigerian Export Processing Zones Authority (NEPZA) whose legal authority is derived from the Nigerian Export Processing Zones Decree No. 63 of 1992 which regulates the establishment and operation of FZs in Nigeria (NEPZA, 1992). Thus, NEPZA is primarily responsible for promoting and facilitating local and international investments into licensed FZs. It does so by collaborating with the concerned state and local government authorities. As part of its roles, NEPZA undertakes promoting zones as well as providing and maintaining services and facilities, and approving development plans and annual budgets for infrastructure development within the zones. Regarding administrative support to the zones, NEPZA is also responsible for the establishment of immigration and other services to allow a 'one-stop shop' for investors. In addition, it facilitates trade-related dispute resolution between employers and employees in the zone as well as supervising companies operating within the SEZs. NEPZA also supervises foreign and local administrators to ensure uniform management of the SEZs, and grants permits and licenses to approved enterprises (UNDP, 2015). In other words, NEPZA works closely with respective stakeholders at state and local government levels, through respective Commerce and Industry ministries to enable the implementation of FZs in their jurisdiction. It, however, holds a macro view of the development processes associated with SEZs at national level (UNDP, 2015).

The Lekki Free Zone (LFZ) and the Lagos Free Trade Zone (LFTZ) case studies which will be discussed herein are located within the jurisdiction of the Lagos State Government and are controlled by the Lagos State

Ministry of Commerce and Industry (UNDP, 2015). To this end, the development of the LFZ, the LFTZ and all associated projects including the new planned international airport and the Lekki Deep Seaport development, which are both critical for further development of the Lekki peninsula, are supervised by the Lagos State Ministry of Commerce and Industry (MOCI) alongside NEPZA (UNDP, 2015). This means the development of the zone was undertaken by Lekki Worldwide Investment Limited, a Special Purpose Vehicle, which ensured that Lagos State Government is involved in the development of the Lekki Zone (UNDP, 2015). For the LFTZ, the Tolaram Group was given additional land measuring 600 hectares to develop the zone. Lagos State Government then provided an additional area of 600 hectares of land to the Tolaram Group to expand the zone (UNDP, 2015). Politically, Lagos State holds regular meetings with the local business community to encourage investment in the FZ while Lagos State Government organises an Annual Eko Expo Trade Fair, and produces promotional material showcased at the trade fair to lure investors (UNDP, 2015). Through a stakeholder forum, Lagos State Government coordinates several large ongoing projects in the Lekki Peninsula: (a) Lekki Free Zone Project that is being run by a Chinese–Nigerian Consortium; (b) LFTZ and Lekki Port Project run by a Singaporean–Nigerian partnership; (c) an oil refinery and petrochemical production facility run by the Nigerian Dangote Group; and (d) the Lekki-Epe International Airport project by public–private partnership arrangement between the Lagos State Government and various private investors.

Lekki Free Zone

This is established on 16,500 hectares of land and is located on the Lekki Peninsula, which is 60 kilometres east of central Lagos. It is 50 kilometres away from the Apapa Port, which is the biggest port in Lagos. LFZ is also 70 kilometres away from the Lagos international airport, and 10 kilometres away from the new Lekki International Airport (UNDP, 2015).

The Chinese consortium established the China–Africa Lekki Investment Company as a follow-up on the Chinese Government's 'going out' strategy, and its decision at the 3rd FOCAC Ministerial meeting in 2006 which established economic trade and cooperation zones in Africa. Later the Lekki Free Zone Development Company (LFZDC) entered into a joint venture with the Nigerian Lekki Worldwide Investment Ltd. and Lagos State Government. Thus, the Chinese consortium holds 60% of shareholding in the joint venture, while Lekki Worldwide Investment Ltd. and Lagos State Government together hold 40% of the shares (Brautigam & Tang, 2011).

One of the critical success factors for the LFZ is the quality of partners in the development of the zone. For example, the China Railway Construction Corporation (CRCC), which is the second biggest construction company in China, together with its subsidiary company China Civil Engineering Construction Corporation (CCECC), which employs more than 10,000 workers in over 60 projects worldwide, were the key partners that steered the LFZ. These companies (CCECC, CRCC) hold a 50% stake in the LFZ project (UNDP, 2015). Conversely, the Nanjing Jiangning Economic and Technology Development Company (NJETDC) holds a 15% stake, and brings technical knowledge to the consortium having designed and developed the Nanjing Jiangning Economic and Technology Development Zone in China. In addition, Nanjing Beyond International Investments and Development Company, another Chinese private venture capital company, also holds 15% of the shareholding (UNDP, 2015). The China–Africa Development Fund (CADF), which is a special-purpose investment vehicle established by the China Development Bank, holds the remaining 20% stake (UNDP, 2015). The dominant role of CRCC, CCECC and CADF within the Chinese consortium shows not only the importance the Chinese government attaches to the LFZ but also the quality of both technical and financial support the zone received (UNDP, 2015).

From a funding perspective, the first development was funded by LFDC to the tune of US$265 million (UNDP, 2015). In this regard, the Chinese consortium invested US$200 million while the Nigerian public and private sectors invested injected US$65 million, which was channelled through Lekki Worldwide Investment Ltd. (UNDP, 2015). The zone also follows the one axis and six parks approach, and it hosts textile production, light manufacturing, logistics, car assembly, warehousing and real estate development facilities (UNDP, 2015). With carefully integrated implementation and proper coordination, the LFZ is well positioned to foster synergies from two other large private investments on the Lekki Peninsula, which are the LFTZ with its deep sea port, and the oil refinery and hydrocarbon industrial park proposed by Dangote Industries (UNDP, 2015). More importantly, the Lekki Port is owned by the Tolaram Group, which is a Singaporean–Nigerian investor who could become one of the key players in the ecosystem (World Bank, 2011).

Given the calibre of the partners, it is 'guaranteed' that the zone will play an important role in boosting the Nigerian manufacturing sector by building the necessary bridge between Chinese, Singaporean and African investors who can trek to the LFZ (UNDP, 2015).

As expected, 21 companies including Wanhao Doors, MC Lighting FZE, H&Y FZE, Sinotruck International FZE and Loving Home Furnishing FZE, with an investment capital of US$156 million, have already been attracted to the LFZ (UNDP, 2015). Importantly, some evidence shows that 79 firms have already registered in the LFZ, and it is anticipated that the total investment capital will reach US$ 418 million (UNDP, 2015). Regarding job creation, 551 permanent jobs have already been created within the LFZ.

Lagos Free Trade Zone

The LFTZ was established in 2002 on a 215 hectare land but has since expanded to 850 hectares. It is located about 60 kilometres to the east of central Lagos (UNDP, 2015). The Tolaram Group, although based in Singapore, has been in Nigeria since the 1970s, and has major interests in Nigeria and Ghana. The group is actually one of the leading corporations in both countries, with diversified interests in fast-moving consumer goods, energy, infrastructure, distribution, logistics, digital services, paper and textiles, and is the main sponsor for LFTZ through the Lagos Free Trade Zone Company owned by Tolaram (UNDP, 2015).

The LFTZ is being developed for the entire West African region as a hub for multi-products and logistics (UNDP, 2015). In this regard, a number of petroleum and petrochemical complexes, agro-commodity and other manufacturing industries will be housed in this zone (UNDP, 2015). The proximity to the Lekki Port makes the LFTZ more strategically attractive in addition to the fiscal and non-fiscal incentives offered to the zone which are consistent with a classical EPZ.

The development, construction and operation of this multi-purpose port within the LFTZ is being undertaken by Lekki Port LFTZ Enterprise (LPLE). The Lagos State Government and Nigerian Ports Authority are shareholders in LPLE while the Tolaram Group's equity stake in the Port is held indirectly through the LFTZC (UNDP, 2015). Under the NEPZA Act, the LFTZC has a licence to operate in the FTZ and LPLE is registered in the LFTZ (UNDP, 2015). Companies in the LFTZ, as is the case in other FZs, can repatriate their profits and dividends earned in the zone, and can sell 100% of their goods within Nigerian Customs Territory, without any Federal, State and Government taxes levied, and they do not require any import or export licences (UNDP, 2015).

Companies in services, manufacturing, warehousing and packaging are also allowed to invest in the LFTZ. In order to invest in the zone, a minimum of US$1 million is required (UNDP, 2015). Palm Oil Refinery company, which produces and sells vegetable oil to local and international customers, was the first company to operate in the LFTZ in 2012. To date, the company has invested over US$30 million, and has recruited 250 workers. In complimenting Raffles Oil, Insignia, a company producing flexible packaging for fast-moving consumer goods, was the second company to operate in the zone with an investment cost of US$20 million. Interestingly, Insignia has expanded its operations in West Africa to become a leading player in the packaging industry. Available data show that up to five more companies are expected to invest in the zone imminently (UNDP, 2015).

Zambia

SEZs were identified by the Zambian government as one of the vehicles for achieving successful middle-income national development by 2030 and as a long-term strategy (RoZ, 2006a). Following this, Zambia has a total of 11 SEZs which are operational, under review, and/or under development (UNDP, 2015). The next section discusses the policy and institutional frameworks that are guiding the SEZs in Zambia.

From policy and institutional framework perspectives, following the development of a Multi-Facility Economic Zone (MFEZ) framework in collaboration with Japan in 2005, the country adopted the Zambia Development Agency Act of 2006, which constitutes the main legislation governing the development and management of SEZs today (RoZ, 2006). The Zambia Development Agency Act (ZDA) empowers the ZDA to administer, control and regulate SEZs; facilitate the development of SEZs by investors; monitor and evaluate the activities, performance and development of enterprises operating in SEZs; and prescribes and enforces measures for the activities carried out within the SEZs to market and promote the safety and efficiency of these SEZs (UNDP, 2015).

Zambia also provides incentives, such as reduced income tax, value-added tax (VAT) and custom duties for all investments in national priority sectors. This means that their SEZ programme is closely linked with its national development strategy (UNDP, 2015). Investors are also required to undertake skills development and transfer to local companies and communities, proving that their activities will promote diversification of the economy, which are in line with Zambia's national development objectives. Investors are also required to have a minimum of US$500,000 capital investment and should be ready to meet environmental standards (UNDP, 2015). Incentives are offered equally to local and international investors in order to encourage domestic companies to invest in SEZs (MCTI, 2015).

To date, the Lusaka East, the Lusaka South and the Chambishi Multi-Facility Economic Zones constitute the three fully operational zones in Zambia. Similarly, the Roma Industrial Park, which was established in 2010 on a 130 hectare land for light industries and commercial and residential establishments, is expected to be the country's next operational SEZ (UNDP, 2015).

Lusaka South Multi-Facility Economic Zone

The Lusaka South MFEZ, which was established in 2010, is Zambia's first government-run facility. It comprises a total area of 2100 hectares. This MFEZ focuses on attracting investment in industrial, commercial and residential buildings; recreational facilities; R&D, and logistics. It is located about 10 kilometres south of Lusaka centre (UNDP, 2015). The zone developer, which is the Lusaka South MFEZ Ltd., invested about US$40 million in March 2015, and 11 companies agreed to invest a total of about US$120 million (UNDP, 2015).

The MFEZ Ltd. participated in SEZ management training by Chinese SEZ managers under China's Ministry of Commerce. MFEZ also worked closely with Malaysian and Japanese experts in the designing of the zone. As noted by the UNDP (2015), the successful development of the Zambia–China Economic and Trade Cooperation Zone (ZCCZ) and the training programme significantly contributed to broad political support from the Zambian government, which eventually enabled the creation of the Lusaka South MFEZ. In particular, involvement of representatives of various ministries and parliamentarians in technical training and study tours in China helped not only to foster cross-ministerial collaboration in this area but also to demystify the SEZs among government officials (UNDP, 2015).

Already, with some temporary utility services available, the zone is still operational. It is anticipated that once completed, it will manage to create 30,000 housing units and 100,000 jobs by 2030 (UNDP, 2015).

Zambia–China Economic and Trade Cooperation Zone

The Lusaka East MFEZ and Chambishi MFEZ constitutes the ZCCZ (UNDP, 2015). Through its Zambian subsidiary ZCCZ Development Limited, the ZCCZ was developed and managed by the Chinese state-owned China Nonferrous Metal Mining Group (CNMC) (CNMC, 2015). With international operations in Asia, Africa and Latin America, CNMC is one of China's largest non-ferrous metal mining and processing companies (UNDP, 2015). CNMC had more than US$30 billion revenue in 2014 and is one of the first 500 largest companies in the world (UNDP,

2015). The zone was first established in 2007 as the Chambishi MFEZ but was later extended in 2010 to include the Lusaka East MFEZ (MCTI, 2015). The zone management offers one-stop shopping services to its potential investors, legal advice, market research, financing, visas, travel and accommodation arrangements (UNDP, 2015).

Chambishi Multi-Facility Economic Zone

The Chambishi MFEZ was launched on 4 February 2007 as the first SEZ by Zambia's former President Levy Mwanawasa and China's former President Hu Jintao (Xinhua, 2007). However, following the pledge by China's government in 2006 to establish about five SEZs in Africa between 2007 and 2009, this SEZ is also the first economic and trade cooperation zone under the FOCAC framework in Africa (Xinhua, 2007). The zone covers 1158 hectares of land, and is located adjacent to the Copper-belt Lusaka highway and a single-track narrow-gauge railway connected to the Zambia–Tanzania Railway (UNDP, 2015). The zone developer had invested US$155 million for developing this SEZ (UNDP, 2015). It focuses on mining equipment and services; copper mining and smelting; construction vehicles and materials; logistics and banking, and chemicals.

By the end of 2014, the zone had remarkably attracted 28 companies with a capital investment of well over US$1.2 billion, and created 8735 permanent jobs (CNMC, 2015; UNDP, 2015). In 2013, the total revenue of the zone companies reached around US$7.8 billion (UNDP, 2015).

Lusaka East Multi-Facility Economic Zone

The establishment of the Lusaka East MFEZ, which started in 2011, was prompted by the signing of an MOU by Zambia's former president Rupiah Bwezani Banda and China's former president Hu Jintao in February 2010 (UNDP, 2015). This SEZ lies on a 570 hectare land and is located 25 kilometres north-east of Lusaka centre. Furthermore, it is adjacent to the Lusaka International Airport and is the extension of the ZCCZ (UNDP, 2015). The main focus of the zone is to attract investment in the logistics, processing and manufacturing industries and real estate. To date, companies operating in the fields of construction and materials; agriculture and agro-processing; automobile repair services, and housing and warehousing have invested in the zone (UNDP, 2015). The zone also includes Zambian companies and has a permanent showroom where a wide range of products such as machinery, household goods, solar photovoltaic products, handicraft and art are exhibited. This showroom also acts as an international exhibition centre, which is used outside exhibition periods by 40 Chinese companies (UNDP, 2015).

The zone also has standard workshop buildings, a multifunctional air dome and residential buildings and is fully operational. By the end of 2014, a total of ten firms had contributed US$19 million as investment capital to the zone, with the potential to create 125 permanent jobs (UNDP, 2015).

2.3 Conclusion

This chapter has demonstrated that Africa has 237 SEZs in force, 51 under development and 53 in the pipeline (United Nations Conference for Trade and Development (UNCTAD), 2019).

Essentially, SEZs offer a wide range of incentives to investors. The majority of countries in Sub-Saharan Africa offer tax reliefs to SEZs as common incentives. Beyond tax incentives, Newman and Page (2017) observe that some countries such as South Africa, Ethiopia and Angola offer infrastructure and supporting services in their zones. However, it is apparent that most African countries have financial and infrastructure limitations required for SEZs. Accordingly, China, through the Conference of FOCAC which was established in 2000, announced the establishment of about five SEZs in African countries (FOCAC, 2006). By 2007, China subsequently established SEZs in Egypt, Zambia, Nigeria, Mauritius and Ethiopia.

The financial and technical support given by China to Africa became a game changer in the development and performance of SEZs. Thus, several countries, such as Cabo Verde and Tanzania, expressed interest to found SEZs though their proposals failed due to feasibility issues (Brautigam & Tang, 2011). In addition, the selection criterion used by China to identify winning bids in the host countries depended on previous Chinese FDI, market size and surplus labour, which disadvantaged Tanzania and Cabo Verde (Fu, 2012). On the other hand, Nigeria, Egypt, Mauritius and Zambia were successful because they already had previous substantive FDI from China and their market sizes and surplus labour requirement were positive (Zeng, 2015). The chapter has also established that SEZs are an important vehicle for the relocation of Chinese manufacturing activity to Africa particularly in mature and labour-intensive industries such as textile, shoe manufacturing and leather goods processing (Fu, 2012; Lin & Wang, 2014). To this end, individual Chinese enterprises have created smaller SEZs which included industrial parks and FTZs in Botswana, Nigeria, Sierra Leone, South Africa and Uganda, in addition to the SEZs established under the FOCAC framework (Brautigam, 2009; Brautigam & Tang, 2013).

Annexure 2.1: SEZs in Sub-Saharan Africa

Table 2.1 SEZs in Sub-Saharan Africa

Country	*Zones (year established)*	*Main incentives*
Angola	**Luanda-Bengo ZEE (2009)** *Activities*: 7 industrial reservations, 6 agricultural reservations, 8 mining reservations	• Infrastructure and services
Benin	**Free Processing Zone of Benin** *Activities*: Biotechnology, IT & communications	• No information available
Cameroon	**Industrial Free Zones (1990)**	• Ten-year exemption from taxes • Flat tax of 15% on corporate profits from the 11th year onwards • Tax-free repatriation of all funds earned and invested in Cameroon Exemption from foreign exchange regulations
Côte d'Ivoire	**Free Zone Village of IT and Biotechnology (2008)**	• Exemption from income tax for the first five years • 1% income tax on revenue from the 6th year onwards, with possible tax rebate 0% Custom duties and VAT • Free transfer of funds on salaries and dividends • Long-term visas and work permits for workers and families; limitation on local and foreign
Democratic Republic of Congo	**Malaku SEZ (2012)** *Activities*: Agribusiness, building materials, packaging, metallurgical transformation	• Tax and customs incentives
Djibouti	**Djibouti Free Zone (2004)** **DAM Commercial Free Zone (2013)**	• 100% foreign ownership allowed • Full exemption from direct and indirect taxes • 100% repatriation of capital and profits • No currency restrictions • Flexible recruitment laws
	Massawa Free Zone (2006) *Activities*: Construction materials, batteries, agro-processing	• No taxes on income, profits or dividends • No customs duties on imports • No currency convertibility restrictions • No minimum investment • 100% foreign ownership allowed • 100% repatriation on profits and capital

(*continued*)

Table 2.1 (continued)

Country	*Zones (year established)*	*Main incentives*
Gabon	**Nkok SEZ (2010)** *Activities*: Timber activities, chemicals, agro-industry, construction materials, metallurgy **Mandji Tax-Free Zone (2014)** *Activities*: Oil & gas	• Zero tax on dividends and land properties • Zero tax on income in the first ten years and 10% for the next five years 100% repatriation of funds allowed • 100% exemption on income tax, corporate tax and capital gains tax 100% foreign ownership permitted • No custom duty on import of plant and machinery or spare parts for industries • Electricity at subsidised rates for SEZ-based industry
The Gambia	**Export Processing Zones (2010)** **July 22 Business Park (2005)** *Activities*: Garments, diapers & tissue manufacturing	• Exemption from import or excise duty and sales tax on goods, import duty on capital equipment, corporate and turnover tax, withholding tax on dividends and municipal tax
Ghana	**Tema EPZ** *Activities*: Textiles and garments Ashanti Technology Park ICT Cyber Village Cocoa processing, light industrial manufacturing, heavy industrial manufacturing, warehousing and logistics services, social services centre, bio technology development **Sekondi EPZ** *Activities*: Mineral processing **Shama EPZ** *Activities*: Petrochemical activities	• 100% exemption from payment of direct and indirect duties and levies on all imports for production and exports from FZs • 100% exemption from payment of income tax on profits for ten years and shall not exceed 8% thereafter Total exemption from payment of withholding taxes from dividends arising out of FZ investments • Relief from double taxation for foreign investors and employees. No import licensing requirements minimal customs formalities. 100% ownership of shares by any investor is allowed • No restrictions on repatriation of dividends or net profits, payments for foreign loan servicing, payments of fees and charges for technology transfer agreements; remittance of proceeds from sale of any interest in an FZ investment • FZ investors are permitted to operate foreign currency account with banks in Ghana

(*continued*)

Table 2.1 (continued)

Country	*Zones (year established)*	*Main incentives*
Kenya	**EPZs (52 in total) (1990)** *Activities*: Textile and apparels, business process outsourcing, IT-enabled services **Athi River EPZ** *Activities*: Garments, cotton yarn, pharmaceuticals, gemstones, computers, food processing, tanning products, electrical goods, construction and lease of industrial buildings **Sameer Industrial Park EPZ (1990)** *Activities*: garments and apparel, agro-processing, call centre, relief supplies, gemstones, macadamia The following zones specialize in garments: Kipevu Zone (1996), Balaji EPZ (2001), Mazeras Kenya EPZ (2002), Pwani Industrial Park EPZ (2000), Ammar EPZ (1993), Mvita Industrial Park EPZ (2004)	• Ten-year tax holiday • Duty, stamp duty and VAT exemption • Exemption from withholding tax for ten years • 25% corporate tax for ten years following the first ten years • 100% investment deduction on initial investment applied over 20 years
Madagascar	**Free Zones (2008)**	• Corporate tax at 10% and a minimum tax collection of 5% • FZs are exempted from corporate tax for up to 15 years • Free regime companies operating in the industrial transformation and intensive production are exempted of corporate tax for five years • Free regime companies operating in the service sector are exempted of corporate tax for two years • The income tax for expatriates working for FZ companies cannot exceed 30% • No VAT on imports realized by FZs and free regime companies

(*continued*)

Table 2.1 (continued)

Country	*Zones (year established)*	*Main incentives*
Malawi	**EPZ (1995)**	• Exemption of corporate income tax • No withholding tax on dividends • No duty on capital equipment, machinery and raw materials 0% VAT
Mauritius	**Mauritius Free Port (1992)** **Sameer Industrial Park EPZ (1990)** *Activities*: Garments and apparel, agro-processing, call centre, relief supplies, gemstones, macadamia, warehousing and storage and breaking bulk, shipbuilding, repair and maintenance, storage, maintenance and repair of empty containers, export- and re-export-oriented airport and seaport-based activities, labelling, packing and repackaging, light assembly and minor processing, quality control and inspection services, sorting, grading, cleaning and mixing, freight forwarding services, seafood hub	• 0% corporate tax for trading activities • 15% tax for processing activities • Reduced port handling charges for all goods destined for re-export • 100% foreign ownership allowed access to local market—50% of re-export value • Preferential market access • Exemption from customs duties on all goods imported into the free port zones • Free repatriation of profits

(continued)

Table 2.1 (continued)

Country	*Zones (year established)*	*Main incentives*
Mozambique	**Nacala SEZ (2007)** *Activities*: Textiles and confection, leather and tannery, construction, production of construction materials, cement and iron, ceramics industry, assembly of machines and production lines **Mocuba SEZ and IFZ** *Activities*: Commercial agriculture, aquaculture and agro-processing, mineral processing, lumber industry, livestock and dairy products, manufacturing, textile industry **Beluluane IFZ (1998)** *Activities*: Companies servicing MOZAL, light manufacturing and production, heavy manufacturing, downstream aluminium conversion and processing, service industries, packaging and labelling, manufacturing primarily for export, training providers, industrial linkage companies, professional health, legal, business services, stockpiling raw materials, forwarding manufactured goods, value-adding industries **Manga-Mungassa SEZ (2012)** Crusse & Jamali Integrate Tourism Development Zone (2013) *Activities*: Tourism and entertainment	• Income tax for SEZ developers: – Income tax exemption in the first five fiscal years – 50% reduction in the rate of income tax from sixth to tenth fiscal years – 25% reduction in the rate of income tax for the remaining life of the project • Income tax for SEZ enterprises: – Income tax exemption in the first three fiscal years – 50% reduction in the rate of income tax from the 4th to the 10th tax year • Income tax for SEZ Service Enterprise: – 50% reduction in the rate of income tax for a period of five fiscal years • Industrial free zone developer and enterprises: – Income tax exemption in the first ten fiscal years – 50% reduction in the rate of income tax from the 11th to the 15th tax year – 25% reduction in the rate of income tax for the remaining life of the project • Isolated free zone enterprises: – Income tax exemption in the first ten tax years – 50% reduction in the rate of income tax from the sixth to tenth fiscal years – 25% reduction in the rate of income tax for the remaining life of the project
Namibia	**EPZs (1996)** *Activities*: Minerals beneficiation, diamond cutting and polishing operations Walvis Bay EPZ *Activities*: Textile and garment industries, Manufacturing plastic pallets and products, automotive parts for VW and Audi vehicles, fishing-related accessories, diamond cutting and polishing	• Exemption from corporate income tax, customs duties and VAT on machinery, equipment and raw materials (10% withholding tax on dividends and personal income tax are still payable • EPZ enterprises are allowed to hold foreign currency accounts at commercial banks and repatriate capital and profits • The incentives offered are applicable for an indefinite period or for the lifetime of the approved project

(continued)

Table 2.1 (continued)

Country	*Zones (year established)*	*Main incentives*
Nigeria	**Calabar FTZ (1992)** *Activities*: Manufacturing, oil & gas, logistic services **Kano FTZ (1998)** *Activities*: Manufacturing, logistics services, warehousing **Tinapa Free Zone (2004)** *Activities*: Manufacturing, trade, tourism **Resort Snake Island IFZ (2005)** *Activities*: Steel fabrication, oil & gas, sea port Maigatari Border Free Zone (2000) *Activities*: Manufacturing and warehousing Ladol Logistics Free Zone (2006) *Activities*: Oil & gas fabrication, oil & gas vessels, logistics Aairline Services EPZ (2003) *Activities*: Food processing and packaging ALSCON EPZ (2004) *Activities*: Manufacturing Sebore Farms EPZ (2001) *Activities*: Manufacturing, oil & gas, Petrochemical Ogun Guagdong FTZ (2008) *Activities*: Manufacturing Lekki Free Zone (2008) *Activities*: Manufacturing, logistics Abuja Tech Village Free Zone (2007) *Activities*: Science and technology Ibom Science & Tech Free Zone (2006) *Activities*: Science & technology **Lagos FTZ (2002)** *Activities*: Manufacturing, oil & gas **Petrochemical Olokola FTZ (2004)** *Activities*: Oil & gas, manufacturing **Living Spring Free Zone (2006)** *Activities*: Manufacturing, warehousing, trading **Brass LNG Free Zone (2007)** *Activities*: Liquefied natural gas	• Complete tax holiday for all Federal, State and Local Government taxes, rates, custom duties and levies • One-stop approval for all permits, operating licences and incorporation papers • Duty-free, tax-free import of raw materials for goods destined for re-export • Duty-free introduction of capital goods, consumer goods, components, machinery, equipment and furniture • Permission to sell 100% of manufactured, assembled or imported goods into the domestic Nigerian market • When selling to the domestic market, the amount of import duty on goods manufactured in the FZs is calculated on the basis of the value of the raw material or components used in assembly, not the finished product • 100% foreign ownership of investments • 100% repatriation of capital, profits and dividends • Waiver of all import and export licenses • Waiver on all expatriate quotas for companies operating in the zones • Prohibition of strikes and lockouts • Rent-free land during the first six months of construction • All new industrial undertakings including foreign companies and individuals operating in an EPZ are allowed full tax holidays for three consecutive years

(*continued*)

Table 2.1 (continued)

Country	*Zones (year established)*	*Main incentives*
Rwanda	**Kigali SEZ (2011)** *Activities*: Heavy and light manufacturing industries, large-scale users, industrial plants, commercial wholesalers, chemical, pharmacy and plastics, warehousing, tourism and service industry, ICT, logistics	• Imported goods are free from customs duties • All new industrial undertakings including foreign companies, as well as individuals operating in an EPZ, are allowed full tax holidays for three consecutive years
Senegal	**Dakar Integrated SEZ (2007)** *Activities*: Industrial, offices, tourist resorts, commerce and services	• 100% foreign ownership • One single authority for all licences, permits and authorisation • Availability of serviced land and pre-built units for industrial, commercial, logistics and services use • A relaxed foreign labour regime, freedom to obtain foreign currency • Protection of property rights • Exemption from customs duties and taxes on all imported goods • Exemption from payment of any direct income taxes • A flat 2% rate tax applicable on sales on local market • Full repatriation of profits and capital
Sierra Leone	**First Step (2012)** *Activities*: Agricultural goods, apparel manufacturing, mineral resources, marine resources, export processing	• Duty-free status on all imported goods • Duty-free status on all goods exported • Corporate tax holiday for the first three years

(*continued*)

Table 2.1 (continued)

Country	*Zones (year established)*	*Main incentives*
South Africa	**Coega IDZ (1999)** *Activities*: Agro-processing, automotive, business process outsourcing, chemicals, energy, logistics, manufacturing, metals, textiles **East London IDZ (2003)** *Activities*: Automotive, agro-processing, pharmaceuticals, ICT and BPO, renewable energy, logistics, aquaculture, general manufacturing **Saldanha Bay IDZ (2013)** *Activities*: Oil & gas, marine engineering **Richards Bay IDZ** *Activities*: Agro-processing, metals beneficiation **Dube Trade Port IDZ (2014)** *Activities*: Aerospace- and aviation-linked manufacturing, agriculture and agro-processing, electronics manufacturing and assembly, medical and pharmaceutical production and distribution, clothing and textiles	• For IFZs: Duty-free import of production-related materials, zero VAT on materials sourced from South Africa • Right to sell in South Africa upon payment of normal import duties on finished goods • For SEZs: Reduction in corporate tax from 28% to 15% • Dedicated in-house customs controlled • Area that expedites clearing duty-free imports for production-related raw materials and machinery • VAT exemptions under specific conditions for supplies procured in South Africa • Employment tax incentive—businesses may be eligible for tax relief including the employment tax incentive subject to requirements • Accelerate depreciation allowance on capital equipment and assets

(continued)

Table 2.1 (continued)

Country	*Zones (year established)*	*Main incentives*
Sudan	**Suakin Free Zone (2000)** *Activities*: 41% industrial, 15% commercial, 44% service **Alijaily Free Zone (2009)** *Activities*: Industrial investment and assembly industries, supporting services, logistic centres and distribution services, Food industries trade centres, light transformational industries, packing and packaging requirement industry, petrochemicals and plastic products industry, financial and consultancy services	• Exemption from tax on profits for a 15-year period, renewable by decision of the minister responsible • Salaries of expatriates working in projects within the FZs are exempted from personal income tax • Exemption of products imported into the FZ or exported abroad from all customs fees and taxes except services fees • Real estate establishment inside the zones are exempted from all taxes and fees • Invested capital and profits are transferable from Sudan to abroad through any licensed bank operating in the FZ • Exemption from customs fees money invested in the FZs may not be frozen or confiscated
Tanzania	**EPZs and SEZs (2002): Millennium Business Park; Hifadhi EPZ; Kisongo EPZ; Kamal Industrial Estate EPZ; BWM SEZ; Global Industrial Park** *Activities*: Textiles and garments, agro-processing, leather processing and manufacture of leather products, fish processing, wood products, agriculture and agro-processing, industrial, tourism, commercial forestry, ICT, banking and financial centre	For EPZs: • Exemption from payment of taxes and duties for capital used in development • Exemption from corporate tax for ten years initially, thereafter corporate tax shall be charged at a rate specified by the Income Tax Act Exemption from withholding tax on rent, dividends and interest • Investments in SEZs offer similar incentives but do not include a ten-year exemption from corporate taxes

(*continued*)

Table 2.1 (continued)

Country	*Zones (year established)*	*Main incentives*
Togo	**EPZs (1989)** *Activities*: Food industry and agro-industry and horticulture, wood industry, metallic engineering industry and plastic industry, clothing industry, synthetic hairs, leather craft, pharmaceutical industry, cosmetic industry, textile, light engineering products and electronics, jewellery, diamond polishing, building materials industry stationery	• Exemption from all customs duties and taxes on capital and production materials, as well as exporting goods manufacture within the FZ • Also, a 50% reduction in the same duties and taxes on commercial vehicles • Ten-year exemption from VAT stabilisation of corporate duty at the reduced rate of – 5% duty on taxable profit during the first five years of operation – 10% taxable profit from the 6th year to the 10th year – 15% taxable profit from the 11th to the 20th year – Ordinary law shall apply from the 21st year onwards (regular rate of 30%) – Reduced flat rate of 2% payroll tax for the lifetime of the company (as opposed to the 7% regular rate) • Reduction in business licence tax: – 5% tax from the second to the fifth year of operation – 10% tax from the sixth to the tenth year – 15% tax from the 11th to the 20th year – Ordinary law shall apply from the 21st year onwards • Reduction in land tax: – 5% tax from the second to the fifth year – 10% tax from the sixth to the tenth year – 15% tax from the 11th to the 20th year – Ordinary law shall apply from the 21st year onwards

(*continued*)

Table 2.1 (continued)

Country	*Zones (year established)*	*Main incentives*
Uganda	**Free Zones (2014)** **Nakaseke SEZ (2015)** *Activities*: Agribusiness products	• Exemption from taxes and duties on all imported raw materials and intermediate goods and capital for exclusive use in the development of production output unrestricted remittance of profit after tax • Tax holiday for ten years on finished consumer and capital goods • 100% exemption from tax on income from agro-processing • 100% exemption on income derived from the operation of aircrafts in domestic and international traffic or the leasing of aircraft • Exemption on plant and machinery used in the FZs for five years and one day from customs duty upon disposal. Exemption from all taxes, levies and rates on exports from the FZs, namely excise duty and customs taxes • 100% exemption from tax on income of a person offering technical assistance under a Technical Assistance Agreement • Exemption from import duties and taxes on all goods entering a free port zone • VAT exemption on supply of selected services, e.g. medical services, social welfare services, power generated by solar • Exemption of withholding tax on petroleum, petroleum products, plant and machinery, human or animal drugs and supply/importation of raw materials • Duty-free status

(*continued*)

Table 2.1 (continued)

Country	*Zones (year established)*	*Main incentives*
Zambia	**Chambishi MFEZ (2007/2008)** *Activities*: Copper smelting, manufacture of household appliances, manufacture of bars, wires, electric cables and motor parts Agro-processing, Lusaka East MFEZ (2009) *Activities*: Light manufacturing activities, provision of services such as conference facilities and hotel accommodation **Lusaka South MFEZ (2012)** Sub-Saharan Gemstone Exchange Industrial *Park Activities*: warehousing and storage, light industry, oil refinery, residential, gemstone processing Roma Industrial Park (2011) *Activities*: Light industries, retail parks, office park, warehousing	MFEZ: Profits on tax: • 0% for the first five years profits are made • 50% of profits taxed for sixth to eighth years • 75% of profits taxed for years nine and ten • 0% tax rate on dividends of companies operating under the MFEZ for a period of five years from the year of first declaration of dividends • 0% import duty rate on raw materials, capital goods, machinery including trucks and specialised vehicles for five years • Deferment of VAT on machinery and equipment including trucks and specialised motor vehicles imported for investment in MFEZ
Zimbabwe	**EPZs (1996)** *Activities*: Mining, agro-processing	• Five-year tax holiday • Following the initial five-year period, tax is paid at a rate of 25%, rather than the normal rate of 35% • Duty-free importation of raw materials and capital equipment for use in the EPZ • No tax liability from capital gains arising from the sale of capital invested • Mining sectors investors in EPZs: – Reduced corporation tax of 20% – Import duty exemption on imported capital goods

Source: Newman and Page (2017)

References

Addis Fortune. (2012). Industrial Zones Development Corporation Wins Formation Approval. http://www. addisfortune.com/Vol_13_No_639_Archive/Industrial%20Zones%20Development%20Corporation%20 Wins%20 Formation%20Approval.htm. Accessed on 22 September 2020.

Brautigam, D. (2009). *The Dragon's Gift: The Real Story of China in Africa*. England: Oxford University Press.

Brautigam, D., & Tang, X. (2011). African Shenzhen: China's Special Economic Zones in Africa. *Journal of Modern African Studies, 49*(1), 27–54.

Brautigam, D., & Tang, X. (2013). Going Global in Groups: Structural Transformation and China's Special Economic Zones Overseas. *World Development, 63*, 78–91.

China Nonferrous Metal Mining Group (CNMC). (2015). Organizational Structure. http://www.cnmc.com

Farole, T. (2011). *Special Economic Zones in Africa: Comparing Performance and Learning from Global Experience*. World Bank.

Forum on China-Africa Cooperation (FOCAC). (2000, October 10–12). *Beijing Declaration of the Forum on China-Africa Cooperation*, Beijing, China.

Forum on China-Africa Cooperation (FOCAC). (2006, November 4–5). *Declaration of the Beijing Summit of the Forum on China-Africa Cooperation*, Beijing, China.

Fu, X. (2012). *Promoting Manufacturing Foreign Direct Investment From China to Ethiopia*. http://www.hks.harvard.edu/index.php/content/download/66862/1240258/version/1/file/SYPA_XiaochenFu_2012.pdf. Harvard University. Accessed 23 Mar 2015.

Geda & Meskel. (2009). *Impact of China-Africa Investment Relations: Case Study of Ethiopia*. Nairobi: African Economic Research Consortium. AERC.

Lin, Y., & Wang, Y. (2014). *China-Africa Co-Operation in Structural Transformation: Ideas, Opportunities and Finances* (Wider Working Paper 2014/046). WIDER.

Ministry of Commerce, Trade and Industry of the Republic of Zambia (MCTI). (2015). *Multi-Facility Economic Zones*. http://www.mcti.gov.zm/index.php/investing-in-zambia/multifacility-economic-zones. Accessed 10 May 2015.

Newman, C., & Page, J. (2017). *Industrial Clusters: The Case for Special Economic Zones in Africa* (WIDER Working Paper 2017/15). United Nations Wide University.

Nigeria Export Zones Authority (NEPZA). (1992). *Nigeria Export Zones Authority Decree No. 63*. http://www.nepza.gov.ng/downloads/NEPZA631992.pdf. Accessed 10 May 2015.

Republic of Zambia (RoZ). (2006). *The Zambia Development Agency Act*, Lusaka, Zambia. http://www.zda.org.zm/?q=download/file/fid/74. Accessed 10 May 2015.

Republic of Zambia (RoZ). (2006a). *Vision 2030 – A Prosperous Middle-income Nation by 2030*. Lusaka, Zambia 2006. http://www.mcti.gov.zm/index.php/quarterly-newsletters/doc_details/12-zambia-vision-2030. Accessed on 15 June 2020.

UNDP. (2015). *Comparative Study on Special Economic Zones in Africa and China*. Beijing, China: UNDP.

UNCTAD. (2019). *World Investment Report: Special Economic Zones*. Geneva, Switzerland.

World Bank. (2011). *Chinese Investments in Special Economic Zones in Africa: Progress, Challenges and Lessons Learned*.

World Bank. (2014). Ethiopia – Competitiveness and Job Creation Project, Project Appraisal Document. http://www.gtai.de/GTAI/Content/DE/Trade/Fachdaten/PRO/2014/08/Anlagen/PRO201408205005.pdf. Accessed on 9 November 2020.

Xinhua. (2007, February 5). *China Launches First Economic, Trade Cooperation Zone in Africa*. http://news.xinhuanet.com/English/2007-02/05/content_5696348.htm. Accessed 10 May 2015.

Zeng, D. Z. (2015, April). *Global Experiences with Special Economic Zones: Focus on China and Africa*. https://openknowledge.worldbank.org/bitstream/handle/10986/21854/WPS7240.pdf?sequence=2. Accessed 10 July 2015.

PART II

Role of Governments and Policy Compatibility

CHAPTER 3

Regulatory and Institutional Framework of Special Economic Zones

3.1 Introduction

SEZs, including their establishment, operation and eventual dissolution, are regulated by legal frameworks enacted at different levels of governance. National SEZ policies around the world differ considerably, reflecting countries' specific industrial structures, current developments and growth opportunities. Nonetheless, they all include a special regulatory regime for SEZs and a separate institutional set-up. The SEZ regulatory framework deals with a variety of policy issues, mainly on trade, investment promotion and facilitation, establishment of investment, access to land, taxation, as well as labour and environmental issues. Rules and regulations that apply in SEZs are contained in countries' general regulatory frameworks, and in SEZ-specific legislation, such as SEZ laws and decrees (UNCTAD, 2019; World Bank, 2010; Zeng, 2010, 2015a, 2015b). SEZ-specific rules are generally more favourable for zone users, as they offer certain benefits and privileges not available outside the zones. The manner in which this special regime and the general legislation interact, as well as the degree to which SEZ rules differ from the general legal framework, varies considerably between countries.

This chapter reviews specific aspects of these regulatory frameworks at the national and international levels. Literature on domestic SEZ laws for 115 countries and models of institutional set-up are discussed. For

G. Mugano, *Special Economic Zones*,
https://doi.org/10.1007/978-3-030-82311-5_3

international economic law, this chapter reviews relevant rules contained in three bodies of international economic law, which include the International Investment Agreements (IIAs), the Agreements of the WTO and Regional Trade Agreements (RTAs). In addition, various SEZ legislations are discussed.

3.2 The National Regulatory Framework

The overall regulatory framework is discussed under this section together with the SEZ laws.

Overall Regulatory Framework

Globally, countries have enacted a special regulatory regime and a separate institutional set-up which is contextualised within the countries' specific growth opportunities, current development stages and industrial structures (UNCTAD, 2019).

Policy issues covered in the SEZ regulatory framework include trade facilitation, establishment of investment, investment promotion and facilitation, taxation, access to land, environmental issues and labour (UNCTAD, 2019; Zeng, 2015a, b). These regulations inter alia include tax incentives, trade facilitation, labour and environment laws, access to land and trade and investment laws (see Table 3.1).

Because rules and regulatory frameworks of the SEZ offer benefits and privileges which are not available to outsiders, they are therefore more attractive to zone users. Policy aspects such as trade rules, establishment of investment, investment promotion and facilitation, taxation, access to land, environmental issues and labour have been used as frameworks through which the zone creates a unique business environment different from the one outside the zone (Farole, 2011).

Regarding trade rules, in order to simplify and streamline procedures and processes, countries stipulate non-tariff measures and administrative procedures and establish tariff systems for both imports and exports. For example, investors in SEZs are mostly exempted from paying custom duties for inputs, equipment and machines. At the same time, evidence from United Nations Economic Commission for Africa (UNECA) (2021),

Table 3.1 Main elements of regulatory framework of Special Economic Zones

SEZ Legal Framework	General Legal Framework
• Specific rights and obligations of Zone users • Tax incentives and tax breaks • Preferential land access • Additional entry liberalisation • SEZ one stop shop, investor targeting • Customs benefits, trade facilitation	• Labour and environmental regulations • General tax code • Real estate laws • FDI investment establishment rules in investment and sectoral laws • Investment promotion and facilitation • Trade rules

Source: UNCTAD (2019)

Zeng (2012a) and Farole (2011) demonstrate that most countries provide trade facilitation by expediting customs clearance procedures, and in some cases establishing special warehouses for zone users.

Similarly, countries working with investment promotion agencies protect investments against political risk, grant attractive incentives and provide investment facilitation services to attract investors (Farole, 2011). Furthermore, countries normally relax entry restrictions in traditionally protected sectors through mechanisms such as local content requirements or regulations or empowerment laws (UNECA, 2021). These investment incentives and facilitation services normally exceed those offered in the rest of the country.

Regarding access to land, a number of countries have adopted various strategies such as relaxing access to land laws; provision of land for free as in the case of Rwanda or at reduced prices; permitting foreign ownership and/or preferential long-term leases that are otherwise not available; and exempting investors from real estate taxes (UNCTAD, 2019).

Relative to fiscal incentives, investors in the zones enjoy preferential treatment on payment of taxes. Although this varies from country to country, UNECA (2021), Zeng (2015a, b, 2016) and Farole (2011) reveal that investors are commonly exempted from paying taxes such as corporate taxes and import duties for a defined period of time (see Box 3.1 and Table 3.2).

Box 3.1 Fiscal Incentives Offered in Special Economic Zones in Zimbabwe

Fiscal Incentives

- Zero-rated Corporate Income Tax for the first five years of operation with a corporate tax rate of 15% applying thereafter.
- Duty-free importation on capital equipment.
- Special initial allowance of 50% of cost from year one and 25% in the subsequent two years.
- Exemption from non-resident tax on fees for services that are not locally available.
- Exemption from non-resident tax on royalties.
- Inputs which include raw materials for use by companies set up in the SEZs will be imported free of duty. The duty exemption will, however, not apply where such raw materials are produced in Zimbabwe.
- Zero-rated Capital Gains Tax.

Source: Zimbabwe Special Economic Zone Authority

Table 3.2 Summary of fiscal incentives offered in Special Economic Zones

Country	*Corporate tax holidays or reductions*	*Other fiscal incentives*
Bangladesh	0 years exempt + five years at 50% of normal rate (v. 35% national rate)	No dividend tax; accelerated depreciation; experts pay no income tax for three years
Dominican Republic	Unlimited exemption (v. 25% national rate)	No VAT, business tax or municipal taxes
Honduras	Unlimited exemption (v. 25% national rate)	No local sales tax, excise tax, tax on net assets or municipal taxes
Vietnam	Four years exempt, 50% reduction for next nine years, then 25% (v. 28% national rate)	N/A
Ghana	Ten years exempt, then 8% (v. 25% nationally)	Permanent exemption from withholding taxes on dividends
Kenya	Ten years exempt, then ten years at 25% (v. 30% national rate)	No VAT or stamp duty (perpetual); ten-year holiday on dividend tax; investment in new equipment 100% deductible

(*continued*)

Table 3.2 (continued)

Country	*Corporate tax holidays or reductions*	*Other fiscal incentives*
Lesotho	Exempt for sales outside Southern African Customs Union (SACU); 15% inside SACU	No withholding tax on dividends; training expenses deductible
	Unlimited exemption (v. 30% national rate)	Unlimited exemption from local taxes and VAT; rent-free land during construction phase
Senegal	15% rate (v. 35% national rate originally, now 25%)	No withholding tax on dividends, employers' taxes on staff, property taxes, licensing fees, or stamp duties
Tanzania	Ten years exempt, then revert to national rate (30%)	Ten-year exemption on local taxes, withholding on rents, dividends, and interest; no VAT on utilities

Source: Individual country SEZ authorities and World Bank Doing Business data (online data, http://www.doingbusiness.org) for national corporate tax rates

On labour regulations, investors in the zones are normally provided with rules which stipulate friendly labour-related obligations that go beyond existing rules in other parts of the country in exchange for certain commitments by the investors such as knowledge transfer and skills development (UNECA, 2021). For example, concessions may be granted to investors in the zones to have flexibility in hiring and firing of workers.

On environmental regulations, governments stipulate measures which must be adhered to by investors on issues such as pollution or excessive noise, or related to water treatment and waste disposal (Karambakuwa et al., 2020).

The Special Economic Zones Laws

Farole (2011) argues that laws and regulations accompanying SEZs are the critical foundation for any zone programme. These laws must be comprehensive and transparent, without any ambiguous ground rules established for all actors.

SEZ laws are thus an important element of the regulatory framework. These laws provide a distinct regulatory framework for the formation and operation of SEZs and categorically outline the rights and obligations of SEZ authorities, zone developers, operators and users (Kweka & teVelde, 2020). The establishment of each SEZ is implemented through executive decrees. These decrees stipulate the peculiarities of an SEZ which include detailed objectives, targeted industries or activities, allocation of land to be developed and other zone-specific regulations. The absence of good laws and regulations inevitably leads to failure although their presence may not be sufficient and enough to guarantee success (Farole, 2011).

In order to broaden the understanding of SEZ laws, the succeeding section discusses the content of SEZ laws, their definition, the objectives of the SEZs and targeted areas, investment attraction tools in SEZs and their establishment, as well as operational requirements for SEZ users.

Content of the Special Economic Zones Laws

According to Farole (2011), Zeng (2015a, b), the World Bank (2020) and UNCTAD (2019), globally, SEZ laws have many common features. These elements include provisions on definitions of a SEZ, objectives of SEZs and the sectors targeted, different types of SEZs and various incentives offered. Furthermore, the SEZ laws also provide institutional framework and regulations for establishment procedures and working conditions for zone users (UNCTAD, 2019).

Definition of Special Economic Zones

Globally, 90% of SEZ laws provide for a common definition of SEZs of which 30% explicitly state the types of specific zones as well as their respective definitions (UNCTAD, 2019; Zeng, 2012a, 2015a, b; Farole, 2011; World Bank, 2010). The core criteria used by countries in defining SEZs are generally similar to the ones presented in Table 3.3.

Objectives of Special Economic Zones and Targeted Sectors

According to UNCTAD (2019) 61% of SEZ laws indicate the zone's objectives. In these laws, the quantitative growth goals and dynamic growth objectives are frequently mentioned. Socio-economic objectives also feature in SEZ laws albeit with less emphasis (Zeng, 2015a, b; Farole, 2011).

Table 3.3 General definitions and types of Special Economic Zones

General definitions	**Examples**
Geographical location Special regulatory regime Economic activity	**Poland:** a separated, uninhabited part of the territory, on which a business activity may be conducted in accordance with the rules of the Act **Pakistan:** a geographically defined and delimited area that has been notified and approved for economic, industrial and commercial activities **Indonesia:** zones with certain boundaries within the territory that are designated to carry out an economic function, and are granted certain facilities and incentives **The Gambia:** any area designated as a free zone where goods and services are deemed, insofar as import duties and taxes are concerned, as being outside the customs territory, where the benefits provided under the law apply
Types	**Examples**
Broad coverage of many zone types	**Botswana:** free trade zone or commercial special economic zone, export-processing zone, enterprise zone, free port, single-factory economic zone, specialised zones and others
Typology based on specific purposes of each zone	**Uzbekistan:** free trade zones (trade-focused); free production areas (stimulating entrepreneurship and priority sectors), free scientific and technical zones (development of scientific and production potential)
Typology based on geographical considerations	**Dominican Republic:** other free zones of border character (at the frontier with Haiti), special free zones (proximity to natural resources processed), industrial free zones or services (any location)

Source: UNCTAD (2019)

Quantitative growth goals place much emphasis on attracting investments, export promotion and job creation, while dynamic growth objectives aim to foster innovation, knowledge transfer and skills development; industrial upgrading, economic diversification; structural change and integration into local value chains (Cheesman, 2012; Brautigam & Xiaoyang, 2011; Aggarwal, 2004). On the other hand, socio-economic objectives place significant emphasis on the quality of the work, environmental protection, sustainable development and gender issues, even though there has been little reference to gender issues (see Box 3.2).

Box 3.2 Examples of Socio-economic Objectives

- **In Mexico**, the Federal Law on Special Economic Zones specifies that the purpose of establishing SEZs is to promote sustainable economic growth, reduce poverty, allow the provision of basic services and expand opportunities for healthy and productive lives in the regions of the country where social development is lagging.
- **In South Africa**, the Special Economic Zones Act states that the creation of decent work and other economic and social benefits, including the broadening of economic participation by promoting medium-size enterprises and cooperatives, as well as skills and technology transfer, are among the purposes of SEZ establishment.
- **In Liberia**, the Special Economic Zone Act declares that its purpose is to carry out de-urbanization of highly populated cities; achieve long-term environmental, labour, and gender sustainability; promote the advancement of human rights; increase the standard of living; reduce poverty levels and achieve sustainable economic development.

Source: UNCTAD (2019)

Investment Attraction Tools in Special Economic Zones Laws

About 80% of the SEZ laws offer fiscal incentives such as exemptions on corporate tax and import duties for a stipulated period (often 5–10 years) or the application of a reduced tax rate (see Box 3.1 and Table 3.2) (World Bank, 2020; UNCTAD, 2019; Zeng, 2015a, b). Other tax exemptions which are offered by countries such as Kenya, as provided for in the country's SEZ Act and EPZ Act, include VAT invoiced by local suppliers of goods, services and works necessary for carrying out SEZ activities, and wages and salaries taxes (UNCTAD, 2019). In order to foster dynamic gains, countries such as Mali and Mexico allow for the deduction of a defined percentage on training expenses for local workers from their tax bill, and set performance targets such as minimum thresholds on local content or export targets in order to be granted fiscal incentives (UNCTAD, 2019).

Likewise, Zimbabwe, Azerbaijan and others provide for SEZ laws with a special customs framework which is characterised by elimination of and/

or tariff reductions on goods, plants or machinery imported into the zone (see Box 3.1) (UNCTAD, 2019). Besides this, customs offices are situated in the zone to expedite and simplify customs procedures.

According to UNCTAD (2019), nearly 30% of the SEZ laws cover investment facilitation. International best practices have shown that the most frequently used tool to facilitate investment is the streamlining of registration procedures through the one-stop shop where all the registration procedures and the necessary documents can be obtained under one roof (World Bank, 2020; UNCTAD, 2019; Zeng, 2015a, b, 2012a; Farole, 2011). Similarly, some countries such as Kosovo and Nigeria have enacted laws which attract investments. Kosovo, for example, established business incubators in zones with a view to offer them technical services and ensure the availability of physical work space. Nigeria, on the other hand, eliminated restrictions on recruitment and employment of foreign personnel within the zones to support investors in their initial phases (UNCTAD, 2019).

It is argued that investment protection constitutes approximately 25% of SEZ laws (UNCTAD, 2019). Countries such as Yemen, for example, through its Free Zones Law, enacted laws which guarantee that investors operating in the zones will not be expropriated or nationalised (e.g. Republic of Yemen, Free Zones Law). Likewise, some countries such as Turkmenistan have enacted SEZ laws which guarantee against future changes of the existing laws (UNCTAD, 2019). Furthermore, Lao People's Democratic Republic have made provisions which ensure that the SEZ Act prevails in cases of any conflict or discrepancies between the SEZ law and other domestic legislation (UNCTAD, 2019).

Regarding land use in zones, UNCTAD (2019) and Zeng (2018) reveal that about 30% of the SEZ laws make provision for preferential land use. These provisions provide for either permanent ownership of land or payment of reduced rent of temporary exemption from lease payment.

On trade facilitation, evidence shows that it constitutes 20% of total SEZ laws (UNCTAD, 2019; Zeng, 2015a, b; World Bank, 2010). Although these regulations vary from one country to another, core elements include the simplification and streamlining of import and export procedures, and simplified taxation systems.

Conversely, less than 20% of the SEZ laws makes reference to the provision of infrastructure as an investment promotion tool (Zeng, 2018). A number of countries such as Iran, Zambia, Togo, South Africa and China supply zones with telecommunication services, water, electricity and fuel at a subsidised rate (Zeng, 2018).

Establishment and Operational Requirements for Special Economic Zone Users

Evidence shows that 38% of all SEZ laws set a minimum requirement that enterprises must meet in order to invest and operate in that zone (Zeng, 2015a, b, 2018). Three categories of establishment and operational requirements are (i) minimum amount of investment, (ii) expected contribution to certain development goals, and (iii) specific performance requirements, which typically focus on employment-related obligations, export performance and skills transfer (Box 3.3).

Box 3.3 Establishment and Operational Requirements of Special Economic Zone Users

Minimum Investment Requirements

- In Jamaica, the Special Economic Zones Act 2016 stipulates that investment in machines, equipment, facilities, buildings and other assets during the first year must exceed $50,000.
- In Turkmenistan, a participant in a free economic zone must invest an amount fixed in the investment contract.
- In Costa Rica, companies may settle in a zone only with initial new investment in fixed assets of at least $150,000 (or its equivalent in local currency).

Expectation to Contribute to Certain Development Goals

- In Northern Macedonia, the Law on Technological Industrial Development Zones requires zone users to meet the following criteria: job creation, compliance with high environmental standards, production based on new technologies and high energy efficiency.
- In Botswana SEZ applicants must meet "indicative performance standards" such as exports, target export volumes, values and their markets, and expected benefits from the investment in terms of production and exports.
- In Eswathini, investors must generate new and innovative economic activities, create employment and other economic and

(*continued*)

Box 3.3 (continued)

social benefits, promote integration with local industry and increase value-added production.

Specific Performance Requirements

Employment-related obligations:

- In Djibouti, 30% of SEZ workforce must be Djiboutian by the end of the first year of operation, and at least 70% after five years of activity.
- In Cambodia, foreign managers, technicians or experts may be employed, provided that the number of foreign staff does not exceed 10% of total personnel.

Export requirements:

- In Nepal, at least 75% of services and materials produced within a zone must be exported.
- In Malaysia, goods manufactured in a free industrial zone may be transported from the zone only for export or with the approval of the relevant authority.
- In Gabon, the law requires that at least 75% of production in a zone must be exported.

Skills transfer:

- In Ethiopia, an industrial park enterprise is obliged to replace expatriate personnel or professionals with Ethiopian nationals by transferring the required knowledge and skills through specialised trainings.
- In Madagascar, the law on SEZs obliges zone users to report to zone developers on training provided to local staff.
- In Maldives, under the Special Economic Zones Act, approval from an SEZ authority to employ expatriate staff above statutory limits may be granted only temporarily and under the condition that a zone user provides for adequate training for Maldivians to fill the position.

Source: UNCTAD (2019)

3.3 Institutional Set-up of Special Economic Zones

This section discusses key stakeholders in SEZs, and institutional models used in establishing SEZs.

Key Stakeholders in Special Economic Zones

Because it involves a multitude of both public and private actors, the institutional set-up of SEZs is complicated. The complexities are further worsened by the fact that the institutional framework of SEZs is highly dependent on country-specific economic, political, regulatory and administrative systems (Tao et al., 2016; Farole, 2011). While there is no uniform institutional model for SEZs, existing SEZ regimes have some similarities with main stakeholders such as government, SEZ authority, zone developer, zone operator and zone user (see Table 3.4).

Government as a key stakeholder takes responsibility of setting overall economic development goals, developing key policies such as industrial, trade policies and SEZ laws (Zeng, 2015a, b). In addition, government is responsible for the coordination of SEZ policies with other relevant policies such as fiscal and monetary policies while harmonising its SEZ Act and regulations with international obligations (UNCTAD, 2019). The government is also responsible for the overall administration of the SEZ regime.

An SEZ authority is either a specialised agency or a state-owned enterprise which is supervised by the highest government officials, such as the president or the prime minister, as is the case of South Korea, or a minister from economic ministries such as the ministry of finance or trade (UNCTAD, 2019). Evidence has also shown that the majority of countries have established a separate SEZ authority whose mandate will be to support or complement government role in the zone (UNCTAD, 2019; Farole, 2011). Accordingly, SEZ authorities assist government in the coordination of policies in the zones and initiate related programmes. In addition to this, SEZ authorities are also responsible for strategic and operational planning, carrying out feasibility studies for planned zones and evaluating applications for zone development. Furthermore, they promote and enforce policies and standards; monitor the SEZ regime and collect relevant data on the effectiveness of individual zones and the entire system (UNCTAD, 2019). They also assist government in planning; executing the integration of SEZs into local economy; making key decisions such as the selection of zone developers and contract negotiations with successful candidates.

Table 3.4 Summary of roles and responsibilities in Special Economic Zones

Stakeholder	*Primary responsibilities*
Government	• Conduct strategic planning • Select site(s) and package land • Establish land use guidelines • Conduct initial feasibility studies • Select developer and enter development agreement • Develop site infrastructure • Training/workforce development and social services • Regulation and administration of the SEZ programme (see later)
Regulator	• *Designate SEZs:* designate public and private land as SEZs and public or private landowners or their agents as SEZ developers/operators • *Facilitate government services:* licensing, permits and regulatory services within the SEZs. These concern land use, business licensing, environmental permit, building permit, labour regulation (including foreign work permits) and inspections. They may also include business registration, utility regulation and dispute resolution. The regulator may set fees commensurate with the cost of service delivery in these areas • *Monitor compliance:* monitor compliance according to SEZ legal framework, policies, standards and requirements, and enforce compliance through appropriate penalties independently from other public agencies
Developer	• *Land use planning*: create a final land use master plan and prepare the land accordingly (grading, levelling and other preconstruction activity) • *Provision of infrastructure:* internal road networks, drainage and sewerage systems, and conduits and infrastructure for utilities However, in most cases, offsite infrastructure is the responsibility of the government
Operator	• *Facility leasing:* manage lease and rental agreements with the investors and assume responsibilities for main services for the zone (for example, security and maintenance) • *Utilities provision:* ensure provision of onsite utilities (electricity, gas, water, telecommunications) via domestic providers or through own provision • *Marketing:* experienced private developers often have a network of multinational clients across a range of industries to which they can market new SEZ opportunities SEZ authority/regulator and other parts of government (a national or local investment promotion agency) typically carry out some marketing activities

Source: Farole (2011)

Furthermore, SEZ authorities provide services such as issuance of permits and approvals within the zones, including construction permits, work permits and visas for foreigners; approval of landownership; and environmental impact assessments (UNCTAD, 2019). In addition to this, through training, liaising with utility companies, customs and tax authorities and local authorities, SEZ authorities assist and facilitate the operations of SEZ users and developers (UNCTAD, 2019; Zeng, 2015a, b). Consequently, SEZ authorities because of the nature of their work are normally physically situated within the SEZs.

Zone developers are an integral part of an ecosystem of main stakeholders of the SEZs whose main functions include provision of essential infrastructure and land arrangements (Zeng, 2015a, b). In this regard, zone developers initiate and participate in zoning and land use processes which lead to the production and adoption of a master plan for the zones. Zone developers also build onsite networks and utilities, and connect them to existing infrastructure. Moreover, zone developers are responsible for the smooth running of a zone by providing essential infrastructure services such as water supply, electricity and telecommunication; security; and maintenance services (Zeng, 2016). Zone developers may also provide one-stop shops, consultancy desks, training centres, focal points for recruitment, provision of conference facilities and office spaces (Farole, 2011). Working jointly with local authorities, they may provide education, healthcare services, transport, housing and recreation facilities.

International experience has shown that success or failure of SEZs depends on the technical and financial capacities and expertise of zone developers (World Bank, 2020 and UNCTAD, 2019). In recent years, a number of developing countries have used the private sector to develop the zones using frameworks such as public– private partnerships (UNCTAD, 2019). Following this, in 2008, about 62% of the SEZs in developing countries were developed and operated by the private sector due to lack of state resources. However, in the 1980s, only 25% of the zone developers were run by the private sector (FIAS, 2008).

The zone users are the investors who are direct beneficiaries of the SEZ laws for specific zones. The roles and functions of the main stakeholders discussed earlier are established in such a way that they provide an environment that is conducive to business, and enhance productivity of the SEZs for them to achieve the intended goals (UNCTAD, 2019).

Institutional Models in Establishing Special Economic Zones

While broad institutional establishment of the SEZs is similar in many countries in terms of structure and the main key stakeholders involved, the legal status and responsibilities of zone developers differ (UNCTAD, 2019; Zeng, 2012b, 2016; World Bank, 2010). Public, private and hybrid models have been extensively noted by UNCTAD (2019) as the basic frameworks through which most institutional set-ups of zones were built upon.

The public model is one in which all institutions both at the zone and national levels are public or publicly controlled (Zeng, 2015a, b). In this case, the zone developers are often called zone administrations. Countries such as Tajikistan, Russia and Vietnam widely use this model.

Conversely, using a competitive process based on statutory criteria, countries engage private zone developers to develop and operate the zones (Farole, 2011). Private developers thus have broad operational autonomy, and they report to the SEZ authorities, which have limited and strictly defined regulatory powers. These zone developers are then responsible for the admittance of investors into the zones. This way, they sign investment contracts which regulate land leases, fees and charges and other operational issues (UNCTAD, 2019). The advantage of this model is that it creates an opportunity for investors to link with the private developer's existing business networks, which then results in dynamic gains (UNDP, 2015; World Bank, 2010). This model is commonly found in countries such as Serbia, Georgia and Uruguay.

The hybrid model, which is a combination of the two models, provides for the possibility of public or private zone developers that retain relatively broad autonomy in their operations (Zeng, 2016). SEZ authorities license all private actors thereby retaining control over the admission processes. Nonetheless, the admission of investors at the zone level is done by zone developers, and the investor status in the zone is administered mainly through contracts (UNCTAD, 2019). The advantage of this model is that it gives broad flexibility to governments to shape SEZ regimes according to specific investment projects and zone activities. It also allows for greater involvement of local governments as they can be the sole zone developers in a particular SEZ (UNCTAD, 2019). China, Ethiopia and Poland are among countries which widely use this model (Zeng, 2012a).

3.4 International Regulations and Special Economic Zones

Governments, in crafting the SEZ regime, must be mindful of their international obligations notwithstanding the fact that it is a domestic policy framework (Farole, 2011). International rules can either constrain or facilitate SEZs. Two key areas of SEZ laws which interact with the countries' international obligations are:

- Support measures given to companies in the SEZ such as tax and other benefits; exemptions from customs and duties; relaxed regulatory requirements; foreign ownership requirements; and streamlined administrative services among others.
- Requirements placed on SEZ investors (e.g. certain performance requirements or duties applicable to imports).

International rules can either facilitate (allowing or requiring) or constrain (prohibiting or requiring phasing out) such measures. Governments are thus required to design and administer SEZ laws which are in compliance with their international obligations, while maximising the benefits these obligations may provide (Cheng, 2019). Specific international treaties which must be taken into account are the IIAs, WTO provisions and RTAs (Cheng, 2019; UNCTAD, 2019).

Nexus between International Investment Agreements (IIA) and Special Economic Zones

The IIA basically guides countries' behaviour with respect to investment protection and, to some extent, investment liberalisation (investor entry rights); facilitation, promotion and investor obligations (UNCTAD, 2019; Cheng, 2019). Most international investment treaties, which host countries have signed, are aimed at attracting investment, which is the main objective of SEZs. Hence, in a number of cases, most IIAs such as Bilateral Investment Treaties (BITs) and Treaties Investment Provisions (TIPs) have provisions which are in sync with SEZs law.

Nonetheless, most BITs allow investors to seek substantive protection in cases of disputes through international arbitration against host governments (Cheng, 2019). Evidence shows that there have been nearly 11 cases of disputes related to SEZs investments (Cheng, 2019). The disputes which were challenged at international courts concerned Kyrgyz, Egypt and Moldova, and these countries revoked benefits such as tax benefits or FZ status (7 cases), and the imposition of restrictions or additional requirements on investors (4 cases) (Cheng, 2019). These cases were tried through international arbitration jurisdiction. Recently, 3 disputes were decided in favour of the government; 4 went in favour of the investors; 2 in which both parties settled, while the other 2 cases are still pending (Cheng, 2019).

Nexus between World Trade Organization and Special Economic Zones

Like BITs, WTO rules do not single out SEZs. As such, member states must promulgate SEZ laws in line with the provision of the WTO (Defever & Riaño, 2017).

The WTO Agreement on Subsidies and Countervailing Measures (SCM) is one such provision which must be taken into account when developing laws governing SEZs. Although SCM do not explicitly refer to SEZ, they prohibits export subsidies and subsidies that are contingent on the use of domestic goods over imported goods (UNCTAD, 2019). In this regard, if SEZs employ such measures, there will be incompatibilities with the WTO provisions such that disputes will arise.

Interestingly, the SCM provides flexibility for certain subsidy-related measures possibly applied in the SEZ context (Coppens, 2013). For example, general infrastructure that is available to all within SEZs is not deemed a subsidy, and hence is not subject to the rules of the SCM Agreement. Likewise, exempting an exported product from duties or taxes borne by the likes of domestically consumed products, or the remission of such duties under duty-drawback schemes are also not subject to the rules of the SCM Agreement (Coppens, 2013).

Furthermore, although the WTO Agreement on Trade-Related Investment Measures (TRIMs) does not mention SEZs, it can affect SEZ laws (Cheng, 2019). For example, laws such as local content requirements or import–export balancing requirements may violate the TRIMS provisions. The violation, if not carefully considered, may arise when governments, as part of the SEZ laws, stipulate minimum thresholds of local content and foreign ownership requirements which are incompatible with WTO provisions on TRIMS (UNCTAD, 2019).

Customs facilitation, which is one of the policy measures within the SEZ laws, is part of the WTO Trade Facilitation Agreement (WTOTFA) that has serious implications on SEZ policies (UNCTAD, 2019). The WTOTFA was signed in 2013 and enforced in February 2017. It establishes rules that seek to expedite the movement, release and clearance of goods (including goods in transit) with flexibility for developing and least developed countries. When developing SEZ laws, countries must align their laws with WTOTFA.

Nexus between Regional Trade Agreements and Special Economic Zones

A modern RTA has a complex agreement that focuses on issues concerning trade in goods and services. It extensively covers investment issues, government procurement, entry of businesspeople, intellectual property, competition policy, labour, environment and regulatory cooperation (UNCTAD, 2019). These rules interact to different degrees with SEZ laws. Thus, when designing SEZ laws, considerable effort must be made to ensure that the SEZ Act and its regulations are harmonised with regional commitments.

3.5 Conclusion

This chapter has reviewed specific aspects of regulatory frameworks at the national and international levels. Drawing from literature on domestic SEZ laws for 115 countries, the chapter discussed models of institutional set-up in SEZs. Regarding international economic law, the chapter reviewed relevant rules contained in three bodies of international economic law which are IIAs, WTOTFA and RTAs.

The chapter also argued that governments are required to design and administer SEZ laws which comply with their international obligations and seek to maximise the benefits these obligations may provide (Cheng, 2019).

The chapter has further demonstrated that because rules and regulatory frameworks of the SEZ offer privileges which are not available to outside users, they are therefore much more attractive to zone users. Policy aspects such as trade rules, establishment of investment, investment promotion and facilitation, taxation, access to land, environmental issues and labour have been used as frameworks through which the zone creates a unique business environment different from the one outside the zone (Farole, 2011).

Importantly, in order to simplify and streamline procedures and processes, countries stipulate non-tariff measures, administrative procedures and establish tariff systems for both imports and exports. For example, investors in SEZs may be exempted from paying customs duties for inputs, equipment and machines. At the same time, evidence from UNCTAD (2019), Zeng (2012a) and Farole (2011) reveals that most countries facilitate trade through expedited customs clearance procedures and establish special warehouses for zone users.

Countries also work with investment promotion agencies, protect investment against political risk, grant attractive incentives and provide investment facilitation services to attract inward investment (Farole, 2011). Furthermore, countries normally relax entry restrictions in traditionally protected sectors through mechanism such as local content regulations or empowerment laws (UNCTAD, 2019). These investment incentives and facilitation services normally exceed those offered in the rest of the country.

Besides this, a number of countries have adopted various strategies such as relaxing access to land; provision of land for free as is the case in Rwanda, offering land at a reduced price, permitting foreign ownership or preferential long-term leases that are otherwise not available and exempting investors from real estate taxes (UNCTAD, 2019). Moreover, investors in these zones enjoy preferential treatment on payment of taxes although it varies from country to country (UNCTAD, 2019; Zeng, 2015a, b, 2016; Farole, 2011). Even though these depend on individual countries, evidence shows that investors are commonly exempted from paying corporate taxes and import duties for a defined period of time.

The chapter has also shown that, because establishing SEZs involves public and private actors, the institutional set-up of SEZs is equally complicated. The complexities are further worsened by the fact that institutional framework of SEZs are highly dependent on a country's economic, political, regulatory and administrative systems (Tao et al., 2016). Thus, there is no uniform institutional model for SEZs. Nevertheless, existing SEZ regimes have some similarities in terms of their main stakeholders, which include government, SEZ authority, zone developer, zone operator and zone users.

References

Aggarwal, A. (2004). *Export Processing Zones in India: Analysis of the Export Performance* (Working Paper No. 148). Indian Council for Research on International Economic Relations (ICRIER).

Brautigam, D., & Xiaoyang, T. (2011). African Shenzhen: China's Special Economic Zones in Africa. *Modern African Studies, 49*(1), 27–54.

Cheesman, A. (2012). *Special Economic Zones and Development: Geography and Linkages in the Indian EOU Scheme* (Working Paper No. 145). Development Planning Unit, The Bartlett, University College London.

Cheng, T. (2019). Special Economic Zones: A Catalyst for International Trade and Investment in Unsettling Times? *The Journal of World Investment and Trade, 20*(1), 32–67.

Coppens, D. (2013). How Special Is the Special and Differential Treatment Under the SCM Agreement? A Legal and Normative Analysis of WTO Subsidy Disciplines on Developing Countries. *World Trade Review, 12*(1), 79–109.

Defever, F., & Riaño, A. (2017). Subsidies with Export Share Requirements in China. *Journal of Development Economics, 126*, 33–51.

Farole, T. (2011). *Special Economic Zones in Africa: Comparing Performance and Learning from Global Experience*. World Bank.

FIAS. (2008). *Special Economic Zones: Performance, Lessons Learned, and Implications for Zone Development*. World Bank.

Karambakuwa, R. T., Matekenya, W., Mishi, S., Jeke, L., & Ncwadi, R. M. (2020). *Special Economic Zones and Transnational Zones as Tools for Southern Africa's Growth: Lessons from International Best Practices* (No. 2020/170). UN WIDER Working Paper.

Kweka, J., & teVelde, D. (2020). Industrialisation and Industrial Hub: Experience in Kenya, Tanzania and Rwanda. In A. Oqubay & J. Lins (Eds.), *The Oxford Handbook of Industrial Hubs and Economic Development*. Oxford University Press.

Tao, Y., Yuan, Y., & Li, M. (2016). Chinese Special Economic Zones: Lessons for Africa. *Africa Economic Brief, 7*(6), 1–11.

UNCTAD. (2019). *World Investment Report: Special Economic Zones*. United Nations.

UNDP. (2015). *Comparative Study on Special Economic Zones in Africa and China*. UNDP.

UNECA. (2021). *Harnessing the Potential of Special Economic Zones for Private Sector Development and Inclusive Industrialisation in Southern Africa*. UNECA.

World Bank. (2010). *Chinese Investments in Special Economic Zones in Africa: Progress, Challenges, and Lessons Learned*. World Bank.

Zeng, D. Z. (2010). *Building Engines for Growth and Competitiveness in China: Experience with Special Economic Zones and Industrial Clusters*. World Bank.

Zeng, D. Z. (2012a). *SEZs in Africa: Putting the Cart in Front of Horse?* World Bank.

Zeng, D. Z. (2012b). *An Overview of Six Economic Zones in Nigeria: Challenges and Opportunities* (World Bank Policy Note). World Bank.

Zeng, D. Z. (2015a). *Global Experiences with Special Economic Zones – With a Focus on China and Africa*. World Bank.

Zeng, D. Z. (2015b). *Global Experiences with Special Economic Zones: Focus on China and Africa* (World Bank Policy Research Working Paper 7240). World Bank.

Zeng, D. Z. (2016). Global Experiences of Special Economic Zones with Focus on China and Africa: Policy Insights. *Journal of International Commerce, Economics and Policy, 7*(3), 1–27.

Zeng, D. Z. (2018). *Special Economic Zones: Lessons from the Global Experience*. World Bank.

CHAPTER 4

Guidelines for Special Economic Zones Development and Collaboration: Evidence from Asia

4.1 Introduction

Many countries in Asia are increasingly using SEZs which include industrial parks, EPZs, technology parks, eco-industrial parks and innovation districts as economic development strategies (UNCTAD, 2019; Zeng, 2018; ASEAN, 2016; Farole, 2011).

SEZs were adopted by most Association of Southeast Asian Nations (ASEAN) Member States (AMS) as a vehicle for luring investors with a view to increasing export earnings and job creation (ASEAN, 2016). Like in other countries, the SEZs in Asia have similar characteristics such as a geographically demarcated area, streamlined procedures such as tax holidays, exemptions on customs duties, special customs services and special regulations (ASEAN, 2016). Additionally, SEZs in Asia enjoy adequate infrastructure, services and duty-free capital access for equipment and raw materials, and efficient administrative services to attract investors (ASEAN, 2016). Consequently, SEZs have been effective in attracting investment in Asia as well as meeting macroeconomic goals (see Box 4.1).

Evidence further shows that designing and implementing successful SEZ strategies as well as improving their operations is extremely difficult (UNCTAD, 2019, Zeng, 2016, 2018; Farole, 2011; Aggarwal, 2004). Ironically, in order to attract investment, create jobs and generate spillover effects for the rest of the economy, literature shows that a compelling master plan, favourable regulatory regime and excellent infrastructure are

G. Mugano, *Special Economic Zones*,
https://doi.org/10.1007/978-3-030-82311-5_4

Box 4.1 Special Economic Zones' Experience in Asia

The Government of Vietnam uses SEZs as an effective vehicle for attracting FDI. From an administrative point of view, central government plays a coordinating role while respective provinces take the responsibility of overseeing the management of SEZs (UNIDO, 2015). In order to have a balanced growth, the Government of Vietnam made a policy decision that all 58 provinces must have at least one zone (UNIDO, 2015).

In 2016, the country had established 15 economic zones, 295 industrial parks and 3 technology parks, which constituted 80% of manufacturing FDI, and over 50% of total FDI (ASEAN, 2016). In 2016 also, SEZs contributed 45% of export value and 40% of GDP (ASEAN, 2016). SEZs also contributed about 2.5% of the total workforce, which, when compared with regional countries, is higher (for example, SEZs contribute 1.1% and 1.25% of total labour force in Thailand and Philippines, respectively). Thus, to consolidate the initial gains of SEZs, in 2015, the Government of Vietnam launched a master plan on SEZs whose main targets were to create a total of 18 economic zones and 400 industrial parks by 2020 (ASEAN, 2016).

In Lao PDR, although SEZs were developed in the early 2000s, they have remained a relatively new concept. In 2016, the country created ten economic zones, two of which were fully operational (ASEAN, 2016). The first SEZ to be established in 2002 was Savan-Seno in Savannakhet whose main goal was to appeal to companies intending to locate on the East–West economic corridor linking Vietnam, Lao PDR and Thailand. This emerging zone development had the potential to attract investors from a broader range of economic sectors, thereby contributing to the transformation and diversification of the Lao PDR economy, which is traditionally driven by natural resources (ASEAN, 2016). The government was preparing a new SEZ law to ensure that zones had their own regulatory framework which reflected good international practices.

In South-east Asia, a number of countries such as Malaysia were using SEZ strategy to develop a less trade-distorting framework for the support of strategic sectors, and comprehensive strategy of cluster development (UNIDO, 2015). As part of the SEZ strategy, in order to link industrial and enterprise development policies, more

(*continued*)

Box 4.1 (continued)
emphasis was given to small to medium-sized enterprise (SME) development (ASEAN, 2016). Penang, which hosted one of Malaysia's most developed technology clusters in the manufacturing of semiconductor-based electronic components, is a classic example of an SEZ which has had mainstream SMEs within it. This way, the Penang SME Centre was established to act as an incubator and encourage SMEs to take advantage of the facility, for which rental subsidies were provided (UNIDO, 2015). Likewise, Johor and Klang Valley followed a similar approach to industrial cluster development.

In Indonesia, SEZs were well developed and contributed about 2.5% of the total workforVce (ASEAN, 2016). Batam Free Trade Zone, which used the advantageous position of the Riau Islands Province, has attracted over 150 major international maritime companies. This has contributed to a booming shipbuilding and shipyard industry, thus becoming one of the most successful SEZs in Indonesia (ASEAN, 2016). In addition to this, using its high-quality infrastructure, which is superior to the rest of Indonesia, Batam has attracted global leaders in electronics including Panasonic, Sanyo and Siemens, and has become an electronics-manufacturing hub (ASEAN, 2016).

As of May 2015, the Philippines hosted over 300 economic zones, which were administered by 18 different investment promotion agencies, and these zones have significantly contributed both to export growth and FDI inflows (ASEAN, 2016). The Philippines Economic Zone Authority (PEZA) alone administered the incentives for over 300 privately managed zones, and owned three ecozones (ASEAN, 2016). These zones also included 216 IT parks and centres, 21 agro-industrial economic zones, 64 manufacturing economic zones, 19 tourism economic zones, and two medical tourism zones (ASEAN, 2016). One of the key success factors was the fact that PEZA had a good reputation among investors for its non-stop, one-stop service. Clark Development Corporation and Subic Bay Metropolitan Authority (SBMA) were also other major zones which formed part of the country's network of IPAs. Owing in part to its performance in encouraging reinvestment, the SBMA was the overall winner of the FDI Global Free Zones Award in Asia in 2015 (OECD, 2016).

(*continued*)

Box 4.1 (continued)

A legal framework for SEZs was established in 2005 in Cambodia. As of September 2015, the country approved 34 SEZs, of which 14 were operational (ASEAN, 2016). Most of them were located along the borders with Thailand and Vietnam, particularly in Sihanoukville and Phnom Penh. However, although these brought 1% of total employment and 3.7% of total secondary industry employment, they were nevertheless relatively small compared with other countries in the region. That aside, Cambodia has started diversifying the industrial base away from garments towards electronics and electrical products, as well as household furnishings and car parts (Warr & Menon, 2015).

In order to attract foreign investment in Myanmar, its reform process sought to develop SEZs (ASEAN, 2016). Eventually, the Thilawa Special Economic Zone which became operational in late 2015, was the first SEZ in Myanmar (ASEAN, 2016). Although investors from China, the United States and Thailand, in particular, were present in the Thilawa zone, Japanese investors constituted the majority of the roughly 60 businesses in this country (ASEAN, 2016). Manufacturing of garments and toys, radiators, steel products, packaging, aluminium cans and waste management were major sectors in the Thilawa zone (ASEAN, 2016). Owing to their impressive record, the SEZs in Myanmar, as in the other AMS, can be used as effective pilot schemes for testing new approaches to boost the investment climate, especially in focused areas such as building capacity for streamlining registration and licensing procedures; effectively managing incentives and promoting linkages; monitoring the environment, and socio-economic impact of investments in the zones (ASEAN, 2016).

Overall, for many decades, evidence shows that SEZs have been the nerve centre of export-led development strategies of Asian economies (ASEAN, 2016; OECD, 2016 and UNIDO, 2015). Precisely, SEZs have attracted significant FDI, created millions of jobs such as those engaging women, boosted exports and have helped in both economic diversification and transformation (ASEAN, 2016; OECD, 2016; UNIDO, 2015).

Source: ASEAN (2016)

necessary preconditions but not sufficient for SEZs' survival (Cheesman, 2012; Brautigam & Xiaoyang, 2011; Chen & de'Medici, 2009). In addition to this, successful SEZ programmes, as noted in Asia, were efficiently designed and managed in a flexible manner, and relevant to the specific local, national and regional context in which they operated (ASEAN, 2016). Again, evidence suggests that the balance between costs on infrastructure investment, few linkages with local economies, and forgone tax revenues and benefits of SEZs was not pronounced. SEZs can therefore create distortions within economies (ASEAN, 2016). Moreover, because it is difficult to disentangle the effects of SEZs from other economic forces, measuring performance of SEZs' policies has also been difficult (ASEAN, 2016; Zeng, 2015a, 2015b).

To this end, the successful SEZs presented in Box 4.1 were established on the back of specific guidelines which were aimed at overcoming these challenges. Using ASEAN experience, the subsequent section presents guidelines and policy practices for the would-be SEZ policymakers.

4.2 Guidelines for Special Economic Zones Development and Collaboration

This section presents guidelines that aim to address different aspects of SEZ policymaking, strategy development, regulation, implementation and increased SEZ cooperation. These guidelines are drawn from international experiences and are assumed to help in dealing with the challenges that are faced during the design, implementation and review stages of the SEZs.

Promotion of Clear Development Strategy

This section discusses critical issues which are not adequately addressed in practice. These issues concern explicit assumptions about the role of SEZs within the broader national or regional policy framework, and the setting of clear and measurable targets. As argued by ASEAN (2016), policymakers must avoid pitfalls such as ending up with zones that are poorly linked to the rest of the economy for reasons ranging from formal restrictions on domestic market access to poor capacities of domestic SMEs to meet the rigorous standards of global value chains. To this end, there is need for careful and inclusive strategic planning as well as independent monitoring and evaluation.

Specific Binding Constraints That Must Be Addressed by the Zone
Farole (2011) argues that a number of SEZs have failed to deliver value for money. Research has shown that, in a number of cases, SEZs do not only yield insufficient social returns for the economy, but also distort economic incentives and lead to capital misallocation, although a clear cost–benefit analysis has been difficult due to the complexity of the issues and challenges in measuring spillover effects (UNCTAD, 2019; Zeng, 2015a, b; Farole, 2011). Suboptimal performance of SEZs is largely defined in cases where factors such as forgone tax revenue and marginal infrastructure spending are taken into account (Farole, 2011). Other studies have also demonstrated that SEZs tend to fall into three broad categories, that is, a larger group breaking even or yielding marginal returns for the economy; a long tail of failed zones that either were not sustainable or simply provided investors with tax breaks without leading to additional employment opportunities, and/or export earnings and a few highly visible success stories (UNCTAD, 2019; ASEAN, 2016; Zeng, 2012a, 2012b, 2015a, 2015b; Farole, 2011).

To this end, in order to successfully implement SEZs, changing the mindset and the economic structure may contribute to the SEZ programmes. These must be firmly nestled in an analysis of the market failure the programme wants to address (Cheesman, 2012; Farole, 2011; Brautigam & Xiaoyang, 2011; Chen & de'Medici, 2009). In this regard, policymakers must clearly define the SEZ's objectives while specifying its performance criteria. Based on international experience, the following objectives may fall into one or more of the general categories:

- Compensation for poor business climate; for example, regulatory burdens and deficit of infrastructure
- Promotion of new ventures and activities in the economy
- Promotion of innovative, R&D intensive activities in the economy
- Political reforms and various economic policies before they are rolled out to the rest of the economy

Generally, if designed well and implemented, SEZs can be used as an effective vehicle for promoting the structural change required for sustainable growth and economic development (Cheesman, 2012; Brautigam & Xiaoyang, 2011; Chen & de'Medici, 2009).

Set Measurable and Time-Bound Objectives

Many policymakers are oftentimes overambitious when setting objectives for SEZs. As part of the broader objectives for SEZs, international experience has shown that many governments ambitiously aim to promote investment, encourage the private sector, encourage innovation, transfer modern technologies, protect investors, expand exports, develop human resources, and reduce unemployment (UNCTAD, 2019; Zeng, 2016; Farole, 2011). At a regional level conversely, some countries have been calling for regional development, promoting integrity, streamlining corporate governance and increasing women's participation (ASEAN, 2016). This further complicates the implementation of SEZs.

Furthermore, in a number of cases, although SEZ objectives are laudable, there are just too many objectives which are also often too broad to offer meaningful guidance, and these end up diluting the focus of SEZs (Cheesman, 2012; Brautigam & Xiaoyang, 2011; Chen & de'Medici, 2009). Likewise, conflicts among objectives are apparent even though most objectives are aligned: for example, the nexus between foreign investment and job creation (ASEAN, 2016). International experience has also shown that consumer goods manufacturers may produce goods for the local market at the expense of exporting them, hence threatening employment opportunities. This is the case because a high-tech company unlike a local competitor may end up concentrating on technology transfers while minimising job creation just to keep away competition (ASEAN, 2016; World Bank, 2010).

Given these realities, a clear focus on decision-making, investments and supporting initiatives can be made considerably easier if efforts aimed at attracting foreign investment are clearly defined, and the characteristics are well aligned with the factor endowments on offer (ASEAN, 2016). Other objectives, such as the establishment of an industrial base that may spawn strong exporting companies and employment creation may be easily attainable goals but, as argued by ASEAN (2016), must not be key decision-making criteria. For UNCTAD (2019), Zeng (2015a, b) and Farole (2011) regional development objectives such as the desire to locate SEZs in rural areas, where there are deficits in infrastructures and connectivity, are a common mistake policymakers should avoid since it pushes investors away.

Beyond this, in cases where the planned targets are new and in untested sectors, policymakers should make educated guesses about the success of a planned SEZ (ASEAN, 2016). There is need for clear and measurable objectives that are integrated into wider economic development policies, which must be subjected to continuous monitoring and evaluation if the SEZs are to be successful (Zeng, 2016; ASEAN, 2016; Farole, 2011). The most sustainable way of ensuring success of the SEZs is to ensure that their objectives help investors undertake activities that are competitive rather than dependent on direct or indirect incentives (ASEAN, 2016; Zeng, 2015a, b; World Bank, 2010).

Special Economic Zones as a Framework for Testing and Catalysing Economic Reforms

In many cases, direct and indirect incentives which may be offered by SEZs to investors may become entrenched. Because the zone residents have more advantages than other firms within the economy for an indefinite period, this sometimes distorts competition (ASEAN, 2016). Furthermore, it may also lower the political momentum for reforms of the overall business environment since the option to locate in the zones may be sufficient for the private sector players who would otherwise lobby for further reforms. In addition, the creation of SEZs may aggravate the gap between the rest of the economy and enclaves of foreign investment which act as offshore entities, thereby hampering the potential to create linkages between foreign and domestic and SMEs on the one hand, and large companies on the other (UNCTAD, 2019). Furthermore, by providing advantages to some companies, this may de facto only benefit large foreign companies, while established zone enclaves may disadvantage domestic SMEs.

For these reasons, when considering various types of SEZs, policymakers should use clear time frames and special regulatory regimes. They should also not use SEZs as a permanent solution to economic reforms and development but rather as a testing ground that may be expanded to the rest of the economy with time (UNCTAD, 2019; ASEAN, 2016). Precisely, as argued by ASEAN (2016), SEZs could indeed alleviate the burdens imposed by regulation and infrastructure in several ways (see Table 4.1).

Foster Coherence Between Investment Policy Framework and Special Economic Zones

Contrary to the view that SEZs and associated incentives should be panacea and game changers in attracting investments, they must be coherent with the overall investment policy framework, and should complement the

Table 4.1 Indicative list of issues that SEZs can alleviate among residents

Category	*Issues*	*How SEZs can alleviate them*
Infrastructure	Limited land available	Undertaking feasibility studies to increase availability
	Inadequate and unreliable supply of utilities; bureaucracy in contracting with state utility	Provision of utilities to a limited area at high standard of service and adoption of an expedited process administered by the zone operator and based on an MoU with the utility companies
	Deficits in transport infrastructure	Locating SEZs in areas with excellent connections over air, road and sea where possible
Regulation Burden	Cumbersome business licensing and registration procedures	Establishment of one-stop shop in the zone
	Difficulties in securing work permits and immigration visas	Expediting procedures in securing permits and visas, and provision of specific exceptions for zone residents to bring in expertise from abroad under defined conditions
	Delays in customs clearing procedures	Simplify and expedite customs procedures by locating customs office inside the zone
	Costly, lengthy and unpredictable construction licensing and property registration process	Fixing property rights in the contract with SEZ tenants. Setting up automatic approval of standard types of structures such as factory shells through establishment of clear zoning restrictions construction
	Slow, costly, unpredictable customs procedures and restrictions makes it difficult to trade across borders	Establishment of one-stop shop within the zone which is run by the zone operator with a view to expedite export procedures
	Insufficient legal framework to enforce property rights	Legislating property rights law with a view to assure property rights to residents

Source: ASEAN (2016)

overall economic development strategy (UNCTAD, 2019; Zeng, 2016; Tao et al., 2016; Farole, 2011).

For instance, investment promotion and concessional finance instruments could help generate strategic zone investments while enterprise support policies could help suppliers to anchor investors in the zone

(ASEAN, 2016; Tao et al., 2016). Likewise, since supplier linkage programmes could also help strengthen local companies, infrastructure and utilities must therefore be provided in a reliable and affordable fashion. For example, in the Philippines, because of trade restrictions imposed on merchandise produced in the zones, SEZs have failed to build linkages with the local economy (ASEAN, 2016). On infrastructure many SEZs worldwide have failed to attract investors because the road networks and electricity services were unreliable, hence imposing inordinate costs on entrepreneurs (ASEAN, 2016; Zeng, 2016; Farole, 2011).

- Given these discourses, policymakers must come up with an SEZ legislative framework which is in line with the overall policies affecting investment following the Organization for Economic Cooperation and Development (OECD) policy framework (ASEAN, 2016). Additionally, respect for laws and international standards protecting labour rights and regulations, the environment and general business climate must also be considered when establishing SEZs (UNCTAD, 2019; Zeng, 2016).

Promote Linkages Between Investors and the Domestic Economy

SEZs, FZs and EPZs have been largely criticised for their failure to positively influence economies (UNCTAD, 2019; Zeng, 2012a; Farole, 2011). Although this phenomenon is due to customs and other exemptions, integrating SEZs with the rest of the economy is important as it creates huge business opportunities through supplying zone tenants with services, raw materials and intermediate goods among others (Tao et al., 2016; OECD, 2016). Other positive spillover effects have included supporting company upgrading and specialisation, introduction of new technologies and establishment of new sectors, which is key in avoiding the "middle-income trap" (Tao et al., 2016; OECD, 2016).

In order to integrate SEZs with the economy, countries have crafted mandatory local content in exports which have been observed to have distorted economic incentives and investment (UNCTAD, 2019; World Bank, 2010). International experience, as observed by UNCTAD (2019) and the World Bank (2010), has shown that business linkage programmes could help local companies develop and upgrade so that they meet the standards set by the firms in the SEZs. In addition to this, incubator programmes can also help entrepreneurs take advantage of supply chain opportunities. Moreover, while governments can support joint research efforts involving firms in the SEZs and local companies, incubator programmes could also help promote the integration of SEZs with the economy. Some governments are also encouraging linkages with local universities in R&D in order to spur innovation and creativity (UNCTAD, 2019; Farole, 2011; World Bank, 2010). For new industrialised countries such as South Korea and China, SEZs have been easily integrated with their economies through promotion of large domestic investments within the SEZs (ASEAN, 2016).

Ensure Coherence and Cost-Efficiency of Incentives
Frequently, tax exemptions and in-kind incentives are used as a policy package to attract investors to SEZs (UNCTAD, 2019; ASEAN, 2016). Because of inter-country competition, a package of fiscal incentives has become almost standardised among zones across the world through duty-free imports, corporate tax exemptions and foreign exchange control exemptions (UNCTAD, 2019). Like with other economic development policies, these incentives have been captured by the political elite and other interest groups, and have had harmful consequences on the economies (Zeng, 2018; UNCTAD, 2019). Furthermore, tax incentives have sometimes drained the already scarce and thin public resources.

The OECD, the International Monetary Fund (IMF), the World Bank and the United Nations have often argued that tax exemptions are ineffective in countries with deficits in infrastructure and governance. Some studies have also shown that tax incentives are mostly poorly designed and redundant (UNCTAD, 2019; Zeng, 2016, 2018; Farole, 2011). For example, income tax exemptions and tax holidays are commonly used but have been subjected to widespread abuse, hence their ability to attract investment in higher-risk areas has been limited since they are only relevant when profits are made (UNCTAD, 2019; Zeng, 2018; Farole, 2011). In situations like these, accelerated depreciation and investment tax credits have been the most effective in stimulating investment (UNCTAD, 2019; Zeng, 2016, 2018).

Furthermore, fiscal incentives have ended up fostering competition among countries, which has seen some countries racing to the bottom, thereby narrowing the fiscal space required to invest in public goods for long-term sustainable development. To this end, countries are encouraged to be fully compliant with the requirements of the OECD/G20 base erosion and profit shifting (BEPS) project and, in particular, the minimum standard on countering harmful tax practices, in order to reduce opportunities for tax avoidance and limit negative spillovers (ASEAN, 2016). In this regard, policymakers must be guided by the OECD checklist for Foreign Direct Investment Incentive Policies of 2003 (OECD, 2003), which postulates the following:

- Incentive should have a date of expiration, and signal all investors when the incentives are available or expires.
- Incentive regimes should be simple, easy to understand and apply for, and transparent as opposed to regimes which are often complex, requiring multiple interactions with different agencies.
- Incentives must include the totality of benefits, regulations and exemptions that favour economic activity. In addition, a pre-feasibility study for a specific project, land access or concessional finance secured through government guarantees should be included as part of the incentives where possible.
- Incentives must target new sectors and new activities where the risks of cost recovery are prohibitively high for investors instead of just benefiting established industries.
- The impact and performance of incentives must be monitored closely in order to ensure that vested interests are not entrenched to the detriment of developmental goals.

Engaging Anchor Investors and Other Stakeholders in the Design Phase
In order to guarantee the effectiveness of zone development, marketing, promotion and negotiation with potential anchor investors are crucial (Cheesman, 2012; Zeng, 2016, 2018; Cheesman, 2012; Farole, 2011). Through a stable revenue flow, and by signalling potential users that the SEZ is a serious investment destination, anchor investors can then defray zone development risk considerably (UNCTAD, 2019; Farole, 2011). For example, in Turkey, Cisco in the METU Technopark in Ankara, which initially focused on manufacturing-related goods and services and later moved into R&D, gave much traction to the zone (ASEAN, 2016).

Likewise, during the process of discovery, developers can engage with anchor investors, which will help tailor SEZ offerings to private sector needs (ASEAN, 2016). Moreover, to accommodate the needs of the users and adapt to market conditions, pilot SEZs should have flexible designs. Internationally, early investors have insisted on having a say in the legislative and institutional framework of SEZs at the design stage (Chen & de'Medici, 2009). Similarly, governments which also provide significant amount of resources have a say on the design and costs involved to ensure the expected social returns are possible from such major investors within the SEZs. Concurrently, the design of the zone should include an ecosystem of potential investors, civil society and government agencies as key stakeholders.

Clarification and Separation of Roles and Responsibilities of Institutions
This section discusses the importance of separating the roles and responsibilities in the SEZ programme to regulate potential conflict of interest and efficiency. As argued by UNCTAD (2019), ASEAN (2016) and Zeng (2015a, b), at a very basic minimum level, a SEZ programme should include the roles of the developer, zone owner, operator and regulator. Traditionally, one single agency used to take the responsibilities of developing zones, regulating and operating them (ASEAN, 2016). Nevertheless, from 2000, many governments have increased private sector involvement in zone development and operation to benefit from their expertise, and share the risks more efficiently although this has been problematic through impeding the licensing of competing private zones (ASEAN, 2016).

According to Farole and Kweka (2011), separating roles and responsibilities which must inform right institutional incentives in a typical zone programme may not only require separating the functions but also efficient monitoring and evaluation (see Table 4.2).

Synchronising Legislation with Institutions and Regulations
Governments may use a dedicated SEZ law which is accompanied by operating procedures and regulations for effective governance and implementation of the SEZ programme. This approach has been adopted by several governments as an alternative to amending existing frameworks because it ensures sustainable legal reforms, and makes bold statements of departure from the "business as usual" ones (UNCTAD, 2019; Chen & de'Medici, 2009).

SEZ regulations and associated laws operate at a high level and are edicts that give effect and weight to policy. Because operating procedures provides SEZ staff with clear interpretation and guidance on the application of policy and law, combined with relevant legal instruments such as the SEZ Act, they provide a solid foundation for the success of the SEZ programme (UNCTAD, 2019).

Table 4.2 Roles and responsibilities in a zone programme

Stakeholders	*Primary responsibilities*
Government	• Carry out strategic planning • Choose site(s) and establish land use guidelines/package land • Undertake initial feasibility studies • Choose and enter into agreement with developer for the development of the zone • Develop or establish offsite infrastructure • Capacity building, development of workforce and social services • Regulation and administration of the SEZ programme (see later)
Regulator	• *Designate SEZs:* Designate private and public land as zones and private or public zone operators and/or developers • *Expedite government services:* Facilitate registration, licensing and permits (building, environmental, work permits, etc.); regulate services within the zones such as utilities; provide for dispute resolution; set fees which are commensurate with the cost of service delivery • *Monitor compliance:* Monitor compliance with the SEZ legal framework, which includes SEZ policies, standards and requirements, and through appropriate penalties independent from other public agencies; enforce compliance
Developer	• *Land use planning:* Develop a final land use master plan and prepare the land (levelling, grading and other pre-construction activity) • *Provision of key infrastructure:* Drainage and sewerage, internal road networks and infrastructure for provision of utilities
Operator (Can be under a contractual agreement with the owner/ developer or may be the same as developer)	• *Facility leasing:* Manage lease and rental agreements with individual investors and take full responsibility for main services of the zone such as security and maintenance • *Transacting utilities:* Through own provision or via domestic providers, ensure provision of on-site utilities (gas, electricity, water, telecommunications) • *Provision of other value-added services:* These include a variety of services such as transport, medical and childcare, recruiting, business and training centres • *Marketing:* Evidence has shown that experienced private developers have a network of multinational clients across a variety of industries to which they can market new SEZ opportunities. However, marketing of the zone is complemented by SEZ authority/regulator and other parts of government such as an investment promotion agency
Zone users/ tenants	• Resident firms' key responsibility is to set up operations in the SEZ • Some zone users are large firms or "anchor tenants", which agree to operate in the zone and help attract other, smaller tenants, in exchange for concessions

Source: Farole and Kweka (2011)

Ensure Compliance of Infrastructure Investors in SEZs Domestic Regulations with Regional Trade Agreements

Provision of attractive infrastructure is required when developing SEZs. International experience has shown that, to attract an investor to fund infrastructure development, the investors, under regular corporate governance standards and in full compliance with the domestic regulations, must retain full control of the investment (UNCTAD, 2019; ASEAN, 2016). For publicly funded corporations, ASEAN (2016) argues that it may hold a specific mandate, within certain predefined limits and can be modified at regular intervals, but such decisions must be commercial in nature. If this is not done, as has been the case with many developing countries, either directly (through cheap land and/or incentives) or indirectly (by limiting competition, trade barriers or the creation of natural monopolies), governments may subsidise unproductive investments, as often is the case with industrial policy, leading to a net destruction of capital from the economy (UNCTAD, 2019). In order to avoid such destructive dynamics even when such funds are public, there is a need to ensure that zone development is seen as a commercial investment by instituting appropriate corporate governance, and ensuring that investor interests are represented (UNCTAD, 2019; Zeng, 2015a, b; Farole, 2011).

Ensure Measurable and Sustainable Monitoring and Evaluation of the Zone Programme

Absence of effective monitoring and evaluation has been cited as one of the major weaknesses of SEZ programmes (UNCTAD, 2019). Because M and E links results back to the overall strategy and objectives, they should be part of an essential decision making and sustainable zone governance. It is against this background that it should be clear as to how success will be measured and defined. For completeness' sake, the M and E process should include zone residents, auditors and the private sector (ASEAN, 2016).

The regulator should also set up a series of indicators to monitor the success of the project. From the onset, tools and methodologies as well as indicators which will be used to monitor progress must be put in place. The real monitoring must be regular, stringent and should match the political commitments. Since the investment zones offer incentives, performance and effectiveness of these incentives should be prioritised, and a carrot and stick approach should be enforced. Thus, it must be clear to all parties involved from the onset that any activity which fails to meet certain performance criteria will be stopped (World Bank, 2010). Similarly, a private developer who fails to attract a minimum number of zone residents must face consequences.

4.3 Conclusion

This chapter has drawn some experiences from Asian countries which are increasingly using SEZs such as industrial parks, EPZs, technology parks, eco-industrial parks and innovation districts as economic development strategies (UNCTAD, 2019; Zeng, 2016, 2018; ASEAN, 2016).

This discourse has also shown that SEZs were adopted by most AMS as a vehicle for attracting investors to increase export earnings and job creation (ASEAN, 2016). Like many countries, the SEZs in Asia have similar characteristics such as a geographically demarcated area, streamlined procedures including tax holidays, exemptions on customs duties and special customs, and special regulations (ASEAN, 2016). In addition, SEZs here enjoy adequate infrastructure, and duty-free capital access for capital goods, raw materials and efficient administrative services to attract investors (ASEAN, 2016). Therefore, SEZs have been effective in attracting investments and meeting macroeconomic goals.

Evidence has also shown that designing and implementing successful SEZ strategies and improving the operation of existing SEZs is extremely difficult (UNCTAD, 2019, Zeng, 2016, 2018; Farole, 2011) among others. Ironically, in order to attract and sustain investment; create jobs and generate spillover effects for the rest of the economy, literature has also demonstrated that a compelling master plan, favourable regulatory regime and excellent infrastructure are necessary but not sufficient for SEZs (Cheesman, 2012; Chen & de'Medici, 2009). In addition to this, successful SEZ programmes were also efficiently designed and managed in a flexible manner and were relevant to the different contexts in which they were used (ASEAN, 2016). Again, the literature has revealed that there is no clear-cut line for costs on infrastructure investment, linkages with local economies and forgone tax revenues against the benefits of the SEZs. To this end, SEZs can create distortions within the economies (ASEAN, 2016). Moreover, because it is difficult to separate the effects of SEZs from other economic forces, measuring the performance of the SEZs' policies is often difficult (ASEAN, 2016; Zeng, 2015; Farole, 2011).

Lastly, this has shown that in order to adequately address challenges faced in the design, implementation and review of the existing SEZs operation, strategy development, regulation, implementation and increased SEZ cooperation should be considered as key in fostering the success of SEZs.

References

Aggarwal, A. (2004). *Export Processing Zones in India: Analysis of the Export Performance* (Working Paper No. 148). Indian Council for Research on International Economic Relations (ICRIER).

ASEAN. (2016). *Guidelines for ASEAN Special Economic Zones Development and Collaboration*, Jakarta, Indonesia.

Brautigam, D., & Xiaoyang, T. (2011). African Shenzhen: China's Special Economic Zones in Africa. *Modern African Studies, 49*(1), 27–54.

Cheesman, A. (2012). *Special Economic Zones and Development: Geography and Linkages in the Indian EOU Scheme* (Working Paper No. 145). Development Planning Unit, The Bartlett, University College London.

Chen, X., & de'Medici, T. (2009). *The "Instant City" Coming of Age: China's Shenzhen Special Economic Zone in Thirty Years* (Working Paper No. 2). Centre for Urban and Global Studies at Trinity College.

Farole, T. (2011). *Special Economic Zones in Africa: Comparing Performance and Learning from Global Experience*. World Bank.

Farole, T., & Kweka, J. (2011). *Institutional Best Practices for Special Economic Zones: An Application to Tanzania* (World Bank Africa Trade Policy Notes No. 25). World Bank.

OECD. (2003). *Checklist for Foreign Direct Investment Incentives Policies.* Paris: OECD.

OECD. (2016). *Investment Policy Reviews, Philippines.*

Tao, Y., Yuan, Y., & Li, M. (2016). Chinese Special Economic Zones: Lessons for Africa. *Africa Economic Brief, 7*(6), 1–11.

UNCTAD. (2019). *World Investment Report: Special Economic Zones.* United Nations.

UNIDO. (2015). *Economic Zones in the ASEAN*. https://www.unido.org/fileadmin/user_media_upgrade/Resources/Publications/UCO_Viet_Nam_Study_FINAL.pdf

Warr, P., & Menon, J. (2015). *Cambodia's Special Economic Zones* (ADB Economics Working Paper Series). Asian Development Bank.

World Bank. (2010). *Chinese Investments in Special Economic Zones in Africa: Progress, Challenges, and Lessons Learned*. World Bank.

Zeng, D. Z. (2012a). *SEZs in Africa: Putting the Cart in Front of Horse?* World Bank.

Zeng, D. Z. (2012b). *An Overview of Six Economic Zones in Nigeria: Challenges and Opportunities* (World Bank Policy Note). World Bank.

Zeng, D. Z. (2015a). *Global Experiences with Special Economic Zones – With a Focus on China and Africa*. World Bank.

Zeng, D. Z. (2015b). *Global Experiences with Special Economic Zones: Focus on China and Africa* (World Bank Policy Research Working Paper 7240). World Bank.

Zeng, D. Z. (2016). Global Experiences of Special Economic Zones with Focus on China and Africa: Policy Insights. *Journal of International Commerce, Economics and Policy*, *7*(3), 1–27.

Zeng, D. Z. (2018). *Special Economic Zones: Lessons from the Global Experience*. World Bank.

CHAPTER 5

The Nexus Between Investment Policy Framework and Sustainable Development

5.1 Introduction

In order to foster effectiveness and sustainable impact of SEZs on national economies, UNCTAD (2015a, b) has argued that the national investment policy framework, which covers aspects of SEZs, must be anchored in sustainable development.

In this regard, this chapter discusses various approaches which national economies can adopt in line with the observations made by UNCTAD (2015a, b) and the OECD (2009). These include embedding investment policy in development strategy, defining the role of public, private, domestic and foreign direct investment; harnessing investment for productive capacity building and enhancing international competitiveness; and designing policies for responsible investment and sustainable development and national policy guidelines.

5.2 Embedding Investment Policy in Development Strategy

To strengthen international competitiveness and achieve economic and social objectives, studies have shown that many countries have developed explicit development strategies which integrate the investment policy (UNCTAD, 2015a, b; OECD, 2009). This is the case because investment

G. Mugano, *Special Economic Zones*,
https://doi.org/10.1007/978-3-030-82311-5_5

is a prerequisite to the build-up of productive capacity, an enabler of industrial development and upgrading as well as the key driver of economic growth (World Bank, 2009).

Defining the Role of Public, Private, Domestic and Foreign Direct Investment

The capacity to mobilise investment for sustainable development especially in least developed countries remains a major challenge (UNCTAD, 2015a, b). Foreign investment can provide a necessary complement to domestic investment given the often huge development financing gaps in these countries, and it can also be beneficial when it interacts in a synergistic way with all domestic investments (UNCTAD, 2015a, b). In most developing countries, infrastructure, agriculture and climate change–related investments hold significant potential for mutually beneficial interaction between public and private investment as well as domestic and foreign investment (UNCTAD, 2015a, b). Although experience has shown that high-quality regulatory and institutional settings are critical to ensure the development benefits of infrastructure, public–private partnerships (PPPs) have become important avenues for infrastructure development in many developing countries (UNCTAD, 2008).

Given the specific development contributions expected from private and public investments, domestic and foreign investments, policymakers should carefully consider the role of each player in the context of their development strategies (UNCTAD, 2015a, b). Specifically, because investment flows and willingness to open up sectors and industries to foreign investors vary among countries, governments must consider the needs and opportunities for foreign investment with a specific focus on direct investment in productive assets (UNCTAD, 2015a, b; OECD, 2015). However, for most developing countries, evidence suggests that there is convergence on the need to attract investments in infrastructure development, skills and education development, agricultural development and mining sectors (OECD, 2015).

In view of the different types of investments and their respective impacts, policymakers should be aware of these differences and the role of foreign investment (UNCTAD, 2015a, b). For example, greenfield investments have different impacts from investments that are driven by mergers and acquisitions (M and As). Further evidence reveals that greenfield investments have immediate and significant impact on job creation and productivity. On the other hand, while M and As may bring benefits such as access to international markets (or survival in case of troubled acquisition targets) and technology upgrading, such benefits may have negative effects on employment through restructuring, retrenchments and redundancies (UNCTAD, 2015a, b; OECD, 2015). Likewise, market-seeking investments will have different development impacts than efficiency-seeking investments, both of which have potential positive and negative contributions (UNCTAD, 2015a, b). It is also important to note that foreign investment comes in different financial guises. For example, FDI may not always translate into actual capital expenditures for the build-up of productive assets (e.g. retained earnings); nor do they always imply an influx of physical capital (e.g. reinvested earnings). Moreover, they can sometimes behave in a manner not different from portfolio investment (UNCTAD, 2015a, b).

In addition, the role of multinational firms and foreign investors in an economy is not limited to FDI. Both multinational firms and foreign investors can contribute to economic development through non-equity modes (NEMs) of international production. These may include services outsourcing, contract manufacturing, contract farming or other economic activities within global value chains, and licensing and franchising (UNCTAD, 2015a, b, UNCTAD, 2011a, b, c, 2013). Additionally, policies on investment, enterprise development and human resource development must be coordinated since such involvement is based on a contractual relationship between the foreign company and domestic business partners, and requires the host country to have enough qualified local entrepreneurs (UNCTAD, 2011a, b, c, 2013).

There is also the need for calibrated policies to stimulate job creation and to maximise the job content of investment. Thus, both quantitative and qualitative aspects have been used for defining the role of investment in economic growth and development strategies (ILO, 2012). This has therefore become an extremely urgent matter for policymakers following the global recession, slow economic growth, cumulative job losses and low job creation opportunities which led to a global employment deficit estimated at over 200 million workers (ILO, 2012).

Harnessing Investment for Productive Capacity Building and Enhancing International Competitiveness

In situations where investment is intended to play a central role in industrial upgrading and structural transformation in developing economies, the investment policy framework and its respective targets must take into account the potential contributions of foreign investment to reinforce local productive capacities (UNCTAD, 2015a, b). As noted by OECD (2015) and UNCTAD (2015a, b), the most crucial aspects which must be covered by the investment policy framework on productive capacity building should include technology and its technical know-how, human resources and skills development, enterprise development and infrastructure development.

Human Resources and Skills Development

Literature shows that human resources development is one of the key determinants of countries' economic growth and long-term economic prospects (UNCTAD, 2015a, b). Interestingly, trainable and productive labour at competitive costs and the availability of skilled workforce are major concerns for efficiency-seeking foreign investors (OECD, 2015; UNCTAD, 2015a, b). To this end, human resource development and education policy should be considered by policymakers as key elements to investment policy. In this regard, due care should be given to matching skills development and skills needs obtained through technical and vocational training. Thus, to enhance the capacity of local suppliers, policymakers use vocational training as an effective tool for preparing trainees for jobs involving practical or manual activities (UNCTAD, 2015a, b).

Admittedly, skills needs and job opportunities evolve as economies develop; hence making constant adaptations of education and human development policies becomes necessary (UNCTAD, 2015a, b). Job opportunities are essential as they ensure that the population gains access to decent job opportunities as well as gaining necessary skills from investors (UNCTAD, 2015a, b).

Evidence shows that both FDI and NEMs are sensitive to the availability of local skills, hence investment location decisions are frequently influenced by the availability of local skills (UNCTAD, 2015a, b; OECD, 2015). Where local skills are limited, foreign and national investors have resorted to using expatriate workers. International experience has also shown that due care is paid to promote employment of locals for national security and development. Nevertheless, where such locals lack skills, governments have deliberately designed policies that allow investors to bring foreign expatriates, who in turn can transfer their skills to the local staff (OECD, 2015). In this regard, governments must design immigration and labour policies which strike a balance between the need to recruit foreign skills and hiring of local employees in line with the skills gaps (UNCTAD, 2015a, b). Besides this, knowledge spillovers may also occur as a direct benefit from hiring foreign experts (UNCTAD, 2015a, b). In order to support and complement the national human resource development policy through education and hiring of expatriates as a coping mechanism during skills shortages, it is essential that maximum transparency and openness in granting work permits to skilled expatriates be observed (UNCTAD, 2015a, b).

Technology and Technical Know-How

Dissemination of technology should be at the heart of investment policy framework. Governments, for example, by bringing together technology firms, suppliers and research institutes, can promote technology clusters that promote R&D in a particular industry to help upgrade industrial activities (UNCTAD, 2015a, b). The involvement of domestic producers in GVCs, such as contract farmers, business processing operators and call centres, can be improved by disseminating and facilitating the acquisition of technology (UNCTAD, 2015a, b).

Likewise, policymakers must place emphasis on intellectual property rights in order to protect and encourage international investors in technologies. Policymakers must require such investors to disclose their technologies to licensing authorities, especially those working on peerless technologies such as software and pharmaceuticals. This is important because such technologies can significantly attract and sustain equity investments (joint ventures) or non-equity investments (licensing) (UNCTAD, 2015a, b). Most importantly, the level of a country's development and its technological capacities should be considered when deciding the level of protection (UNCTAD, 2015a, b). Arguably, businesses are more likely to invest resources in both R&D and technologies if their innovations are protected. This then subsumes that intellectual property rights may serve as the means of encouraging research activities undertaken by local companies (UNCTAD, 2015a, b).

Infrastructure

The development of key domestic infrastructure such as telecommunications, transport, energy and water are important enablers of investments. Technological skills and technical know-how may be required in infrastructure development, which local firms may lack, especially in areas such as energy, telecommunication and mining (UNCTAD, 2015a, b). Importantly, the demands for low carbon economy, which requires green technologies, may obviously need foreign investors' participation. However, many developing countries lack even water, electricity, transport and telecommunications infrastructure, which is essential for basic investments (UNCTAD, 2015a, b).

Conversely, with changes in regulatory attitudes and technological progress, some countries have succeeded in introducing private participation of domestic and foreign investors in traditional monopolies such as power generation and telecommunications (UNCTAD, 2015a, b). In view of the potential role of FDI in the development of high-quality infrastructure, UNCTAD (2015a, b) has argued that governments, using balanced public service provisions, affordability and accessibility, should consider the extent to which certain sectors could be opened up to (foreign) private investment. This way, using screening procedures and national security issues, liberalisation of critical infrastructure can be guided (UNCTAD, 2015a, b). Similarly, a clear vision is essential since economic growth and infrastructure development are also shaped by socio-economic realities as well as technical and business contexts (UNCTAD, 2015a, b).

Interestingly, international experience has shown that most developing countries have attempted to privatise public services but failed to achieve the desired outcomes (UNCTAD, 2011a, b, c). One major reason privatisation has failed is governments' lack of capacity to develop not only a comprehensive understanding of the complex technicalities involved in infrastructure development and their long-term cost implications, as well as quality, availability and affordability of services, but also poor assessment of the goals and their associated costs (UNCTAD, 2008). In this regard, as part of the infrastructure development and investment strategies, governments must develop a sound legal framework to guide management contracts, concessions and all forms of PPPs (UNCTAD, 2008).

Enterprise Development

A dynamic and robust domestic enterprise development is an important mechanism and a priori requirement for the transfers' development benefits of investments (UNCTAD, 2015a, b). Likewise, the presence of viable local enterprise is an important determinant for further investment, especially by foreign investors and for partnerships in NEMs. From a policy perspective, UNCTAD (2015a, b) has argued that governments must hatch a comprehensive entrepreneurship policy framework which can foster domestic entrepreneurial development. This must cover aspects such as access to finance, regulatory environment, education and training and technological development. Furthermore, in order to improve international competitiveness, absorb and adapt technology and technical know-how, governments must develop enterprise development policies aimed at enhancing the benefits from investments that focus on building capacity (UNCTAD, 2015a, b). Thus, governments should do so by cooperating with multinational firms.

In addition, the national investment policy framework must aim to promote linkages and spillover effects between domestic enterprises and foreign investments (UNCTAD, 2001). Besides the development of the national investment policy framework which considers linkages, there is the need for policy coordination that harnesses investment promotion among those industries that could have the biggest impact in terms of creating backward and forward linkages, as well as contributing to both direct and indirect employment creation (UNCTAD, 2001). Simultaneously, governments must also pay attention to the traditional risk of domestic enterprises such as SMEs being swallowed by foreign investments (UNCTAD, 2015a, b). To this end, using industrial policies, governments can limit foreign firms from accessing certain activities within the local economy to protect infant and sensitive industries (UNCTAD, 2013, 2015a, b).

According to UNCTAD (2015a, b), the interaction between investment policy and other elements within the economic development and growth strategies is usually complex. Such elements may include infrastructure, human resource development, technology and enterprise developments. As part of the balancing act to guarantee sustainability, governments must work coherently towards the common national objective of inclusive growth and sustainable development (UNCTAD, 2015a, b). This way, policy coordination at the design stage should involve relevant stakeholders such as the private sector, foreign investors and civil society.

5.3 Designing Policies for Responsible Investment and Sustainable Development

Since FDI comprises a package of assets such as long-term capital, technology, market access, skills and technical know-how, stimulating economic growth would require more than the flow of capital (UNCTAD, 1999). As such, by providing enough financial resources, generating employment, transferring skills and disseminating technology, strengthening export capacities, adding to GDP through investment and value added (directly and indirectly) and generating fiscal revenues, FDI can contribute to sustainable development (UNCTAD, 1994, 2002, 2015a, b). Furthermore, FDI can support industrial and agricultural diversification, enhance productive capacity and improve infrastructure development (UNCTAD, 2008, 2009). Importantly, by providing access to GVCs, FDI can contribute to local enterprise development through linkages with suppliers which is important for sustainable development. This is true because GVCs are mostly aligned with pro-poor dynamics such that marginalised communities and SMES can penetrate the global or regional value chains as suppliers or producers of goods and services (UNCTAD, 2001, 2013). However, evidence suggests that these positive developments do not always materialise automatically (UNCTAD, 2008, 2009, 2013, 2015a, b).

Coincidentally, in each of the impact areas listed earlier, the effect of FDI has also been negative (UNCTAD, 2015a, b). For instance, FDI has crowded out domestic investment and domestic enterprises, and also led to outflows of financial resources through repatriated earnings. These have increased imports more than exports or indeed yielded limited net export gains. For example, in the case of investment operations requiring intermediate inputs or market-seeking investments, FDI has sometimes reduced job opportunities by introducing more efficient work practices, restructuring and retrenchments. Moreover, the jobs created have sometimes been unstable due to the footloose nature of some investment types, and the skills transferred have also been limited to the nature of jobs created. Furthermore, technology dissemination has in many cases not taken place, or occurred but at a high cost (e.g. through licensing fees), hence slowing down local technological development. Finally, fiscal gains have been limited by tax exemption schemes and transfer pricing which are accorded to international investors (UNCTAD, 1994, 2000, 2002, 2011a, b, c).

The debates on the positive and negative contributions of FDI show evidence that there is need for an investment project which seeks to maximise the positives while minimising the negatives. To reap the development benefits from investment, UNCTAD (2015a, b) has argued for a two-pronged approach, that is (1) development of an enabling policy framework which combines elements of investment promotion and regulations that provides clear, unequivocal and transparent rules for the entry and operation of foreign investors and (2) development of adequate regulations aimed at minimising possible risks associated with investment.

Going by these discourses, it is evident that if a country is to address these impacts, specific regulations which cover a broad range of policy areas beyond investment policies such as taxation, trade, intellectual property, labour market regulation, social issues, environmental policies and access to land must be developed (UNCTAD, 2015a, b; OECD, 2015). The call to cover such different policy areas is based on the premise that the overall investment policy framework, which reinforces sustainable development, must foster consistency in policymaking across government (UNCTAD, 2015a, b).

Most importantly, a balance of regulation and promotion is required if sustainable development and inclusive growth are to be fostered through investment (UNCTAD, 2015a, b). Likewise, governments may also undertake direct assistance alongside tax incentives and marketing strategies, such as establishing new policy frameworks for a nascent renewable energy sector and so on, to attract low-carbon investment (UNCTAD, 2010). In addition, by building sound regulatory frameworks and facilitation of responsible investment in agriculture (including contract farming), governments may also encourage investment in sectors such as agriculture since evidence shows this sector is the main source of income for the poor in many developing countries (UNCTAD, 2009).

On the regulatory side, when deciding on the granting of investment incentives, sustainability should be a key consideration (UNCTAD, 2015a, b). In this regard, as argued by UNCTAD (2010 and 2015a, b), short-term benefits of an investment must be weighed against the potential long-term environmental effects. Likewise, balancing of the rights and obligations of agricultural investors alongside those of the locals must be considered whenever dealing with land issues (UNCTAD, 2015a, b). Equally, when infrastructural services are opened for private investment, there is a need to ensure that they are accessible and affordable to the people (UNCTAD, 2015a, b). Many developing countries find it difficult to strike a balance between the desire to strengthen social and environmental protection with maintenance of an attractive investment climate (UNCTAD, 2015a, b).

Accordingly, UNCTAD (2015a, b) has argued that investment policy framework should be anchored in sustainability, hence any investment contracts between the host country and investors should consider these facts. These kinds of contracts can help investors commit to social or environmental standards beyond the level established by the host country's general legislation as such legislation usually considers international laws.

Although laws and regulations are the basis of investor responsibility, voluntary corporate social responsibility (CSR) initiatives and standards, which have become mechanisms for influencing corporate practices and investment decisions, have proliferated in recent years (UNCTAD, 2011a, b, c). In order to maximise the development benefits of investment, governments can build on them to complement the regulatory framework (UNCTAD, 2011a, b, c).

Management of CSRs and their policy implications is a challenge for many developing countries because CSR initiatives are voluntary and a relatively new area, but one that is developing and evolving quickly (UNCTAD, 2015a, b). Specifically, the potential interactions between hard law and soft law can be complex and, in a number of cases, because of lack of monitoring capacity and limited comparability, the value of standards is difficult to extract (UNCTAD, 2015a, b). However, through recognising the benefits of CSR initiatives and voluntary dissemination of standards, CSRs have helped promote responsible business behaviour such as accountability, transparency and investment, which have in turn promoted low-carbon and environmentally sound investment among others (UNCTAD, 2015a, b).

Some studies have also shown that reporting by private investors on their social and environmental performance and impact measurement may promote CSRs and mobilise resources, and re-channel them towards other investments (UNCTAD, 2015a, b; OECD, 2015). Likewise, publicising CSR functions may also help policymakers monitor the effectiveness of incentive structures and policies while also acting as a beacon for resource mobilisation to be invested in priority sectors (UNCTAD, 2015a, b).

Because of the importance of sustainability reporting, the United Nations High-Level Panel of Eminent Persons on the Post-2015 Development Agenda proposed that

> *at latest by 2030 – all large businesses should be reporting on their environmental and social impact – or explain why if they are not doing so.* (UNCTAD, 2013)

In line with this directive, the European Parliament adopted a directive in 2014 which compels large public-interest companies (500+ employees) to disclose environmental and social information (UNCTAD, 2015a, b). Individual UN member states around the world have also taken steps to promote sustainability reporting. For example, India's 100 largest listed companies are required to report on environmental and social impacts (UNCTAD, 2015a, b). Elsewhere, apart from regulatory initiatives, some stock exchanges such as the Johannesburg Stock Exchange and BM & FBOVESPA in Brazil have implemented mandatory listing requirements in the area of sustainability reporting, and have actively promoted voluntary mechanisms such as reporting standards and indices to incentivise corporate sustainability reporting (UNCTAD, 2015a, b).

Given the importance that has been attached to sustainable development debates, from 2013, many countries began promoting reporting practices, standards and frameworks which have then influenced the approach to the preparation of sustainability reports. Recent examples of such initiatives have included the Carbon Disclosure Project (CDP), the International Integrated Reporting Council (IIRC), Global Reporting Initiative (GRI), the Accounting for Sustainability (A4S) and the Sustainability Accounting Standards Board (SASB) (UNCTAD, 2015a, b; KPMG, 2013).

5.4 Implementation and Institutional Mechanisms for Policy Effectiveness

Important for any policy effectiveness is the need for investment policy to be adequately enforced by impartial, competent and efficient public institutions (UNCTAD, 2015a, b). Integral to investment strategies are policies aimed at addressing implementation issues. These policies must endeavour to both achieve integrity across government and regulatory institutions and, wherever possible, be service-orientated (UNCTAD, 2015a, b). Regulatory agencies should be free from political pressure subject to accountability and transparency to elected officials or representatives (UNCTAD, 2015a, b, 2019). These principles are mainly relevant for investors in institutions which involve sector regulators (e.g. transport, electricity, telecommunications, banking), courts and judiciary systems, investment promotion agencies, tax administration or revenue authorities, and licensing bodies (OECD, 2015; UNCTAD, 2015a, b; World Bank, 2009).

According to UNCTAD (2015a, b), the effectiveness of investment policy must be based on a set of explicitly formulated policy objectives which have clear priorities, a time frame and key measures to support the objectives. Thus, the principal yardstick for measuring policy effectiveness will be the objectives.

To this end, the UNCTAD's Investment Contribution Index for the measurement of policy effectiveness contends that policymakers should use a focused set of key indicators that are the most direct expression of the core development contributions of private investments such as capital formation and export generation, direct contributions to GDP growth through value addition, entrepreneurial development and development of the formal sector and tax base, job creation and social, environmental and development sustainability aspects (UNCTAD, 2015a, b) (see Table 5.1).

Table 5.1 Possible indicators for the definition of investment impact objectives and the measurement of policy effectiveness

Area	*Indicators*	*Detail and examples*
Economic value added	1. Total value added	• Gross output (GDP contribution) of the new/additional economic activity resulting from the investment (direct and induced)
	2. Value of capital formation	• Contribution to gross fixed capital formation
	3. Total and net export generation	• Total export generation; net export generation (net of imports) is also captured by the value added indicator
	4. Number of formal business entities	• Number of businesses in the value chain supported by the investment; this is a proxy for entrepreneurial development and expansion of the formal (tax-paying) economy
	5. Total fiscal revenues	• Total fiscal revenue taken from the economic activity resulting from the investment, through all forms of taxation
Job creation	6. Employment (number)	• Total number of jobs generated by the investment, both direct and indirect (value chain view), dependent and self-employed
	7. Wages	• Total household income generated, direct and indirect
	8. Typologies of employee skills levels	• Number of jobs generated, by ILO job type, as a proxy for job quality and technology levels (including technology dissemination)
Sustainable development	9. Labour impact indicators	• Employment of women (and comparable pay) and of disadvantaged groups • Skills upgrading, training provided • Health and safety effects, occupational injuries
	10. Social impact indicators	• Number of families lifted out of poverty, wages above subsistence level • Expansion of goods and services offered, access to and affordability of basic goods and services
	11. Environmental impact indicators	• Greenhouse gas emissions, carbon offset/credits, carbon credit revenues • Energy and water consumption/efficiency hazardous materials • Enterprise development in eco-sectors
	12. Development impact indicators	• Development of local resources • Technology dissemination

Source: UNCTAD (2011)

5.5 National Policy Guidelines

Best practices, as noted by UNCTAD (2015a, b), have shown that the national investment policy guidelines are organised into four sections: (i) the strategic level which aims to ensure integration of overall development strategy and the investment policy; (ii) the investment policy; (iii) investment-related policy areas such as taxation, labour, trade, environmental regulations and intellectual property policies; and (iv) investment policy effectiveness (Table 5.2).

It is important to note that the national policy framework guidelines are meant to establish a generally applicable setting for investment-related policymaking, and cannot provide a "one-size-fits-all" solution for all economies (UNCTAD, 2015a, b). This is particularly so because countries have different development strategies. Hence, any policy guide must take into account these diversities. To this end, policymakers may have different perceptions about what role foreign investors should play in their contexts, and which industries to promote and in what manner (UNCTAD, 2015a, b).

In addition, cultural, social, geographical and historical differences may also play important roles in shaping the national investment policy guideline. More so, policymakers must take into account their specific investment climate and the country's strengths and weaknesses, and build their policies based on the existing realities while reducing perceived

Table 5.2 Structure of national policy guidelines

Investment and sustainable development strategy	• Integrating investment policy in sustainable development strategy • Maximizing the contribution of investment to productive capacity building and international competitiveness
Investment regulation and promotion	Designing investment-specific policies regarding: • Establishment and operations • Treatment and protection of investments Investor responsibilities • Investment promotion and facilitation
Investment related policy areas	• Ensuring coherence with other policy areas, including: trade, taxation, intellectual property, competition, labour market regulation, access to land, corporate responsibility and governance, environmental protection, infrastructure and PPPs
Investment policy effectiveness	• Building effective public institutions to implement investment policy • Measuring investment policy effectiveness and feeding back lessons learned into new rounds of policymaking

Source: UNCTAD (2015)

deficiencies (UNCTAD, 2015a, b). Accordingly, investment policies must be designed based on sector investment priorities, specific economic contexts and development issues faced by individual countries (UNCTAD, 2015a, b).

5.6 Conclusion

This chapter has discussed various policy approaches and strategies which must be undertaken by policymakers to foster effectiveness and sustainable impact of SEZs on national economies.

In line with the observations of UNCTAD (2015a, b) and OECD (2015), this chapter has also discussed various approaches which national economies can adopt when designing policies for responsible investment and sustainable development. These have included embedding investment policy in development strategy, defining the role of public, private, domestic and foreign direct investment, harnessing investment for productive capacity building and enhancing international competitiveness. In addition, the need to design policies which nurture responsible investment and sustainable development has been treated. From a development perspective, because FDI comprises a package of assets that includes long-term capital, technology, market access, skills and technical know-how, stimulating the economy may require more than a flow of capital (UNCTAD, 1999). Thus, provision of financial resources, generating employment, transferring skills and disseminating technology, among many other factors, may help FDI contribute towards sustainable development (UNCTAD, 2002, 2015a, b).

Furthermore, FDI can support industrial and agricultural diversification as well as enhance productive capacity and infrastructure development (UNCTAD, 2009). By providing access to GVCs, FDI can also contribute to local enterprise development through linkages with suppliers, which is important for sustainable development. This is the case because GVCs are usually pro-poor dynamic so that they can help the marginalised communities and small suppliers penetrate the global or regional markets through provision of raw materials, goods and services (UNCTAD, 2001, 2013).

This chapter also noted that FDI can have both negative and positive consequences (UNCTAD, 2015a, b). For instance, FDI can crowd out domestic investments and lead to outflows of financial resources in the form of repatriated earnings. FDI can also increase imports more than exports in case of investments requiring intermediate inputs or for market-seeking investments which may end up reducing job opportunities as they tend to adopt efficient work practices, restructurings and retrenchments. Similarly, the jobs created may be transient due to the footloose nature of some investment types and the skills transferred may also be limited. Importantly, technology dissemination might fail, or only happen at a high cost, hence slowing local technological developments. Finally, the fiscal gains may equally be limited by tax exemption schemes given to international investors (see UNCTAD, 1994, 2000, 2002, 2011a, b, c).

On the regulatory side, when granting investment incentives, sustainability should be a key consideration (UNCTAD, 2015a, b). Thus UNCTAD (2010 and 2015a, b) observes that short-term benefits of an investment must be weighed against the potential long-term environmental effects. For example, balancing the rights and obligations of agricultural investors must be considered alongside those of the communities whenever dealing with issues of access to land (UNCTAD, 2015a, b). Similarly, when services are opened for private investment, accessibility and affordability issues should be prioritised (UNCTAD, 2015a, b). This chapter has also shown that many developing countries fail to balance between the desire to strengthen social and environmental protection and maintaining an attractive investment climate (UNCTAD, 2015a, b).

The chapter further argued that the investment policy framework should be anchored in sustainability; hence investment contracts between the host country and individual investors should consider this fact. These kinds of contracts should be aligned with international standards and practices as they will help investors commit to social or environmental standards established by the host country's general legislation.

With respect to the need for effective implementation of policy, this chapter has argued that there is a need for investment policy and regulations to be adequately enforced by impartial, competent and efficient public institutions (UNCTAD, 2015a, b). Moreover, investment strategy must aim to address implementation issues, hence must help achieve integrity across regulatory institutions (UNCTAD, 2015a, b). Regulatory agencies should therefore be adequately free and independent of political interests and seek to be accountable and transparent to all stakeholders (UNCTAD, 2015a, b, 2019). These principles are relevant for investors who may be interested in sector regulators (e.g. transport, electricity, telecommunications, banking), courts and judiciary systems, investment promotion agencies, tax administration or revenue authorities, and licensing bodies (OECD, 2015; UNCTAD, 2015a, b; World Bank, 2009).

On national policy guidelines, as noted by UNCTAD (2015a, b), this chapter has revealed that the national investment policy guidelines are organised into four sections, which include (i) the strategic level which aims to ensure integration of overall development strategy and the investment policy; (ii) the investment policy; (iii) investment-related policy areas such as taxation, labour, trade, environmental regulations and intellectual property rights; and (iv) investment policy effectiveness.

References

ILO. (2012). *Global Employment Trends 2012*. Available on www.ilo.org

KPMG. (2013). *Survey of Corporate Responsibility Reporting*. UK, KPMG.

OECD. (2009). *Private Sector Participation in Infrastructure*. OECD.

OECD. (2015). *Policy Framework for Investment (PFI), and Instruments Developed by Various Regional Organizations and NGOs*. OECD.

UNCTAD. (1994). *World Investment Report*. United Nations.

UNCTAD. (1999). *World Investment Report*. United Nations.

UNCTAD. (2000). *World Investment Report*. United Nations.

UNCTAD. (2001). *World Investment Report*. United Nations.

UNCTAD. (2002). *World Investment Report*. United Nations.

UNCTAD. (2008). *World Investment Report*. United Nations.

UNCTAD. (2009). *World Investment Report*. United Nations.

UNCTAD. (2010). *World Investment Report*. United Nations.

UNCTAD. (2011a). *Promoting Investment for Development: Best Practices in Strengthening Investment in Basic Infrastructure in Developing Countries*. Investment, Enterprise and Development Commission, UNCTAD, TD/B/C. II/14. www.unctad.org

UNCTAD. (2011b). *Indicators for Measuring and Maximizing Economic Value Added and Job Creation Arising from Private Sector Investment in Value Chains*. United Nations.

UNCTAD. (2011c). *World Investment Report*. United Nations.

UNCTAD. (2013). *World Investment Report*. United Nations.

UNCTAD. (2015a). *Investment Framework for Sustainable Development*. United Nations.

UNCTAD. (2015b). Recent Trends in IIAs and ISDS. *IIA Issues Note No. 1*.

UNCTAD. (2019). *World Investment Report: Special Economic Zones*. Geneva, Switzerland: UNCTAD.

World Bank. (2009). *Public-Private Partnerships: Reference Guide*. World Bank.

PART III

Impacts of Special Economic Zones

CHAPTER 6

The Impact of Special Economic Zones

6.1 Introduction

Countries have embraced SEZs on the basis that they bring both direct and indirect economic benefits including job creation, investment attraction, export growth, diversification and economic growth. Ironically, if not properly managed, the economic costs associated with the establishment of the SEZs alongside social costs may outweigh the intended benefits of SEZs.

In order to unpack the impact of SEZs, this chapter discusses the conceptual framework of the sustainable development impact of SEZs; direct and indirect economic contributions of SEZs; the nexus between SEZ costs and revenues; the dynamic contribution of SEZs, and their social and environmental impacts.

6.2 Conceptual Framework of a Sustainable Development Impact Assessment of Special Economic Zones

The performance of SEZs, as noted by the UNCTAD (2019), can be assessed through reviewing the "profit and loss statement of the SEZs" which evaluate their contribution to FDI attraction, export growth and diversification, job creation, income generation and improvement in foreign exchange earnings (see Table 6.1).

G. Mugano, *Special Economic Zones*,
https://doi.org/10.1007/978-3-030-82311-5_6

Table 6.1 Profit and loss statement of Special Economic Zones

Cost Benefit Areas	Key Elements
Direct economic contributions	• Attraction of FDI • Job creation • Export growth • Foreign exchange earnings • Supplier linkages beyond the zones • Indirect and induced job creation
+	
Indirect contributions	• Supplier linkages beyond the zones • Indirect and induced job creation
=	
Combined economic impact	• Additional GDP growth
+/-	
Net cost of/revenue from zones	• Investment expenditures • Operating costs • Foregone revenues and subsidies • Income from zones
Fiscal/ financial viability of zones	• Payback time of zone investment • Fiscal burden
+	
Dynamic economic contributions	• Technology dissemination • Skills and know-how transfers • Industrial diversification and upgrading • Enhanced regional economic cooperation
+/-	
Social and environmental impacts and externalities	• Labour conditions • Environmental impact • Appropriation or misuse of land • Illicit flows
+/-	
Policy learning and broader reform impact	• Pilot function of zones • Catalyst function for reforms • Reduced motivation to reform
=	
Overall sustainable development impact	• Evolution of the role of zones in the economy • Long-term zone transformations

Source: UNCTAD (2019)

Although indirect economic benefits are more difficult to measure, they are an essential component of the sustainable development impact of zones beyond their confines. Key elements covered under the indirect economic benefits include supplier linkages beyond the zones, and the indirect employment they create, as well as induced income and jobs resulting from zone-based wages being spent in the surrounding economy (UNCTAD, 2019; Cheng, 2019).

Eventually, the combination of direct and indirect economic contributions should result in higher economic growth (Cheng, 2019). The establishment and early development of zones provide a temporary boost to

GDP growth. Yet given the benefits and incentives provided to investors in SEZs, they should also provide a sustained stimulus to growth. In other words, the growth of economic activity in the zones should outpace overall economic growth after the zone's early development phase (UNCTAD, 2019; Zeng, 2016; World Bank, 2010).

UNCTAD (2019), Farole (2011) and World Bank (2010) have argued that in order to measure the impact of SEZs, their economic benefits, efficiency and effectiveness should be weighed against the costs of the zones. Zone development also entails financial costs and capital expenditures, including infrastructure development outlays; the costs of operating the zone authority and other operating expenses, and revenues foregone through exemptions on import duties and taxes (UNCTAD, 2019). Some of these costs, however, may increase when existing domestic businesses relocate from the national customs territory to the zone or when they obtain free-point status.

The investment and operating costs of the zones can be recovered through rentals and service charges. Evidence from UNCTAD (2019) and Cheng (2019) has shown that public expenditures on SEZs tend to be the highest where governments develop and manage zones, especially if they provide subsidies. From a theoretical perspective, the combined economic impact of SEZs measured against their development and running costs provides a picture of their fiscal sustainability, including the payback period of initial capital outlays and the burden (or benefit) that zones might generate for the public budget in the long run (UNCTAD, 2019; Zeng, 2016; Aggarwal, 2004).

In addition to the economic benchmarks, the dynamic economic effects, as well as social and environmental factors, play a key role in determining SEZs' overall sustainable development impact (UNCTAD, 2019; Cheng, 2019; Tao et al., 2016; Zeng, 2010). The dynamic effects of SEZs, especially their impact on technology and skills development and spillover effects on the broader economy, are important to industrial development and upgrading. In addition, regional economic cooperation such as cross-border or international cooperation zones is another dynamic benefit of zones that can be important in the context of the development of regional value chains (Zeng, 2015a, b; FIAS, 2008). Furthermore, UNCTAD (2019) has argued that many countries have raised concerns about the zones' dependence on low-skill, low-technology, assembly-type operations and the concentration of their activities in one sector. However, there are examples of zones that have promoted industrial upgrading and economic diversification.

The ILO (2017) has equally argued that SEZs have long been criticised for negative social and environmental impacts. For example, poor treatment of women, labour standards, bad working conditions in the zones, and pollution and misuse of land have been noted as areas of concern. Other concerns have included suppression of core labour rights (e.g. collective bargaining); poor employment conditions (e.g. working long hours, health and safety standards); lack of training or skill upgrading; use of trainees to lower wage costs, and exploitation of women (e.g. lower wage levels, lack of childcare holidays, inadequate rights during pregnancy) and so forth (ILO, 2017).

Finally, social and environmental impacts of SEZs are the potential areas for zones that may support broad-based reforms. On the one hand, as enclaves of differential regulation, zones can reduce the pressure on governments to pursue difficult nationwide structural reforms (UNCTAD, 2019). As noted in the early stages of reforms in China, zones can serve as regulatory laboratories by allowing countries to test different policies with successful experiments serving as a catalyst for countrywide policies (UNCTAD, 2019; Zeng, 2012a, b).

The fiscal and financial viability of SEZs and their overall sustainable development impact are both equally important. Whilst governments may well accept bearing the fiscal burden of zones for some time in order to support industrial development objectives and to spur broader business reforms, they cannot endlessly cover the costs of zones that do not pay for themselves through direct and indirect economic contributions that lead to higher fiscal revenues (UNCTAD, 2019; Cheng, 2019; FIAS, 2008). In this regard, zones that are not run on a cost-recovery basis or that entail significant subsidies are at higher risk of becoming financially unviable (UNCTAD, 2019).

Ultimately, a positive overall sustainable development impact contributes to gradual industrial transformation. This implies that the role of SEZs needs to evolve over time. In addition, the economic activities within zones should change, alongside the emphasis governments place on different parts of the cost–benefit analysis.

6.3 Direct and Indirect Economic Contributions of Special Economic Zones

Investment attraction, export growth and job creation are some of the direct economic contributions of SEZs. However, zones are neither a precondition nor a guarantee for above-average performance on FDI and GVC participation (UNCTAD, 2019). The overall impact on economic growth tends to be temporary, and, after a build-up period, most zones grow at the same rate as the national economies.

Investment Attraction

Evidence shows that through adequate infrastructure and best practices, zones may compensate for an adverse investment climate, and thus zones are a key investment promotion as they can help attract FDI (UNCTAD, 2019; Cheng, 2019; Tao et al., 2016; Zeng, 2010, 2018). Sadly, the impact of zones on FDI—especially on additional FDI that would not have otherwise been attracted—is hard to measure because data are scarce. Countries and international statistics (including UNCTAD's FDI data) do not track investment in zones separately from investment outside the zones, and SEZs themselves mostly do not register foreign investment flows separately.

Research on China, however, has shown that SEZs can have a strong positive effect on FDI, including on new greenfield investments (Zeng, 2012a, 2015a, b, 2018; Tao et al., 2016; UNDP, 2015). Importantly, SEZs do not seem to crowd out domestic investment (World Bank, 2017). Some studies in Philippines has also showed that the share of FDI flows going to SEZs increased from 30% in 1997 to over 81% in 2000 (UNCTAD, 2002). Limited data available for current zone programmes demonstrate that SEZs are an important destination for FDI in many countries. In China, SEZs account for over 80% of cumulative FDI. In Malaysia, almost 90% of total investment found in SEZs originates from foreign investors (UNCTAD, 2002). In Vietnam, between 60% and 70% of all FDI is located in SEZs (UNCTAD, 2002). In Myanmar, conversely, 80% of investors in the Thilawa SEZ are foreign-owned while 15% are joint ventures with foreign firms (UNCTAD, 2002). In the other low-income countries such as Cambodia and the Lao People's Democratic Republic, zones also exclusively attract foreign investment, and do account for a significant share of total FDI (UNCTAD, 2013). Similarly, in Bangladesh, foreign investors represent 72% of zone tenants in eight publicly owned zones. In some countries, zones either have failed to attract significant investment or have attracted primarily domestic investors rather than FDI. In Colombia, for example, the free-point scheme has resulted in many domestic SMEs obtaining FZ status.

Export Generation and Diversification

Another primary goal of SEZs is to develop exports focusing not only on export growth but also on diversification. The export diversification is particularly important for developing countries that rely on the export of commodities and aim to add value to these exports.

In many countries, zone programmes account for a major share of exports such as manufactured exports. In Latin America and the Caribbean, SEZs contribute more than 50% of total exports in Costa Rica, the Dominican Republic and Nicaragua; 31% in Mexico; and 13% in Colombia (UNCTAD, 2019) (see Box 6.1). In Asia, SEZs are credited with more than 60% of the Philippines' exports, and close to 10% of India's (UNCTAD, 2019). In Bangladesh, just eight publicly owned zones account for about 20% of the country's exports of goods (UNCTAD, 2019).

Box 6.1 Impacts of Special Economic Zones

Boosting Investment, Exports and Jobs

Although there is little systematic research on the impact of SEZs, evidence shows that the effectiveness of SEZs on investment, exports and jobs has been mixed. Case studies show that the impact of SEZs on FDI attraction, export performance and job creation is positive. For example, in China, as noted by the World Bank (2017), while not crowding out domestic investment, SEZs account for over 80% of cumulative FDI, and are found to have a particularly strong effect on greenfield investments. Similarly, in Costa Rica, through the use of SEZs, the country diversified its production from garments to electronic components which resulted in the contribution of SEZs in manufacturing exports to increase from 10% in 1990 to 55% in 2003 (Gereffi et al., 2019). Job creation averaged 7% per year since 2013 in the US FTZ programme compared to 2% for the wider economy. When juxtaposing the construction and running costs, evidence also shows that benefits of zones especially boosting FDI, jobs and exports outweighs the establishment and running costs (Mongé-Gonzalez et al., 2005; Jayanthakumaran, 2003).

At the same time, anecdotal evidence shows that zones that did not attract the expected influx of investors, or while delivering limited employment and exports gains, has resulted in some investors

(*continued*)

Box 6.1 (continued)

profiting from generous fiscal incentives (Farole & Akinci, 2011). In some countries, as noted by the OECD (2018), decentralised policymaking for developing zones has led to excessive competition between provinces, and a misuse of resources and land, especially in instances where zones are only partially occupied. Moreover, in a number of cases, SEZs have been criticised for negative social and environmental impacts, which include low environmental, health and safety standards and exploitation of workers (ILO, 2017). In Sub-Saharan Africa, SEZ programmes have been largely unsuccessful mainly due to lack of effective strategic planning, weak regulatory and institutional frameworks, insufficient governance and implementation capacity, and inadequate infrastructure (Zeng, 2015a, b). International experience has also shown that before SEZs yield the desired impacts, they require many years of nurturing with consistent support from the government (OECD, 2018).

Experimenting with Policy Reform

In the process of economic liberalisation and reforms, SEZs can play a catalytic role. The enclave nature of SEZs can be an asset wherein governance is relatively weak or economic reforms are politically sensitive to implement (OECD, 2020). China, for example, effectively used its numerous SEZs as a testing lab for the market economy. In this regard, the government of China, since the 1980s, before gradually introducing them to the wider economy, experimented with liberal economic reforms and new institutions in Shenzhen and other coastal SEZs. Recently, in 2013, Shanghai tested the more liberal negative list approach for foreign investment (that restricts access only in explicitly listed industries) by establishing an FTZ and, after its success, it was extended to other pilot zones in 2015, and ultimately adopted as national policy in 2018 (UNCTAD, 2019). Likewise, in Mauritius, the success of the EPZ was mainly due to its role in economic and political reform processes that it catalysed, and the ensuing structural transformation of the economy as opposed to its impact on job creation, investment or exports (Farole & Akinci, 2011).

(continued)

Box 6.1 (continued)

Moreover, SEZs can be used as effective pilot schemes for testing policies to boost the investment climate. For example, these pilots can be applied in the area of one-stop services, environmental impact assessment, supplier development initiatives and business matchmaking programmes (OECD, 2014). However, it is important to consider the framework conditions that allowed SEZs to serve a catalytic role in the policy reform process. For instance, as noted by Cheesman (2012), Shenzhen was only part of the country's overall economic reform landscape. The OECD (2020) further argued that what worked for China over this period will not necessarily work in other contexts. However, there is convergence of thoughts around the need to build local capabilities (both in public and private sectors) if SEZs are to impact the wider economy (OECD, 2020; UNCTAD, 2019; World Bank, 2017).

Source: OECD (2020)

In West Asia and North Africa, a number of countries have relied on oil and gas exports. Conversely, in Morocco SEZs have accounted for approximately 60% of net non-oil exports while in Egypt they have accounted for 25% and 40% in the United Arab Emirates (UNCTAD, 2019). Even in Sub-Saharan Africa, where the proportion of manufactured goods tends to be low, zones have accounted for nearly 10% of exports in Kenya and Ghana (UNCTAD, 2019).

Some African governments have also used SEZs as part of export promotion strategies, backed by trade preferences. EPZs have also become the epicentres for Kenya's export strategy. These have been enabled by the AGOA, which sought to attract foreign investors in the apparel industry, urging them to target exports to the United States (UNCTAD, 2019; Zeng, 2015a, b) (see Box 6.2).

Strategically, focusing SEZs on specific trade preferences does carry risks. Changes in trade preferences may require strategic refocusing of zone specialisation, as was the case with the Dominican Republic after the end of the Multi-fibre Arrangement (see Box 6.3).

SEZ programmes have been a key component of export diversification efforts in many countries. For example, countries in Central America and

Box 6.2 Special Economic Zones and Trade Preferences: Kenya's EPZ and AGOA

Kenya actively pursues a strategy based on AGOAs, which provide duty-free market access to the United States for qualifying countries in Sub-Saharan Africa. Since the AGOA was enacted in 2000, Kenya has increased the value of its exports to the United States from US$110 million to $550 million in 2016. Kenya was one of the first countries to establish SEZs. By the time the AGOA came into force, zones already had a well-functioning manufacturing ecosystem, including adequate infrastructure. EPZs were given a pivotal role in the AGOA-based strategy by targeting foreign investors in the apparel industry seeking to export to the United States. Kenya currently has 71 EPZs (including 10 single-firm zones). They account for over 55,000 jobs, an annual sales turnover of about $650 million and more than 90% through exports (compared with national exports of approximately $6 billion). In 2017, EPZs accounted for 94% of the $340 million in apparel exports from Kenya to the United States. EPZs have made Kenya the biggest exporter of apparel and textiles to the United States, with an estimated $4.3 billion worth of garments exported duty-free since 2000. Most of the apparel firms in EPZs are foreign-owned, and foreign companies have invested an estimated $460 million since 2017. The deliberate targeting of FDI in the apparel industry has generated not only large-scale employment, but also integration in manufacturing GVCs and utilisation of local textiles and raw materials. Moreover, using the industrial capacities developed, apparel firms in Kenya's EPZs have now started to diversify their markets, and are increasing exports to other developed economies, such as the EU and Canada. In recent years, as part of broader economic planning, Kenya has issued a five-year National AGOA Strategy and Action Plan, which prominently features the role of SEZs. It also announced the intention to increase the value of total exports of SEZs in non-apparel industries to the United States. The targeted products will include processed food, coffee, tea, fresh fruit and cut flowers.

Source: UNCTAD (2019)

Box 6.3 Refocusing and Turning Around Special Economic Zones: Evidence from the Dominican Republic

The Dominican Republic is one of the world's pioneers in SEZs. The programme is widely considered a success, attracting FDI and fuelling sustained economic growth in the 1990s. At its peak in 2003, SEZ companies accounted for 7.5% of GDP in the country. The key factors driving this performance included the country's proximity to the US consumer market, preferential trade agreements, incentives granted to SEZs and the availability of low-cost labour.

At the turn of the century, however, the country faced several external shocks such as a global economic meltdown and a rise in oil prices; the end of the Multi-fibre Arrangement in 2005 and China's accession to the WTO in 2001. This meant that the number of companies exporting from SEZs fell, and the programme stagnated until 2010 (Burgaud & Farole, 2011).

In this context, local SEZ investors pushed at the national and regional (Caribbean) levels towards expanded market access in the United States. Through the leadership of the SEZs' official trade association (the Asociacion Dominicana de Zonas Francais, ADOZONA) and the SEZ regulating body, the National Free Zones Council, they lobbied successfully for the Dominican Republic's accession to the Central America Free Trade Agreement (2007) and to the Economic Partnership Agreement between the Caribbean and the EU (2008).

In collaboration with workforce development agencies, human resource development was encouraged so as to support the upgrading of the country's production. While foreign manufacturers in the textiles industry relocated to lower-cost economies, local firms invested in new technology (new types of fibres) and human capital to be able to integrate vertically and stay competitive with low-cost producers.

Local investors also developed inter-industry linkages and diversified production. Some shifted production from apparel to footwear, others opened call centres and pursued joint ventures with Indian IT

(*continued*)

Box 6.3 (continued)

companies (Schrank, 2008), while others opened factories and SEZs in neighbouring Haiti. As part of this private engagement, the National Free Zones Council and ADOZONA increased their efforts to attract new investors from emerging industries, including services (call centres and business process outsourcing), surgical equipment, pharmaceuticals, jewellery and electrical appliances.

Since 2010, SEZ exports, output and employees have rebounded and are continuing to grow, although not yet to the levels of the early 2000s in terms of relative contribution to GDP. Their contribution to total exports and GDP has stabilised at 55% for exports and 3.2% for GDP—lower than the past levels of 85% and 8%, respectively—indicating that the non-SEZ economy is also growing.

The number of industrial parks has grown by a third since 2012, standing at 72 zones today. Production in SEZs has also grown more diversified, with exports of medical and pharmaceutical products representing over a quarter of total exports; and electrical and electronics products representing about the same share (16%) as the traditional garment and textile industry in 2018. The United States also still represents the biggest market, with the majority of companies exporting there (58%), even though that share has declined since 2000 (from 86%).

In 2017, SEZs provided about 166,000 direct jobs and an estimated 250,000 indirect ones, the majority of which were still low-skilled workers (blue collar, 71%), even though the share of technical workers has steadily grown since 2012 (ASEAN, 2017). A growing number of SEZs are entering into collaboration agreements with local universities. Training through a programme, offered by the National Institute of Technical-Vocational Training and ADOZONA, enables reaching increasing shares of SEZ workers. In 2018, the Ministry of Education signed an agreement with ADOZONA and the National Council for Export Free Zones (CNZFE) to improve the quality of tertiary education, making it more relevant for SEZ companies.

Source: UNCTAD, Based on information from the National Council for Export Free Zones (CNZFE)

the Caribbean have used SEZs to reduce their reliance on fruit and vegetable exports. In Costa Rica, the SEZ share of manufactured exports increased from less than 10% in 1990 to 55% in 2003 (Gereffi et al., 2019; FIAS, 2008). At the same time, SEZs have diversified production from apparel and textile to electronic components.

Evidence from UNCTAD (2019) and World Bank (2010) have shown that SEZs have been instrumental in the development of GVCs and, as policy tools, in boosting countries' participation in GVCs. Trade costs such as tariffs, transportation and insurance, as well as other border taxes and fees, accumulate when intermediate goods are imported, processed and then re-exported downstream in complex GVCs, going through various transformation steps in different countries. By lowering such transaction costs within GVCs, SEZs have contributed to the profitability of multinational enterprise (MNE) operations, which explains much of the zones' success (UNCTAD, 2019).

Table 6.2 shows the three developing regions and transition economies, the top- and bottom-ranked economies in terms of trade growth, GVC integration and FDI attraction, as well as the number of SEZs they host.

Looking at the growth in exports of goods, the top-ranked economies tend to have a higher number of SEZs relative to both bottom-ranked ones and the regional median. This is particularly clear for Asia, Latin America and the Caribbean. In these two regions, the countries with the fastest growth in exports generally show a number of SEZs aligned or significantly higher than the regional median. Yet, both groups include countries with high growth rates in exports and little use of SEZs. This then suggests that while SEZs can support trade expansion, they are not necessarily a precondition.

In Africa, which has the largest number of economies with no SEZs to date, the impact is less clear. However, all the countries whose exports are growing fast have one or more SEZ. In this region, the presence of SEZs, at the very least, signals policy efforts to stimulate international trade and investment (UNCTAD, 2019). Some countries such as Ghana and Ethiopia have gone further, explicitly pursuing an SEZ-driven strategy to fuel their trade growth. It is important therefore to note that, across the three developing regions, SEZ statistics for the countries with the lowest growth rates in exports show that the mere establishment of SEZs is not a sufficient condition. Ironically, a number of countries show no growth in trade despite a relevant number of SEZs.

Table 6.2 Analysis of the impact of Special Economic Zones

A. Trade Growth. Economies ranked by average annual growth of trade goods, CARG 2007 – 2017						
	Africa			Asia		
	Economies	CAGR07-17 (%)	SEZs (Number)	Economies	CAGR07-17 (%)	SEZs (Number)
Top Five Economies	Rwanda	20	2	Lao People's Dem. Rep.	18	12
	Burkina Faso	17	2	Viet Nam	16	19
	Ghana	13	4	Cambodia	13	31
	Ethiopia	9	18	Mongolia	12	3
	Madagascar	9	4	Bangladesh	11	39
Bottom Five Economies	Angola	-2	1	Malaysia	1	45
	Gabon	-3	2	Saudi Arabia	-0	10
	Nigeria	-4	38	Iraq	-1	4
	Algeria	-5	1	Kuwait	-1	4
	Equatorial Guinea	-9	2	Brunei Darussalam	-3	1
Median		4	2		4	16

B. GVC Integration. Economies ranked by foreign value added share, 2017						
	Africa			Asia		
	Economies	FVA share (%)	SEZs (Number)	Economies	FVA share (%)	SEZs (Number)
Top Five Economies	Eswatini	43	2	Singapore	62	10
	United Republic of Tanzania	39	8	Korea, Republic of	37	47
	Namibia	27	0	Malaysia	35	45
	Tunisia	27	0	Viet Nam	32	19
	Botswana	27	8	Thailand	31	74
Bottom Five Economies	Ghana	8	4	Pakistan	6	7
	Gabon	8	2	Kuwait	3	4
	Cote d Ivoire	7	1	Qatar	3	2
	Nigeria	6	38	Iraq	2	4
	Angola	5	1	Myanmar	0	3
Median		13	2		14	19

C. FDI Attraction. Economies ranked by ratio of inward FDI stock to GDP, 2017						
	Africa			Asia		
	Economies	FDI/GDP (%)	SEZs (Number)	Economies	FDI/GDP (%)	SEZs (Number)
Top Five Economies	Mozambique	301	2	Singapore	397	10
	Congo	239	4	Mongolia	162	3
	Mauritania	142	1	Cambodia	94	31
	Equatorial Guinea	110	2	Jordan	83	16
	Tunisia	72	0	Viet Nam	58	19
Bottom Five Economies	Cameroon	19	9	Sri Lanka	13	12
	Eswatini	17	2	China	12	2 543
	Algeria	17	1	Iran, Islamic Republic of	12	23
	Kenya	16	61	Bangladesh	6	39
	Angola	10	1	Iraq	6	4
Median		38	2		25	19

(continued)

Table 6.2 (continued)

A. Trade Growth. Economies ranked by average annual growth of trade goods, CARG 2007 – 2017						
	Latin America and the Caribbean			Transition		
	Economies	CAGR07-17	SEZs	Economies	CAGR07-17	SEZs
		(%)	(Number)		(%)	(Number)
Top Five Economies	Guyana	8	0	Bosnia and Herzegovina	8	4
	Nicaragua	7	52	Armenia	7	4
	Uruguay	7	23	Moldova, Republic of	6	8
	Haiti	7	13	North Macedonia	6	15
	Honduras	6	39	Georgia	6	4
Bottom Five Economies	Barbados	-1	0	Belarus	2	7
	Cuba	-1	1	Kazakhstan	0	10
	Trinidad and Tobago	-3	1	Russian Federation	0	130
	Jamaica	-6	17	Turkmenistan	-2	7
	Venezuela, Bolivarian Republic of	-8	14	Azerbaijan	-3	6
Median		4	14		3	7

B. GVC Integration. Economies ranked by foreign value added share, 2017						
	Latin America and the Caribbean			Transition		
	Economies	FVA share	SEZs	Economies	FVA share	SEZs
		(%)	(Number)		(%)	(Number)
Top Five Economies	Mexico	30	17	North Macedonia	36	15
	Barbados	29	0	Turkmenistan	24	7
	El Salvador	26	17	Bosnia and Herzegovina	21	4
	Jamaica	24	17	Armenia	20	4
	Chile	23	4	Georgia	16	4
Bottom Five Economies	Paraguay	10	2	Kazakhstan	14	10
	Peru	10	4	Russian Federation	9	130
	Colombia	9	39	Azerbaijan	9	6
	Trinidad and Tobago	8	1	Uzbekistan	6	7
	Venezuela, Bolivarian Republic of	7	14			
Median		16	14		16	7

C. FDI Attraction. Economies ranked by ratio of inward FDI stock to GDP, 2017						
	Latin America and the Caribbean			Transition		
	Economies	FDI/GDP	SEZs	Economies	FDI/GDP	SEZs
		(%)	(Number)		(%)	(Number)
Top Five Economies	Barbados	150	0	Georgia	115	4
	Jamaica	108	17	Kazakhstan	92	10
	Chile	99	4	Turkmenistan	90	7
	Guyana	90	0	Serbia	86	14
	Nicaragua	78	52	Azerbaijan	73	6
Bottom Five Economies	Haiti	20	13	Moldova, Republic of	45	8
	Paraguay	19	2	Armenia	41	4
	Ecuador	17	12	Belarus	36	7

(*continued*)

Table 6.2 (continued)

	Argentina	12	14	Russian Federation	28	130
	Venezuela, Bolivarian Republic of	9	14	Uzbekistan	19	7
Median		46	14		49	7

Source: UNCTAD (2019)

The relationship between the number of SEZs and GVC integration confirms these findings as well. In Asia and in Latin America and the Caribbean, some champions of GVC integration such as the Republic of Korea, Malaysia or Mexico have heavily relied on SEZs to sustain their GVC integration strategy, but others have achieved good results with a limited presence of SEZs (e.g. Chile). In Africa, the results are again mixed. Some countries with relatively high GVC participation, such as Tanzania and Botswana have a significant number of SEZs relative to the median, while Namibia has no SEZs. Likewise, Tunisia used SEZs to achieve its relatively high GVC participation and has since extended SEZ benefits to the broader economy. With some exceptions, the least integrated countries in each developing region have a few SEZs.

Direct and Indirect Employment Creation

One of the key rationales for SEZ development is to generate employment. Zones are generally considered an effective tool for job generation, particularly for women entering the workforce. Evidence from UNCTAD (2019) and Zeng (2016) reveal that, worldwide, an estimated 90–100 million people are directly employed in SEZs and FZ programmes. Likewise, SEZs have significance impact on indirect employment (World Bank, 2010). UNCTAD studies also show that the ratio of indirect to direct jobs created ranges from one fourth in countries where zones function as relative enclaves to multiples of two in countries where zones are significantly linked to the domestic economy. Precisely, UNCTAD (2019) observed that the indirect employment effect of SEZs globally could range from 50 million to 200 million jobs.

SEZs can also play a major role in employment creation in individual countries. In several countries, the rate of job creation in national SEZ programmes has significantly outpaced employment growth in their total economies. For example, job creation in the United States FTZ programme since 2013 has averaged over 7% per year, compared to less than 2% for the wider economy (UNCTAD, 2019). Employment in Tunisia's SEZs has grown from 8% of the workforce in 2008 to 8.7% in 2019 (UNCTAD, 2019). Ethiopia has been able to generate nearly 50,000 jobs within a few years through its SEZs, with a high proportion of the jobs going to women, while in Kenya, EPZs account for close to 60,000 jobs (UNCTAD, 2019). In Colombia, FTZs have created more than 65,000 direct jobs and 155,000 indirect jobs. Similarly, in the Dominican Republic, SEZs are credited with generating 166,000 direct jobs and an estimated 250,000 indirect ones, a growing share of which are higher-skilled technical jobs (UNCTAD, 2019).

The impact of these jobs in countries with high rates of unemployment and underemployment is significant. Thus in the poorest countries, SEZs can be an important avenue for formal employment. Although SEZs can be effective tools to boost employment, the jobs created have been observed to be relatively insecure (UNCTAD, 2019). The flexible use of labour can lead to fluctuations in employment levels with shifts in production. Also, MNEs in the industries prevalent in SEZs can be prone to relocations or restructuring when costs in the host economy rise.

Overall Economic Growth Impact

SEZ success can be measured directly by looking at FDI, exports and employment indicators, and overall production growth in the zones.

A recent study by Frick et al. (2019) and the World Bank (2017), based on a sample of 346 SEZs across developing regions over the period 2007–2012, found that the average economic growth rate across all SEZs was about 14.7%, with significant variation, and the median growth rate was only 2.8%. Looking at the SEZs' performance relative to the broader economy in which they are located, evidence has shown that the growth of SEZs was on average 2–5% lower than the national GDP growth. Even in countries where SEZs' absolute growth was relatively high, such as Kenya, Turkey and Ghana, it remained below overall national GDP growth. In 55 other countries with high SEZ growth, such as Vietnam and the Russian Federation, zones grew faster than the national average (Frick et al., 2019). The average difference over national growth, however, never exceeded 5% (UNCTAD, 2019).

A study on SEZs in India by Hyun and Ravi (2018) concluded that they had an overall positive and persistent impact on economic activity that extended well beyond their geographical limits. In addition, it found out that SEZs led to a formalisation of the economy, with resources moving away from the informal sector.

Hyun and Ravi (2018) nevertheless showed that the SEZ growth stimulus mostly benefited workers at the upper end of the income distribution. Those at the lower end of the wage and educational scale did not really benefit significantly. Moreover, the transition towards formalisation did not also occur as a result of upgrading, but rather at the cost of informal firms (UNCTAD, 2019). This then highlights the potential unintended downsides of SEZs for parts of the population, even in cases where SEZs outperform the rest of the economy.

6.4 The Nexus Between Special Economic Zones Costs and Revenues

UNCTAD (2019) has argued that in assessing the success of zones, both direct and indirect economic contributions of SEZs should be weighed against their construction and running costs. Zeng (2016) highlighted factors that can negatively affect the financial and fiscal viability of zones such as high up-front costs due to overspecification, subsidies for zone occupants, transfers to zone regimes of already operating firms and illicit financial flows. And since SEZs may rely on significant government subsidies, the growth of economic activity in an SEZ does not necessarily ensure that the zone makes a net positive contribution to the economy (UNCTAD, 2019; World Bank, 2017). In this regard, in order to effectively evaluate the economic contribution of SEZs, there is a need to weigh economic benefits of SEZs against resources they receive from governments.

The decision to establish a zone programme tends to consider the investment expenditures required to build the SEZs. A recent review of the World Bank portfolio of SEZ projects (World Bank, 2017) shows several projects with capital outlays exceeding US$100 million, although early projects that fell below US$10 million are also cited.

Capital expenditures for the initial construction of the zone depend chiefly on three elements:

(i) The location, which determines the need to build expensive additional transport infrastructure to serve the zone.

(ii) The quality and coverage of the existing utilities and telecommunication infrastructure, as zones in some countries may require dedicated power, water and waste management plants.
(iii) The type and specifications of zones.

The latter element is a key factor that is relatively associated with high costs for many modern zones. On the one hand, with the extensive zone construction experience that developers have today, modern zone programmes tend to ensure that new projects are located close to existing public infrastructure and facilities, thereby reducing government outlays. Many modern zones also offer "plug and play" models for investors with pre-built facilities, warehouses and offices, or they combine residential areas and other amenities with traditional industrial facilities in township (wide-area SEZ) models (World Bank, 2017). Both types of development may multiply the initial capital outlays for zones. In contrast to the high commitments for such modern zones, entry-level zones can be relatively inexpensive to build. In addition, outlays tend to be spread over time, as the site develops gradually with the addition of new tenants.

SEZs' operating costs are also largely associated with the running of the zone authority. Other operating costs are usually recouped from investors in the zone through rentals, fees and service charges. Most zones are thus established on a cost–recovery basis, although government-run SEZs regularly subsidise operating costs and utilities, which can make these zones expensive to run. Experience has also shown that both zone development and zone management are increasingly outsourced to the private sector, however, significantly reducing government outlays and risks (World Bank, 2017).

6.5 Dynamic Zone Contributions: Industrial Development and Upgrading

SEZs are an important instrument of industrial policy because of the opportunity they can provide for technology and skills development and upgrading in GVCs. Linkages with local firms, spillovers, crowding and demonstration effects are key to maximising the industrial development impact of SEZs, though these effects do not occur automatically (UNCTAD, 2019; World Bank, 2017).

SEZs have also been criticised for perpetuating the middle-income trap, due to their typical focus on low labour costs; low value-added activities for exports and their enclave nature with consequent limited spillovers and technology transfer to the domestic industry (UNCTAD, 2019). Various studies have further shown that the average skill level of SEZs' workforce is relatively low and rarely increases over time (FIAS, 2008).

Yet there are numerous examples of how development strategies that incorporate SEZs have contributed to industrial development and upgrading. Early examples include the Republic of Korea and Taiwan Province of China, which successfully developed extensive backward supplier linkages with domestic firms (UNCTAD, 2019). ASEAN countries, such as the Philippines and Malaysia, have also been able to attract FDI to SEZs and upgrade them to higher value-added and technology-intensive industries such as electronic and software development (UNCTAD, 2019). Outside of Asia, zones have also contributed to structural transformation in a number of countries. The Dominican Republic, for instance, was a commodity exporter before SEZs turned it into a hub for export manufacturing (World Bank, 2017).

SEZs' contribution to industrial development strategies is largely driven by workforce upgrading and skills development that occur through formal training and work experience. Since zone-based production processes typically involve basic skills and low technology, such skills development may often be limited. In zones that attract efficiency-seeking investors and focus on processing industries, labour is often primarily considered as a cost to be contained, rather than a resource to develop (UNCTAD, 2002).

SEZ programmes in East and South-East Asia have also increased the domestic value added in exports over time, which indicates both higher value-added activities in the zones and greater linkages with the domestic economy. A number of early Latin American examples, however, illustrate that this process is not automatic. For example, value addition in exports from the Mexican maquiladoras, during their rapid growth in the 1990s and 2000s, did not increase significantly despite their success in attracting FDI and generating employment (FIAS, 2008).

UNCTAD (2019) and the World Bank (2017) have also argued that several factors can explain why some zones tend to remain enclaves with few linkages to the rest of the economy:

(i) The relatively high import intensity of some of the industries common in SEZs, such as apparel, footwear and electronics.

(ii) The tendency of MNE affiliates in zones to rely on internal suppliers or on suppliers that are already in their international network as part of global sourcing strategies.
(iii) The scarcity of competitive local suppliers in relevant industries, or unawareness of their existence by zone-based firms.
(iv) Local firms in many developing countries may lack the capacity to serve zone-based investors, hence may not produce according to the required standards or may struggle to access zone-based firms.

Linkages between zone-based investors and domestic suppliers are important for transmitting technological and skills spillovers that support broader industrial development. They are also important to ensure that zones become bridges to structural reforms in the broader economy, since SEZ investors do interact with the local business environment, thus indirectly inducing the business climate (World Bank, 2010). This is the key rationale for the continued use of SEZs in the recent wave of new industrial policies.

6.6 Social and Environmental Impacts

Modern SEZs can make a positive contribution to the environmental, social and governance (ESG) performance of countries' industrial base. Controls and enforcement, as well as support services (e.g. inspectors, health services, waste management and renewable energy installations), can be provided more easily and cheaply in confined areas. As such, new zones are increasingly competing on the basis of high ESG standards.

Since the earliest EPZs were launched in developing countries, concerns have been raised about working conditions and environmental impacts. SEZs have also been criticised for misappropriating agricultural land in the pursuit of industrialisation, or for fraudulent private gains (Moberg, 2015). As of 2017, the ILO concluded that "problems persist [in zones] in the protection of fundamental principles and rights at work, in particular freedom of association; collective bargaining; gender equality", and other violations of workers' rights such as hours of work and health and safety measures. Most countries with zone programmes have ratified relevant ILO conventions, though some countries have pursued a low-wage strategy for EPZ development, where labour law either does not apply or is not enforced (ILO, 2017). Furthermore, ILO has reported instances of unpaid overtime, unremunerated work at night and lack of social security. The report also shows that such practices are due to the laxity of regulatory standards. Instead, divergent practices have occurred due to insufficient resources for effective inspection and administration of labour laws (ILO, 2017). In contrast, some countries have developed mechanisms to monitor labour practices and avoid disputes, such as involving trade union representatives on SEZ boards (Farole & Akinci, 2011).

It is also important to note that SEZs' working conditions and environmental impacts have sometimes more to do with general conditions in the surrounding economy or within a specific industry than with the SEZ status (UNCTAD, 2019). Wage levels and occupational safety and health standards tend to be higher in SEZ-based foreign affiliates of MNEs than in domestic firms outside the zones. Wages and labour practices depend on the local context, and on prevalent industries and economic activities in the zones. The most cited incidents have generally been associated with zones hosting low value-added manufacturing operations.

Furthermore, SEZs have a significant impact on the formal employment of women. Female workers are estimated to have accounted for more than 60% of zone workforces worldwide (FIAS, 2008). This share is the highest in EPZs focused on light manufacturing (e.g. garments, footwear and electronics). It is also lower in zones focusing on heavy manufacturing or diversified economic activities, although it remains above 50% on average in those zones (UNCTAD, 2019).

Poor environmental practices in SEZs have also been of concern. An oft-cited example of environmental degradation relates to Mexican maquiladoras (FIAS, 2008). Here, their rapid growth caused air and waste pollution that became a health hazard for nearby populations. Weak monitoring and enforcement capabilities compounded the problem. SEZ programmes in other countries, especially free points or single-factory FZs, have also caused environmental concerns.

However, SEZs operating as confined industrial areas, as opposed to dispersed single-FZ programmes, can actually make it easier for governments to enforce environmental standards. More modern zones also offer facilities tailored to the needs of target industries (e.g. high-tech, petrochemicals, software development) (UNCTAD, 2019). Such SEZs tend to have zone-specific environmental regulations and dedicated facilities for waste management. Modern zones also use effective environmental management as their unique selling points for investors, especially those operating in industries perceived to carry higher reputational risks.

Services provided by zone operating companies or shared services among zone investors are increasingly used to support higher social and environmental standards. Many EPZs assist companies operating within the zone with labour-related issues (UNCTAD, 2015b). This assistance comes in a variety of forms, from inspection services (such as labour inspectors) to management assistance (such as on-site labour and human resources bureaus that help resolve labour disputes). Some SEZs set out clear labour standards for companies operating within their confines; addressing minimum wages, hours and conditions for the operation of unions. Mostly, these stated labour standards conform to local and national laws, but in some cases (including SEZs in China and India), standards are higher than those required at the state or national levels (UNCTAD, 2015a, b).

More than half of the SEZs polled in UNCTAD's survey on their sustainable development contribution have policies on environmental standards and regulations, and a few have adopted international environmental standards (UNCTAD, 2015a, b). In some cases, these policies are further developed or controlled through a dedicated committee. It is not uncommon for zones to have relatively well-developed environmental reporting requirements under which companies are required to disclose their anticipated amounts of waste and pollutants, and the decibel level of noise expected to be produced. Examples from UNCTAD's poll include zones in Turkey; two of the three zones in South Africa; several in India, Morocco and the United Arab Emirates; and zones in Argentina and China.

Leading SEZs provide technical assistance, institutional mechanisms and physical infrastructure to assist companies with incorporating environmental standards and promote compliance. Most notable is the availability of hazardous waste management systems in SEZs in, for example, Argentina, the Republic of Korea, Saudi Arabia, South Africa and Turkey (UNCTAD, 2015a, b). This type of service is particularly important because many zones host manufacturing activities that generate significant waste. Whereas numerous zones provide services related to the disposal of hazardous waste, only a few provide recycling services (UNCTAD, 2015a, b). Several EPZs around the world, including in China and India, have also been certified as compliant with the ISO 14001 environmental management system standard. Equally so, the EPZ authority of Kenya launched a strategic plan to achieve the ISO 14001 certification for all of the country's zones. An SEZ in India polled as part of UNCTAD's survey actively encouraged companies operating within the zone to become ISO 14001 certified. The use of these standards by SEZ management companies positively steers companies operating within their zones towards responsible business practices.

6.7 Conclusion

This chapter has provided empirical evidence on the impact of SEZs on job creation, investment attraction, export growth and diversification and economic growth. The chapter has shown that if not properly managed, the economic costs associated in the establishment of the SEZs, together with social costs, may outweigh the intended benefits of SEZs. The chapter also unpacked the impact of SEZs; the conceptual framework of the sustainable development impact of SEZs; direct and indirect economic contributions of SEZs; the nexus between SEZ costs and revenues; dynamic contribution of SEZs; and social and environmental impacts of SEZs.

The chapter also demonstrated that although there is little systematic research on the impact of SEZs, the effectiveness of SEZs on investment, exports and jobs has been mixed. Case studies showed that the impact of SEZs on FDI attraction, export performance and job creation is positive. For Example, in China, as noted by the World Bank (2017), while not crowding out domestic investment, SEZs accounted for over 80% of cumulative FDI and had a strong effect on greenfield investments. Similarly, in Costa Rica, the country diversified its production from garments to electronic components, which resulted in the contribution of SEZs in manufacturing exports to increase from 10% in 1990 to 55% in 2003 (Gereffi et al., 2019). Job creation averaged 7% per year since 2013 in the US FTZ programme compared to 2% for the wider economy. When juxtaposing the construction and running costs, benefits of zones especially boosting FDI, jobs and exports outweighed the establishment and running costs (Mongé-Gonzalez et al., 2005; Jayanthakumaran, 2003).

Anecdotal evidence nevertheless showed that zones that did not attract the expected influx of investors, while delivering limited employment and exports gains, had resulted in some investors profiting from generous fiscal incentives (Farole & Akinci, 2011). As noted by the OECD (2018), decentralised policymaking for developing zones led to excessive competition between provinces, and a misuse of resources and land, especially in instances where zones were only partially occupied. Moreover, SEZs were criticised for negative social and environmental impacts such as low environmental, health and safety standards and exploitation of workers (ILO, 2017). In Sub-Saharan Africa, SEZ programmes were largely unsuccessful mainly due to lack of effective strategic planning, weak regulatory and institutional frameworks, insufficient governance and implementation capacity, and inadequate infrastructure (Zeng, 2015a, b). Moreover, before SEZs yield the desired impacts, they require many years of nurturing with consistent support from the government (OECD, 2018).

The ILO (2017) also noted that SEZs have long been criticised for negative social and environmental impacts. For example, poor treatment of women, labour standards and working conditions in some zones, and pollution and misuse of land had been spotted as areas of concern. Other concerns were also on labour-related issues such as suppression of core labour rights, poor employment conditions, lack of training or skill upgrading, use of trainees to lower wage costs and exploitation of women (ILO, 2017).

References

Aggarwal, A. (2004). *Export Processing Zones in India: Analysis of the Export Performance* (Working Paper No. 148). Indian Council for Research on International Economic Relations (ICRIER).

ASEAN. (2017, October). *ASEAN Investment Report 2017: Foreign Direct Investment and Economic Zones in ASEAN*. ASEAN Secretariat.

Burgaud, J., & Farole, T. (2011). When Trade Preferences and Tax Breaks Are No Longer Enough: The Challenges of Adjustment in the Dominican Republic's Free Zones. In T. Farole & G. Akinci (Eds.), *Special Economic Zones: Progress, Emerging Challenges, and Future Directions*. World Bank.

Cheesman, A. (2012). *Special Economic Zones and Development: Geography and Linkages in the Indian EOU Scheme* (Working Paper No. 145). Development Planning Unit, The Bartlett, University College London.

Cheng, T. (2019). Special Economic Zones: A Catalyst for International Trade and Investment in Unsettling Times? *The Journal of World Investment and Trade, 20*(1), 32–67.

Farole, T. (2011). *Special Economic Zones in Africa: Comparing Performance and Learning from Global Experience*. World Bank.

Farole, T., & Akinci, G. (2011). *Special Economic Zones: Progress, Emerging Challenges, and Future Directions*. World Bank.

FIAS. (2008). *Special Economic Zones: Performance, Lessons Learned, and Implications for Zone Development*. World Bank.

Frick, S. A., Rodríguez-Pose, A., & Wong, M. D. (2019). Toward Economically Dynamic Special Economic Zones in Emerging Countries. *Economic Geography, 95*(1), 30–64.

Gereffi, G., Frederick, S., & Bamber, P. (2019). Diverse Paths of Upgrading in High-Tech Manufacturing: Costa Rica in the Electronics and Medical Devices Global Value Chains. *Transnational Corporations, 26*(1), 1–30. United Nations Conference on Trade and Development, Geneva.

Hyun, Y., & Ravi, S. S. (2018). *Place-based Development: Evidence from Special Economic Zones in India*. Massachusetts: Boston University.

International Labour Organisation (ILO). (2017, November 21–23). *Promoting Decent Work and Protecting Fundamental Principles and Rights at Work in Export Processing Zones*. Report for Discussion at the Meeting of Experts to Promote Decent Work and Protection of Fundamental Principles and Rights at Work for Workers in Export Processing Zones. International Labour Office, Enterprises Department, Geneva, ILO.

Jayanthakumaran, K. (2003). Benefit-Cost Appraisals of Export Processing Zones: A Survey of the Literature. *Development Policy Review, 21*(1), 51–56.

Moberg, L. (2015). The Political Economy of Special Economic Zones. *Journal of Institutions, 11*(1), 167–190.

Mongé-Gonzalez, R., Rosales-Tijerino, J., & Arce-Alpizar, G. (2005). Cost-Benefit Analysis of the Free Trade Zone System: The Impact of Foreign Direct Investment in Costa Rica. *OAS Trade, Growth and Competitive Studies*, Organization of American States.

OECD. (2014). *OECD Investment Policy Reviews: Myanmar 2014* (OECD Investment Policy Reviews). Paris: OECD Publishing. https://doi.org/10.1787/9789264206441-en

OECD. (2018). *OECD Investment Policy Reviews: Cambodia 2018* (OECD Investment Policy Reviews). OECD Publishing.

OECD. (2020). *OECD Investment Policy Reviews: Myanmar 2020* (OECD Investment Policy Reviews). OECD Publishing.

Schrank, A. (2008). Export Processing Zones in the Dominican Republic: Schools or Stopgaps? *World Development 36*(8), 1381–1397.

Tao, Y., Yuan, Y., & Li, M. (2016). Chinese Special Economic Zones: Lessons for Africa. *Africa Economic Brief, 7*(6), 1–11.

UNCTAD. (2002). *World Investment Report*. Geneva, Switzerland.

UNCTAD. (2013). *World Investment Report*. Geneva, Switzerland.

UNCTAD. (2015a). *Investment Framework for Sustainable Development*. Geneva: UNCTAD.

UNCTAD. (2015b). *Recent Trends in IIAs and ISDS. IIA Issues Note No. 1*. Geneva: UNCTAD.

UNCTAD. (2019). *World Investment Report: Special Economic Zones*. Geneva, Switzerland.

UNDP. (2015). *Comparative Study on Special Economic Zones in Africa and China*. UNDP.

World Bank. (2010). *Chinese Investments in Special Economic Zones in Africa: Progress, Challenges, and Lessons Learned*. World Bank.

World Bank. (2017). *Special Economic Zones: An Operational Review of Their Impacts*. World Bank.

Zeng, D. Z. (2010). *Building Engines for Growth and Competitiveness in China: Experience with Special Economic Zones and Industrial Clusters*. World Bank.

Zeng, D. Z. (2012a). *SEZs in Africa: Putting the Cart in Front of Horse?* World Bank.

Zeng, D. Z. (2012b). *An Overview of Six Economic Zones in Nigeria: Challenges and Opportunities* (World Bank Policy Note). World Bank.

Zeng, D. Z. (2015a). *Global Experiences with Special Economic Zones – With a Focus on China and Africa*. World Bank.

Zeng, D. Z. (2015b). *Global Experiences with Special Economic Zones: Focus on China and Africa* (World Bank Policy Research Working Paper 7240). World Bank.

Zeng, D. Z. (2016). Global Experiences of Special Economic Zones with Focus on China and Africa: Policy Insights. *Journal of International Commerce, Economics and Policy*, *7*(3), 1–27.

Zeng, D. Z. (2018). *Special Economic Zones: Lessons from the Global Experience*. World Bank.

CHAPTER 7

Outcomes in Special Economic Zones in Africa

7.1 Introduction

Literature on the impact of SEZs on economic development in Africa is both limited and relatively outdated. This chapter is thus predominantly based on the World Bank research and other studies. Evidence on the performance of SEZs will be drawn from Ghana, Kenya, Lesotho, Nigeria, Senegal and Tanzania. In order to showcase the paradox of SEZs, comparisons will be drawn from Vietnam, Bangladesh and the Dominican Republic because they have similar characteristics to African economies and could foreground SEZs in Africa. SEZs are established for job creation, investment, trade and wider economic growth. In a number of cases, they endeavour to foster competitiveness so as to facilitate the economic transformation in the host countries at a much faster or more effective rate than would be possible without them (Farole, 2011). However, in many countries the objectives of SEZs may vary from attracting FDI and job creation to experimenting with reforms as was the case in China (Farole, 2011). In this chapter, objectives which are based on both static and dynamic outcomes of SEZs will be used to review the possible impact of SEZs in Africa.

As argued by Farole (2011), through the use of investment and trade policies, static economic gains of SEZs are obtained in the relatively short term. These static gains may include attraction of FDI, job creation, the generation of foreign exchange through exports and the creation of

G. Mugano, *Special Economic Zones*,
https://doi.org/10.1007/978-3-030-82311-5_7

economic value-added goods and services (UNCTAD, 2019; Zeng, 2015a, b; World Bank, 2010).

SEZs also have a track record of contributing to long-term development by leveraging on static benefits into dynamic economic benefits, which include hard and soft technology transfer, promotion of non-traditional economic activities, promotion of economic openness and promotion of domestic entrepreneurism (Zeng, 2016; Farole, 2011; World Bank, 2010). While assessing the impact of SEZs in Africa, this chapter will equally analyse the static and dynamic gains and other cross-cutting issues such as social impacts as a measure of success by focusing primarily on the quality of jobs created and the gender mainstreaming in various zones.

7.2 Assessment of the Performance of Special Economic Zones in Africa

In Africa, Liberia, Mauritius and Senegal launched SEZs in the early 1970s (Tao et al., 2016; Farole, 2011). Thereafter nearly 30 African countries with over 80% of the SEZs programmes started to implement the SEZs in the late 1990s and early 2000s (UNCTAD, 2019; Tao et al., 2016; Zeng, 2016; World Bank, 2010). Since most African countries are latecomers to SEZs and considering the fact that SEZs require a long gestation period to make an impact, data on the impact of SEZs on job creation, investments, exports and economic growth are scarce and in some countries, absent (UNCTAD, 2019; Zeng, 2016; Farole, 2011).

Regarding the impact of SEZs on job creation, the ILO has shown that, as of 2006, SEZs in Africa and the Indian Ocean (Mauritius, Madagascar and the Seychelles) employed more than a million workers (Zeng, 2018; Farole, 2011). This is equivalent to 4% of worldwide zone employment (excluding China; 1.6% including China). Ironically, more than 50% of the total employment is in South African SEZs (Farole, 2011).

Some anecdotal evidence (see Tao et al., 2016 and Farole, 2011) shows that the success of SEZs in African economies is largely elusive and very few countries such as South Africa, Mauritius, Kenya, Madagascar and to some extent Ghana have been successful. Likewise, most zones in African countries such as Zimbabwe, Nigeria, Namibia, Senegal, Malawi and Mali have performed dismally due to lack of effective planning and management, lack of political will, poor location and policy inconsistency, huge infrastructure deficit and skills gaps in specific areas of zone management and operations and poor governance (Zeng, 2012a; Auty, 2011; Stein, 2008; Rolfe et al., 2003).

What is striking is that, even in those African countries where SEZs were able to attract investment, create jobs and generate exports, the quality of investment and employment as well as their sustainability remained an area of concern for policymakers (Farole, 2011).

For this reason, the following section compares the performance of African zone programmes with the static, dynamic and socio-economic objectives discussed earlier.

Static Economic Outcomes in African Zones

Using data drawn from UNCTAD's FDI database, UN COMTRADE, World Development Indicators and World Bank studies, the next three sections provide a summary of key outcomes of SEZs. In order to demonstrate the paradox of SEZs, comparisons are made using data from Asian economies. In this regard, the possible impact of SEZs on investment, exports, job creation and economic growth is discussed in detail in the next section.

Impact of Special Economic Zones on Investment

Investment, ceteris paribus, is an a priori and minimum requirement for job creation, exports generation and possible structural benefits of SEZs (Farole, 2011). In this regard, the scale and nature of investment in African SEZs is reviewed.

Evidence suggests that on FDI stock and FDI per capita, the non-African zones, that is, comparator countries such as Vietnam, Bangladesh and the Dominican Republic, outperformed the African SEZs. However, it is important to note that Ghana did exceptionally well in attracting large-scale investment in its SEZ during the 2000s (Tao et al., 2016; Farole, 2011). This is mainly because of the fact that the majority of FDIs in Ghana's programme came through single-unit FZs rather than through investment in firms based in the Tema Free Zone (UNCTAD, 2019; Zeng, 2018). These single-unit firms were licensed as FZ companies but were entitled to operate anywhere in the Ghanaian territory.

Similar SEZs programmes in Kenya, Senegal and Tanzania have shown that, in relative terms and notwithstanding the fact that they performed below regional comparator countries, SEZs still remained a significant source of FDI in these countries (Tao et al., 2016). However, Nigeria's SEZs failed to attract significant investments by almost the least measure (UNCTAD, 2019; Tao et al., 2016). This paradox can be clearly attributed to a poor overall investment environment rather than to the failure of the zone programmes themselves.

A study by Farole (2011), where active SEZ-licensed firms were distinguished as those operating in spatially defined zones against those SEZs which operated as single-factory units, showed that the gap in scale between the African and non-African zones (comparator countries) is evident. Specifically, in Asian economies, enterprises in SEZs are considerably large, for example, SEZs in the Dominican Republic supported 550 firms, Honduras had nearly 350 firms, Bangladesh had nearly 300 and Vietnam had 3500 firms in its export processing and industrial zones (ASEAN, 2017).

In contrast, excluding the single-factory units, empirical evidence from African SEZs shows that all the zones have firms not exceeding 35 on average operating in them (UNCTAD, 2019; Tao et al., 2016; Farole, 2011). Such small-scale operations have a double tragedy, with one centred around the host country's failure to recoup costs associated with infrastructure investments in the zone, while the second one is on the host country's failure to derive reasonable static and dynamic gains of SEZs (UNCTAD, 2019; Tao et al., 2016; Farole, 2011).

In what could be exceptional cases, UNCTAD (2019), Tao et al. (2016) and Farole (2011) have observed that both Senegal and Ghana have large-scale enterprises operating through single-unit FZ programmes totalling around 300 and 180 enterprises, respectively. Single-factory models look attractive in Africa because they provide advantages associated with flexibility in terms of location while offering both trade-related and fiscal incentives (Farole, 2011). The enclave programmes tend to be more advantageous than single-factory models, particularly when significant challenges exist in the broad economy regarding access to infrastructure. Enclave programmes also work better when resources to deliver on the administrative benefits of zone programmes (e.g. licensing, efficient customs administration, value-added services) are limited. Thus concentrating these resources in one location rather than spreading them over a large geographical area will result in superior service delivery (Farole, 2011; World Bank, 2010). However, notwithstanding the benefits of the enclave programmes and their successful outcomes in East Asia, their performance in Africa is elusive (UNCTAD, 2019; Tao et al., 2016; Aggarwal, 2004).

Even though these zones are 'large', the scale of the African programmes appears to be limited. Farole (2011) has further argued that the dismal performance of SEZs in Africa can only be explained from two angles. First, like Bangladesh and Vietnam, most African countries minus Nigeria have a very small economy and population which does not attract investment or guarantee demand. Second, most African zones were established recently, hence require more time to show their potential.

In assessing the impact of SEZs on investment, Farole (2011) evaluated the extent to which companies investing in the zones are foreign or locally controlled, and the source regions of foreign investors. Traditionally, SEZ policy has focused on foreign sources of investment as a priority. While SEZs initially need a substantial volume of FDI to attract the knowledge and technology that can be the basis of structural economic transformation, local investment also plays an important role over time (World Bank, 2010). Evidence has also shown that most successful SEZs started with substantial FDI but eventually became dominated by locally based enterprises (UNCTAD, 2019; Tao et al., 2016). For example, in Mauritius, Malaysia, Korea and China, SEZs were initially dominated by FDI, but later on local investors emerged as significant drivers. Likewise, in comparator countries used here, Farole (2011) noted a moderate share of local ownership in most countries, with substantial levels in Vietnam, Senegal and Tanzania. However, this top-line figure may mask underlying differences in the nature of investment in the African and non-African zones.

Precisely, the non-African zones have shown some evidence of the shift from foreign to local investment. For example, in Vietnam, the local share of investment projects rose steadily from around 23% in 1995 to over 50% in 2008 (ASEAN, 2017). Local investors have also played critical roles in the zone programmes in Honduras and the Dominican Republic (Farole, 2011).

In the case of the African zones, the same pattern does not appear to hold. For example, new programmes such as those in Tanzania have had high shares of local investment from the outset. This, in combination with the low levels of FDI attracted into the African zone programmes to date, suggests that the relatively high share of local investment may reflect a failure to attract FDI as well as local investors. In addition, SEZ programmes in Senegal show the existence of single-unit licences and the propensity of locally based firms to switch into the SEZ programme (Farole, 2011). On a positive note, this may reflect the relative perceived advantage of the SEZ operating environment even to local firms, and perhaps could indicate a pent-up demand for investment opportunities by the domestic private sector.

Impact of Special Economic Zones on Exports

Like investments, the level of exports sustained is one of the most commonly used outcome measures for SEZ programmes. Again, the small scale of the African programmes under study stands out on both an absolute and per capita basis (with the exception of Lesotho). Evidence of success in SEZs was also noted in Ghana's programmes. For instance, the Tema enclave, which hosts a small number of firms, had its exports reaching US$280 million in 2008, and exports from the single-factory units were almost four times as high (UNCTAD, 2019). In 2018 also, four SEZs in Ghana contributed to US$1.25 billion in exports (UNCTAD, 2019). The success of exports under the Ghana programme is partly attributed to cocoa-processing activities, which account for a large share of activity under the FZ programme, and which have grown robustly since the programme was launched in 1995. Nonetheless, the activity goes beyond cocoa, with firms in Tema involved in prefabricated housing (US$64 million in exports) and plastic household products (US$11 million in exports) (UNCTAD, 2019; Zeng, 2018). Outside the enclaves, the FZ includes several exporters, for example, a tuna processor (US$100 million in exports), a processor of fresh fruits and juices (US$33 million in exports) and a number of timber companies (together accounting for up to US$200 million in exports) (UNCTAD, 2019).

Contrary to this, Kenya's SEZs have been often held up as an example of African success although their performance on exports looks rather uninspiring. Simply put, after including the single-factory units, the SEZs, which have been operating for nearly two decades, accounted for just over US$400 million in exports in 2008, that is, US$11 in exports per capita. Moreover, the SEZs' performance in Tanzania, Senegal and Nigeria was even worse than that of Kenya (Farole, 2011). As was the case with investment, while nominal exports from the African zone programmes were extremely small (on average 10–15 times smaller than the corresponding absolute and per capita exports in the non-African SEZs), their contribution to national exports was much more in line with international SEZ norms (Farole, 2011). However, in Nigeria, Tanzania and Kenya, SEZ programmes' relative contribution has been considerably limited (Farole, 2011).

Impact of Special Economic Zones on Employment

While SEZs are often major contributors to FDI and exports in a country, their overall impact on the labour market tends to be rather small. That is not to say that economic zones are not often a major generator of employment; rather, it reflects the relative share of the export sector in most economies. In small countries, SEZs are often large contributors to employment. Thus, Farole (2011) observed that, in absolute and relative terms, the contribution of the SEZs to employment in African economies, save Lesotho, is limited even when measured against the limited scale of their industrial sectors. Briefly put, total jobs supported across all the six African SEZs reviewed (Farole, 2011) show that employment created in the SEZs is equivalent to that in Honduras and the Dominican Republic, countries with a population of less than 10 million. Compared with countries such as Kenya and Ghana, Honduras and the Dominican Republic have generated more than four times as much employment through their zone programmes, and 10–15 times as much on a per capita basis (Farole, 2011). Ironically, SEZs in Nigeria have created virtually no manufacturing employment (Farole, 2011). What is striking also is that in Ghana, notwithstanding the significant impact of the SEZs on exports, their contribution to job creation is elusive.

Moreover, Farole (2011) noted that SEZs' activities in Ghana are concentrated in resource-and capital-intensive sectors which create limited job opportunities. Unlike Ghana, Kenya's EPZ programme created nearly 3.5 times more jobs per US$ of exports while Lesotho's had nearly five times more labour-intensive jobs, owing to its nearly exclusive concentration in the garment sector (Farole, 2011).

Ironically, the comparator countries such as Vietnam and Bangladesh managed to shift to exponential job growth over the past decade, while African SEZs exhibited rapid growth in the first half of the decade followed by a stagnation cliff (Farole, 2011). One explanation for the stagnation of and decline in employment is that most SEZs in Africa depend on the garment (Kenya and Lesotho) and agricultural sectors, which have witnessed slow growth in recent years due to weather and climate changes. For example, employment in Lesotho's export garment sector declined by 15% from its 2004 peak, while in Kenya's EPZ programme, the employment segment declined by more than 20% from the 2003 peak (Farole, 2011). In Ghana, nonetheless, job growth was weak as it remained stuck at around 4.5% since 2004, while job creation remained the same between 2005 and 2008 even though exports grew by 2.5 times (Farole, 2011).

Dynamic Outcomes of Special Economic Zones in Africa

This section explores literature from a study undertaken by Farole (2011) to analyse dynamic gains of SEZs in Africa. In analysing the success of African economic zones against dynamic outcomes, it focuses on two questions: (1) to what extent have the zones played a role in supporting industrialisation or diversification of the host country's exports? and (2) to what extent have the zones contributed towards knowledge and technology spillovers to local markets? The first question can be explored through sector patterns of exports and by analysing the inter- and intra-sector adjustments in the zone programmes over time. The second question measures an intermediate-level outcome—one that, if achieved, should lead the country down the path towards diversification. This outcome can be analysed by looking at the main sources of spillovers between zones and local economies based on product markets and labour markets.

Evidence from Farole (2011) shows that Lesotho (a garment export mono-economy) and Nigeria have experienced no change in their national export structures. Export structures in Senegal and Ghana have nonetheless fluctuated somewhat over recent decades, with no clear discernible patterns (at least none that appear to have any relationship with their zone programmes) (Farole, 2011).

Ironically, Kenya and Tanzania have shown a broad pattern of sector adjustment over time. In Tanzania though, the government focused on increasing growth of non-traditional exports, particularly services and minerals, with no real link to the EPZ programme. Although Kenya has shown a steady rise in manufacturing exports, its agricultural exports have been on the decline (Zeng, 2012b). However, most of this adjustment appears to have taken place before the establishment of the SEZs programme, and, in fact, manufacturing share growth appears to have stagnated in the years following the launch of the SEZs.

One factor at play here may be the timing of the launch of SEZ programmes in the context of global trends in trade and investment. With the exception of Senegal and Lesotho, the African programmes in the study were only operationalised in the 1990s—probably too late to take advantage of the massive globalisation of manufacturing that accelerated during the 1980s and 1990s (Zeng, 2012a). One hypothesis is that the structural adjustment seen in Honduras, the Dominican Republic, Vietnam and Bangladesh is not a story of economic zones but rather of broader macro trends, which African countries were unable to tap into for various reasons (e.g. weak micro competitiveness and lack of fiscal and political stability) (Farole, 2011). An alternative hypothesis is that Africa missed out on these opportunities precisely because most countries lacked an effective instrument like SEZs through which to channel their trade and investment.

In direct contrast, all four of the non-African zones have shown quite dramatic structural changes in export patterns towards greater manufacturing. In the case of Vietnam, the data also show that there was no change in manufacturing shares of exports until the zone programme was established (alongside other policy initiatives linked to the opening of Vietnam's economy), which was followed by a radical shift in export structure towards manufacturing. Moreover, Bangladesh experienced a similar radical shift, which only became apparent 5–10 years after its EPZ programme was launched (Farole, 2011). This shift was driven almost entirely by the growth of the garment sector, which had no more than 50 firms in the early 1980s, and grew to more than 4500 firms employing more than 2 million workers by 2009. In the Dominican Republic and Honduras, the structural changes were equally dramatic, although they occurred after the programmes had been operational for 10 years (ASEAN, 2017).

Analysing structural changes within the SEZs may provide a measure of the extent to which the zone programmes facilitate sector adjustments or hinder them. It is instructive to look at how SEZ programmes have responded to changing competitiveness in the garment sector, particularly in the post-MFA environment. In Jayanthakumaran's (2003) seminal study on EPZs, the author concludes that there is "a strong correlation between the growth of EPZs and the Multi-Fibre Arrangement in general" and that the phasing out of the MFA and guaranteed market access "will eventually result in lower rates of return and could act as a threat to the existing and new EPZs". In terms of exports to the US market, East and South Asia (Bangladesh) have grown rapidly at the expense of Central America, the Caribbean and Sub-Saharan Africa, which have experienced declines of up to 40% over four years (World Bank, 2017). There is also evidence of erosion of competitiveness in the sector.

For SEZ programmes that rely on the garment sector, the impact has been significant. While the Bangladesh and Vietnam programmes have experienced rapid growth in exports (16% and 34% annually respectively) and employment (12% annually in each country), programmes in Latin America and Africa (Kenya and Lesotho) have suffered (ASEAN, 2017; Farole, 2011). In Lesotho, exports fell by 25% since 2004 although employment remained steady since 2006, and over 8000 jobs were lost since 2004 (Farole, 2011).

In Kenya, job losses in the SEZs were nearing 10,000 from their peak. Tanzania was unfortunate in launching its programmes just as the MFA was being phased out. The programme originally had commitments from a significant number of garment manufacturers, almost all of whom eventually decided against investing or had shut down.

Interestingly, in the face of these competitiveness challenges, some SEZs have been successful in at least beginning the process of adjustment. In the Dominican Republic, for example, the flat export picture since 2000 masks substantial sector shifts. Although the textile exports declined by more than half between 2000 and 2008, they were offset by 60% growth in non-textile exports. Sectors such as jewellery, electronics, pharmaceuticals and even call centres took over the traditional garment sector. This shift contributed to rapidly increasing value added in the zones. Essentially, value added per worker grew nearly by 12% annually between 2004 and 2008 (Farole, 2011). However, this new transformation came at the cost of the SEZs maintaining their traditional role as a generator of large-scale employment as employment in the FZs declined by more than 70,000 (36%) from its peak of over 195,000 in 2000 (Farole, 2011).

Kenya has also shown some evidence of shifting its sector structures inside the zones. While apparel exports declined by some 10% between 2004 and 2008, non-apparel exports doubled during this period, contributing to steady overall export growth in the SEZs (Farole, 2011). And, while apparel accounted for 84% of Kenya's EPZ exports in 2003, by 2008 it represented less than half. Other sectors such as horticulture and food processing, call centres and pharmaceuticals emerged in the zones (Farole, 2011). Productivity rose steadily in Kenya's EPZ programme due to a shift towards higher value production and also due to growing price competition within the apparel sector. These forced the remaining apparel companies to maintain volumes with fewer workers.

With respect to intermediate measures of SEZs' outcomes, the extent to which SEZs are facilitating spillovers of knowledge and technology to the local economy is discussed in the subsequent section.

The first channel through which these spillovers may occur is through product market links between SEZ firms and firms in the domestic economy. These links can be either forward or backward. As discussed previously, forward links are limited by zone regulations in most markets, so we will focus on supply links. On average, African zones reported higher use of local raw materials than in the non-African zones, primarily because of the relatively larger share of agro-processing activity in the African zones (UNCTAD, 2019; Tao et al., 2016). For example, Kenya appears to benefit from its status as the industrial and commercial hub of the region, which enables its zone-based firms to source more inputs locally.

A second channel for transmitting spillovers occurs via the labour market through the free movement of skilled workers across firms. With the exception of Nigeria (46%) and Ghana (56%), the large majority of managers in all the zones studied were locals (Zeng, 2016, 2018). In general, the African zones appear to rely more on foreign management than the non-African zones do. This is simply true because one-third of the managers in Kenya were foreign, as were one-fourth in Lesotho. In Senegal though, foreign share of management was reported to be below 10% (Zeng, 2016, 2018; Farole, 2011).

The share of the workforce sourced from local vocational training in SEZs is also another measure of the dynamic benefits. This measure is designed to capture the extent to which zone-based firms hire locally trained skilled workers—workers who are most likely to be in a position to transfer knowledge across firms (inside and outside the zones) and/or to employ their knowledge in an entrepreneurial venture. Evidence shows no clear pattern, with most firms reportedly sourcing only a very small share of workers through such programmes. The standout situations here are Tanzania (14%) and Senegal (7%) at one end, and Kenya (less than 1%) at the other end (Farole, 2011). It is important to note that the use of workers from vocational training programmes depends on many factors, including the sector, the nature of firm activities, the availability of vocational training programmes and any specific initiatives and incentives available to zone-based firms to employ vocational workers.

Socio-economic Outcomes in African Zones

Both measures (dynamic and static) of success discussed in this chapter are concerned only with economic efficiency, though the impact of SEZs on their host societies goes further. Critical documentation exists on the social and environmental impacts of zones but, like most research on zones, it is largely based on single-country or small-sample case studies. This section thus focuses on the employment-related social effects of zones. Specifically, it focuses on African SEZ programme outcomes in terms of (1) the quality of employment generated; (2) the extent to which workers' rights are protected; and (3) the gender-differentiated impacts of zones (given that a large majority of workers in most zone programmes are female).

These social issues and economic issues, as discussed earlier, are intertwined and as such they should not be segregated. Zone programmes that fail to offer opportunities for high-quality employment and upward mobility of trained staff, those that derive their competitive advantage from exploitation of workers and those that neglect to provide an environment that addresses the particular concerns of female workers may not achieve the dynamic benefits possible from zone programmes and may find themselves in a "race to the bottom" (ILO, 2017; Farole, 2011). By contrast, SEZs that recognise the value of skilled workers and seek to provide the social infrastructure and working environment in which such workers thrive will be in a position to facilitate upgrading.

Quality of Employment and Protection of Workers' Rights

Overall, workers in the African countries receive relatively higher wages than those in Bangladesh (and, in some countries, more than those in Vietnam) but substantially lower wages than workers in the two Latin American countries. The monthly wage (adjusted for purchasing power) ranged from US$232 in Kenya to US$371 in Senegal, and for the sample overall, it ranged from US$124 in Bangladesh to US$675 in Honduras (Farole, 2011).

Actual monthly wages received by workers in Kenya were reported to average just US$96. This is less than half the average wage reportedly paid by firms in Nigeria. Conversely, it is three times the actual wages received by unskilled workers in Bangladesh's SEZs (US$32), or little more than US$1 per day (Farole, 2011). Overall, the purchasing power parity adjustment is much lower for the African countries in the study, reflecting an average 20% higher cost of living (Farole, 2011). This situation may place significant limitations on African zones' ability to balance the pressures of competitiveness and paying a living wage. This is particularly so in labour-intensive global sectors such as garments where extreme competitive pressure on wages appears to have given rise to a debate over whether a living wage is a reasonable objective (World Bank, 2010).

Alternatively, wage rates in the zones can be compared with national minimum wages or, better, with comparable sector- and task-specific wages outside the zones. In almost all countries, unskilled wages inside the zones were substantially higher than the minimum wage. The main exception was Honduras, where the Maquila sector lobbied successfully to be exempt from a large increase in the national minimum wage in 2009 (Farole, 2011).

And, in the Dominican Republic, firms inside the zones have a lower prescribed minimum wage than the national minimum wage. In all the three zones, unskilled workers typically received wages above the minimum when benefits and bonuses were taken into account. For the African zones in particular, the SEZ wage premium over the minimum wage is very significant. However, anecdotal evidence from most countries indicated that the total of wages and benefits received by workers inside the zones was generally equal to or slightly higher than that for a comparable job outside the zones (with the exceptions of the Dominican Republic, Honduras and possibly Nigeria) (ASEAN, 2017; Farole, 2011).

Another measure of the quality of employment is its security. Evidence shows that temporary workers did not only have less job security but were also not likely to receive the full range of benefits available to permanent staff. Here, the African zones minus those in Nigeria stand out as making substantial use of temporary labour (Farole, 2011). Many African countries have struggled with highly inflexible labour markets, which caused firms to make greater use of temporary workers. In the case of Senegal, for example, SEZ-specific relaxation of the rules for hiring temporary workers has led many firms to rely almost exclusively on temporary workers.

Overall, union participation in zones, as reported by the surveyed firms, is somewhat lower than the national rates, with the exception of Senegal and Bangladesh (Farole, 2011). Within the African programmes, union membership is particularly low in the Kenyan and Nigerian programmes. This is perhaps not surprising, given the historical legal treatment of unions in these zone programmes. The Nigerian free zone law, for example, prohibits strikes and lockouts for a period of 10 years after a company begins its activities in a given EPZ. The law also states that employer–employee disputes are not to be handled by trade unions but rather by the authorities who manage these zones (Farole, 2011). In Kenya, until 2005, workers in the EPZs were prohibited from joining unions or engaging in collective bargaining.

As observed by Farole (2011), a wide range of negative work quality and social consequences was common across many of the zones under study, including the following:

- Lack of job advancement opportunities: a common problem across most SEZs is the lack of mobility of production workers into supervisory positions. This is particularly true for women who dominate the production workforce in many SEZ companies but are poorly represented in supervisory and managerial positions (see later).
- Difficult working hours and shift structures: in Honduras, for example, workers in the Maquila factories typically work 11–12 hours a day, four days in a row, before having four days of rest. This scheme has led to some adverse social implications as many Maquila workers had a second job during off days for additional income.
- Lack of social infrastructure: most of the large zones are located in or near major metropolitan areas but attract their workforces from distant rural communities. This has led to large-scale migration in some countries (e.g. Honduras and Lesotho) and put significant pressure on the already weak social infrastructure, particularly regarding the provision of decent housing, education and health services. It has also contributed to health problems such as HIV and Aids such that in Lesotho, an estimated 40% of the apparel workforce has been affected.

Gender-Differentiated Impacts

Several studies on employment in SEZs have established that firms located inside zones do employ more women than firms in the rest of the country (Milberg & Amengual, 2008; Cling & Letilly, 2001; Kusago & Tzannatos, 1998; ILO-UNCTC 1988). In this regard, zones have created an important avenue for young women to enter the formal economy at much better wages than in the agriculture and domestic services (ILO, 2003).

With the notable exception of Ghana and Nigeria, the share of the workforce that is female is larger in the SEZ firms than in firms in the rest of the non-agricultural economy (Farole, 2011). In most cases, the relative female share of employment in the zones is at least 50% higher than outside the zones, while in Senegal and Bangladesh, SEZ employment is more than twice as female-intensive as employment in the non-agricultural economy overall (Farole, 2011). In Ghana and Nigeria again, female participation in the overall non-agricultural economy is substantially lower than in the other countries (Farole, 2011).

Indeed, evidence from countries such as Costa Rica (Jenkins, 2005) and the Dominican Republic (USAID, 2007) has shown that, as zones move away from a concentration on the garment sector or even upgrade within the sector, the gender mix usually changes towards much greater male participation. This change is driven by changes in production technology that are not accompanied by an equal upgrade in the skills of female workers, as well as the competitive pressure that results when males are attracted to previously overlooked sectors by the higher wages prevalent inside SEZs (Farole, 2011).

Another important issue is the extent to which female workers have opportunities to move up to supervisory and management positions. Outside the zones, gender bias in relation to certain tasks or positions often undermines the potential of female workers to move up the ladder. With the exception of Ghana, there is a clear gap in the number of females at the managerial level in SEZs relative to their participation in the overall workforce (Farole, 2011). The largest gap is in Bangladesh where female workers represent more than half the workforce but account for only 14% of the managers. The African SEZs show, on average, much lower ratios of overall to management staff, though no one knows whether this reflects less bias in the firms based in Africa or not. It can therefore be assumed that this could simply be sector differentiation, and the fact that the African zone programmes are generally less reliant on the garment sector. However, the ratio in Kenya, which has a strong garment sector, is substantial, while in Lesotho, which is dominated by the garment sector, 44% of all managers are reported to be female (Farole, 2011).

7.3 Conclusion

This chapter has provided some evidence on the impact of SEZs on job creation, investment attraction, export growth and diversification and economic growth in Africa. Literature on the impact of SEZs on economic development in Africa is both limited and relatively outdated. However, based on the World Bank research and firm-based surveys, the performance of SEZs has been drawn from SEZs in Ghana, Kenya, Lesotho, Nigeria, Senegal and Tanzania. To showcase the paradox of SEZs, the chapter sought to set benchmarks upon which African SEZs can be analysed with Vietnam, Bangladesh and the Dominican Republic, since they have similar characteristics to those in Africa. The chapter noted that SEZs are established for job creation, investment, trade and wider economic growth. They also endeavour to foster competitiveness so as to facilitate the economic transformation in the host countries at a much faster and effective rate than would be possible without them (Farole, 2011). In

China, however, the objectives of SEZs have demonstrated that they could range from attracting FDI and creating employment to experimenting with reforms (Farole, 2011). This chapter also unearthed both static and dynamic outcomes of SEZs on African economies.

Anecdotal evidence has also shown that the success of SEZs in African economies is largely elusive and very few countries such as South Africa, Mauritius, Kenya, Madagascar and Ghana have been successful (see Tao et al., 2016; Farole, 2011). Likewise, most zones in African countries such as Zimbabwe, Nigeria, Namibia, Senegal, Malawi and Mali have performed dismally due to lack of effective planning and management, lack of political will, poor location and policy inconsistency, infrastructure deficit and skills gaps in specific areas of zone management and operations, and drought of governance (Zeng, 2012; Stein, 2008; Auty, 2011), among others.

References

Aggarwal, A. (2004). *Export Processing Zones in India: Analysis of the Export Performance* (Working Paper No. 148). Indian Council for Research on International Economic Relations (ICRIER).

ASEAN. (2017, October). *ASEAN Investment Report 2017: Foreign Direct Investment and Economic Zones in ASEAN*. ASEAN Secretariat.

Auty, R. (2011). Early Reform Zones: Catalysts for Dynamic Market Economies in Africa. In T. Farole & G. Akinci (Eds.), *Special Economic Zones: Progress, Emerging Challenges, and Future Directions*. World Bank.

Cling, J. P., & Letilly, G. (2001). *Export Processing Zones: A Threatened Instrument for Global Economy Insertion?* (DT/2001/17). Development et Insertion Internationale (DIAL).

Farole, T. (2011). *Special Economic Zones in Africa: Comparing Performance and Learning from Global Experience*. Washington, DC: World Bank.

ILO/United Nations Centre on Transnational Corporations. (1988). *Economic and Social Effects of Multinational Enterprises in Export Processing Zones*. ILO.

International Labour Organisation (ILO). (2003). *Employment and Social Policy in Respect of Export Processing Zones*. ILO.

International Labour Organisation (ILO). (2017, November 21–23). Promoting Decent Work and Protecting Fundamental Principles and Rights at Work in Export Processing Zones. *Report for Discussion at the Meeting of Experts to Promote Decent Work and Protection of Fundamental Principles and Rights at Work for Workers in Export Processing Zones*, International Labour Office, Enterprises Department, Geneva, ILO.

Jayanthakumaran, K. (2003). Benefit-Cost Appraisals of Export Processing Zones: A Survey of the Literature. *Development Policy Review, 21*(1), 51–56.

Jenkins, M. (2005). *Economic and Social Effects of Export Processing Zones in Costa Rica* (Working Paper 97). ILO.

Kusago, T., & Tzannatos, T. (1998). *Export Processing Zones: A Review in Need of Update* (SP Discussion Paper 9802). World Bank.

Milberg, W., & Amengual, M. (2008). *Economic Development and Working Conditions in Export Processing Zones: A Survey of Trends.* ILO.

Rolfe, R. R., Woodward, D. P., & Kagira, B. (2003, September 17–19). Footloose and Tax Free: Incentive Preferences in Kenyan Export Processing Zones. *Paper Presented at the Biennial Conference of the Economic Society of South Africa*, Somerset West, South Africa.

Stein, H. (2008, July 10–11). Africa, Industrial Policy and Export Processing Zones: Lessons from Asia. *Paper Prepared for Africa Task Force Meeting*. Addis Ababa, Ethiopia.

Tao, Y., Yuan, Y., & Li, M. (2016). Chinese Special Economic Zones: Lessons for Africa. *Africa Economic Brief, 7*(6), 1–11.

UNCTAD. (2019). *World Investment Report: Special Economic Zones.* Geneva, Switzerland.

United States Agency for International Development. (2007). *Dinamicas recientes de la produccion, el comercio y el empleo en las zonas francas de exporta- cion de la Republica Dominicana.* USAID Greater Access to Trade Expansion Project. Development and Training Services, Inc.

World Bank. (2010). *Chinese Investments in Special Economic Zones in Africa: Progress, Challenges, and Lessons Learned.* World Bank.

World Bank. (2017). *Special Economic Zones: An Operational Review of Their Impact.* World Bank.

Zeng, D. Z. (2012a). *SEZs in Africa: Putting the Cart in Front of Horse?* World Bank.

Zeng, D. Z. (2012b). *An Overview of Six Economic Zones in Nigeria: Challenges and Opportunities* (World Bank Policy Note). World Bank.

Zeng, D. Z. (2015a). *Global Experiences with Special Economic Zones – With a Focus on China and Africa.* World Bank.

Zeng, D. Z. (2015b). *Global Experiences with Special Economic Zones: Focus on China and Africa* (World Bank Policy Research Working Paper 7240). World Bank.

Zeng, D. Z. (2016). Global Experiences of Special Economic Zones with Focus on China and Africa: Policy Insights. *Journal of International Commerce, Economics and Policy, 7*(3), 1–27.

Zeng, D. Z. (2018). *Special Economic Zones: Lessons from the Global Experience.* World Bank.

PART IV

Critical Factors for Special Economic Zones' Success and Failure

CHAPTER 8

Critical Success Factors of Special Economic Zones

8.1 Introduction

As noted in Chap. 7, most African countries failed to use SEZs to attract high-tech investors into their economies and thus failed to leapfrog into higher value-added activities and accelerate economic growth (UNCTAD, 2019, 2020a, b). For example, the majority of the SEZs in Africa failed dismally just like early zones in Bangladesh were unsuccessful. They later started attracting significant investment only when the authorities allowed garment producers to invest (Farole & Akinci, 2011). In fact, the fastest-growing SEZs in developing countries appear to be those with lower technological components (Frick et al., 2019; World Bank, 2017). This reflects the difficulties that countries face when aiming to transition from low to higher value-added industries. Ironically, countries such as China and South Korea and to some degree Ethiopia and Ghana witnessed significant success. Building on the experience of successful countries, this chapter presents critical success factors for SEZs which can be adopted by African countries.

G. Mugano, *Special Economic Zones*,
https://doi.org/10.1007/978-3-030-82311-5_8

8.2 The Context and the Framework for Sustainable Special Economic Zone Programmes

The performance of SEZs is dependent on external factors such as those that can be managed by governments and zone developers. External factors include high competition for internationally mobile investment and changes in the policy environment, such as shifting trade preferences. Manageable factors revolve around the strategic focus of zones, the regulatory and institutional framework and the infrastructure, and services and benefits provided to investors in zones.

Factors such as poor site locations which require heavy capital expenditures or that are far from infrastructure hubs or cities with sufficient pools of labour, poor zone design with inadequate facilities or maintenance, unreliable power supplies, cumbersome administrative procedures, weak governance structures and/or too many institutions involved in zone management were observed as major impediments for successful implementation of SEZs (UNCTAD, 2019, 2020a, b; Zeng, 2015, 2016).

Evidence based on the interviews carried by UNCTAD with investment promotion agencies (IPAs) shows that, apart from factors that are directly related to SEZs' location, design and management and contextual considerations are also critical for SEZs' success (UNCTAD, 2019). The IPAs argued that proximity to large markets is an important driver for zone performance (Frick et al., 2019), and that traditional advantages attracting FDI to the broader economy, especially a pool of adequately skilled and relatively low-cost labour, remained key determinants of zone success. In addition, infrastructure support to investors and the domestic presence of capable suppliers outside the zones were also top issues, and more than incentives packages, the cost of labour and/or strategic concerns such as zone specialisation were equally listed (UNCTAD, 2019; Frick et al., 2019).

In order to address the binding constraints to effective implementation and success of SEZs, African countries must adopt the standard framework for SEZs which was developed by UNCTAD (2019) (see Table 8.1).

However, the specific impact of these factors on the success of SEZs varies from country to country. To this end, turnaround of unsuccessful SEZs must be contextualised through a timely diagnosis of the factors impeding success and targeted action to address them (UNCTAD, 2019, 2020a, b). Contextualisation of the country's own specific conditions is

Table 8.1 Framework for sustainable Special Economic Zones

General Approach	Policies/Standards	Infrastructure Assistance	Administrative Assistance
	Maintain and enforces policies and standards including:	**Provides services or specialists to ensure compliance/offer assistance including:**	**Provides guidance and training to companies, covering how to:**
General Approach	*Create multi-stakeholder partnerships to identify opportunities and develop an action plan*		
Labour	• Minimum wage • Working hours and benefits • Respecting the right of unions to be active within the zone • Gender equality and related issues • Incentives for third party certifications	• Labour inspectors • Conflict resolution specialists • Reporting hotlines • Gender focal points	• Improve labour conditions • Engage in social dialogue
Environmental	• Emissions • Waste disposal • Energy use • Incentives for third party certifications • Promoting circular economy	• Centralised effluent treatment • Water reclamation systems • Recycling services • Hazardous waste management services • Alternative energy sources • Reporting hotlines • Enabling circular economy	• Further reduce natural resource use • Reduce waste • Increase recycling • Improve energy efficiency • Adopt renewable energy
Health and Safety	• Employee health and safety protection • Incentives for third party certifications	• medical clinic • fire brigade • reporting hotlines	• Prevent health and safety emergencies
Corruption	• Anti – corruption standards and policies	• Hotlines • Information on reporting corruption	• Build capacity to detect and avoid corrupt business practices
Economic Linkages	• Employer support for staff training and development	• Assistance with local sourcing	• Identify and upgrade local suppliers

Source: UNCTAD (2015)

critical if there has been a significant level of public investment to develop zone facilities (see Box 8.1).

Box 8.1 Turning Around Underperforming Special Economic Zones in the Tema Free Zones in Ghana

Ghana has one of the most successful SEZ programmes in Africa today. Only four EPZs generated approximately US$1.25billion of exports in 2018, of the country's estimated total of $14 billion. The biggest and most successful SEZ is the flagship Tema free zone. Yet the programme, which was initiated in 1995, did not always perform well. In 2005, only US$105 million worth of exports could be attributed to the country's FZs, against imports of US$46 million (Farole, 2011). The Tema zone in particular was performing well below expectations, owing to the problems with the developer, high vacancy rates and inactive tenants.

The Ghana Free Zones Board, aided by external experts, launched a three-pronged restructuring of the Tema zone. First of all, firms were clustered on the basis of industry to promote agglomeration economies. This entailed physically collocating firms in the same industry along with suppliers and providing a minimal level of services tailored to specific industry needs. For example, a technology incubator and a garment village were designated within the zone. Second, a renewed effort was undertaken to provide hard and soft infrastructure geared towards exports, including offices for customs, immigration, the environment and the Export Promotion Council. Finally, a multipurpose industrial park was established within the zone, allowing local firms in but not offering them the incentives extended to export-oriented foreign affiliates. This promoted forward and backward linkages between local and foreign firms, improving both zone performance and spillover benefits to the local economy. Within a few years, the performance of the Tema zone improved significantly. World Bank assessments revealed that from June 2008 to June 2009, companies in the FZ generated $281 million in exports and 2085 jobs (Farole, 2011). Since then, the performance of the zone steadily kept improving, and it is now considered a key component of the country's economic strategy and one of the few examples of SEZs done right in Africa.

Source: UNCTAD Based on information from Ghana Free Zones Board and the OECD

8.3 Strategies and Policy Consideration for Effective Implementation of Zones

Current debates on SEZs and what makes them successful have generally focused on policy considerations, which include the need for strategic focus, experimentation and gradual approach, appropriate regulatory frameworks and governance structures, and the value proposition for investors in the zone—thus, the package of advantages that zones provide (UNCTAD, 2019, 2020a, b; Aaron, 2019).

Value Proposition

The overall value proposition of individual SEZs includes a host of locational advantages, some of which are determined or can be influenced by government policy. Focusing on those that depend on active policy decisions, the first and most important feature is the choice of location. SEZ policies often aim to promote the economic development of certain regions, for example areas with high levels of unemployment. At the same time, a strategic location close to key infrastructure hubs (for example, ports and airports) and close to labour pools is fundamental in attracting investors into the zone (UNCTAD, 2019).

Several studies have shown that closeness to ports or large cities is more likely to spur zone dynamism than locating an SEZ in more remote areas (UNCTAD, 2020a, b; Zeng, 2015; Farole, 2011). In fact, in most developing countries with one or very few major urban agglomerations, the distance to the largest city is negatively correlated with zone performance, indicating that SEZs may not be the most effective tool for the development of remote or relatively poor regions (Frick et al., 2019).

The incentives offered in the SEZs are one of the key elements of the value proposition offered by countries (UNCTAD, 2019). Ironically, the use of generous incentive packages to offset locational disadvantages has been observed to be ineffective. For example, studies by Farole (2011) and Frick et al. (2019) established no correlation between fiscal incentives offered to investors and zone growth in terms of jobs and exports. This implies that incentives on their own are insufficient to explain zone performance. UNCTAD (2019) further argued that the absence of correlation may also be explained by the increasing convergence of zone investment incentives and the lack of differentiation. For instance, some variations in fiscal incentives existed and were only at the margin level since most incentive packages included exemptions from corporate taxes and from import duties on machinery and inputs, which in a number of cases applied to firms outside the zones, thus rendering fiscal incentives weak in attracting the FDIs into the zones (UNCTAD, 2019). Furthermore, facilitation of administration procedures for businesses and investors in the zones through regulatory streamlining and one-stop shops was considered more important than the incentives package (UNCTAD, 2019). In India, for example, Moberg (2015) observed that most of the failed zones were the ones that had been negatively affected by excessive bureaucracy.

Given these debates, lessons which arise for African countries are that, in order to successfully implement SEZs, there is need to streamline administration procedures, provide adequate facilities and efficient services as well as differentiated incentives. Equally so, there is need to place emphasis on key elements which are commonly prioritised in business and investment facilitation efforts such as elimination of import and export licences, customs facilitation, simplified investment approvals, expedited work permits and automatic foreign exchange access. Lessons can be drawn from Vietnam's single windows dedicated to SEZs.

Infrastructure and Services Are Key for Zone Success

Most SEZs in developing countries suffer from lack of utilities, telecommunication, water and waste management installations among other basic infrastructure (UNCTAD, 2019). Similarly, there has been lack of basic non-infrastructure services such as dedicated customs offices and inspection units, as well as human resources–related services, security, housing and business.

This being the case, African countries must establish key infrastructures and related services if the SEZs are to be functional. This means African governments must consider using PPPs in building the infrastructure for the zones. Governments could also seek bilateral investment support from countries such as China which have in recent years undertaken significant interest in Africa's infrastructure development and SEZs (see Box 8.2).

Box 8.2 China's Infrastructure Financing in Africa

China recognises that the lack of infrastructure in Africa is a major obstacle to the continent's development. It has therefore prioritised, pronounced and implemented infrastructure development in African platforms such as FOCAC and other bilateral agreements. The Infrastructure Consortium for Africa (2014) estimated that Chinese investment in African infrastructure stood roughly at US$13.9 billion a year between 2011 and 2013 and this made it the largest single source of financing for infrastructure in Africa. China is also financing projects such as the Lamu Port–South Sudan–Ethiopia Transport (LAPSSET) corridor, the standard gauge railway between Nairobi and Mombasa and the Dares-Salaam–Bagamoyo transport corridor, which, once completed, will be the regional game changers in enabling the mobility of goods and people. Furthermore, in 2015, China and the African Union (AU) signed the "most ever substantive project." A memorandum of understanding to jointly develop infrastructure to connect the continent's capitals through road, rail and air transport routes as part of Agenda 2063 was signed. As part of implementing the MoU, China undertook to fund and construct projects which included the 186 km Abuja–Kaduna Railway that was completed at a cost of US$850 million in Nigeria, and which forms part of the larger 1224 km Lagos–Kano railway construction and modernisation project, the $12 billion Nigerian Lagos–Calabar Coastal Railway, the US$1 billion deep-sea port deal between China Harbour Engineering Company and the Cameroonian government, and the construction of the US$200 million Mamamah Airport in Sierra Leone. Once completed, these projects will help address the acute shortage internal trade on the continent, with around 80% of Africa's exports destined for the outside world (Du Plessis, 2016).

Furthermore, at the FOCAC Forum in December 2015 in Johannesburg, China pledged to fund African infrastructure development projects worth US$55 billion, of which $35 billion would go towards preferential loans, export credits and concessional loans, $5 billion would go towards the China–Africa Development Fund—a private equity and venture capital initiative by the China Development Bank—and a further $5 billion was to be reserved for loans for the development of African SMEs.

(*continued*)

Box 8.2 (continued)

Interestingly, at the FOCAC VI, China recognised the need for beneficiation and manufacturing in Africa for the first time, and US$10 billion are to be made available for a China–Africa production capacity co-operation fund. This fund would invest in sectors such as manufacturing, technology, agriculture, energy, infrastructure construction and finance in African countries. This widening of FOCAC's scope indicates that Beijing recognises that Africa's favourable demographics, urbanisation, growing middle class and improvements in transport and electricity infrastructure are making it an increasingly attractive destination for investment. However, FOCAC's financial pledges are no guarantee of actual loans being extended, as they are still subject to conditions such as the feasibility of proposals and the likelihood that these projects can be completed within a reasonable time frame, in which most African countries are found lacking.

Source: Du Plessis (2016)

Experimentation and a Gradual Approach

In China, SEZ policies have taken the shape of a step-by-step approach alongside an experimental mentality (Xing & Zhang, 2013). The first industrial park, Shekou, established in 1979, was very small (11 square kilometres), after which Shenzhen was established in 1980 (328 square kilometres), followed by 14 "opening-up" coastal cities in 1984. According to Zhang (2017), governments "start small" so that any negative spillovers that might accidentally arise from the creation of industrial parks can be quickly corrected and restricted to a narrow locality. The policies which best spur growth can then be identified and gradually scaled up, as they have been in Jamaica, Kuwait, Malaysia and Jordan (Akinci & Crittle, 2008). Moreover, SEZs provide governments with a small-scale area in which to experiment with new regulatory frameworks and institutions which, if they are successful, can act as an effective catalyst for implementing country-wide institutional reforms from which many LDCs could benefit (Khandelwal & Teachout, 2016).

Contrary to most African countries such as Egypt and Senegal, the location of the SEZs and selection of firms in China were not based on political considerations. In Egypt and Senegal most SEZs failed due to tax base erosion, facilitating land speculation, producing white elephants and channelling funds towards politically favoured districts and firms (Saleman & Jordan, 2014). An example of such a failed attempt at establishing an industrial park is where severe information asymmetries persisted between grassroots entrepreneurs and governments, due to the heavy bureaucracy of the SEZ system and constant policy changes in Egypt (Zhang, 2017). In Senegal, excessive bureaucracy, inadequate transportation infrastructure, expensive labour force and high electricity costs inhibited the growth of effective industrial parks (Cling & Letilly, 2001).

Government Commitment

The Hawassa case study showed that genuine commitment on the part of the Ethiopian government towards the development of industrial parks was paramount in attracting PVH to Hawassa Park (see Box 8.3). According to various scholars, there is a close and cooperative relationship between investors and high-level government officials, with strong and genuine commitment from the government (see UNCTAD, 2020a, b; Zeng, 2012a, b, 2015, among others).

Box 8.3 Ethiopia Hawassa Industrial Park

Hawassa Industrial Park (HIP) was established by the Ethiopian Industrial Parks Development Corporation in 2016. HIP has thus far been considered by many as a great success (Hoque, 2017 and Davison, 2017). Hoping to lure manufacturers who are currently suffering from increasing wages in Asia, the Ethiopian government has invested US$250 million into HIP. The park is projected to create 60,000 jobs annually, compared to the mere 250,000 jobs that the country's manufacturing sector has managed to generate over the last 30 years, as well as export revenues worth US$1 billion, generating the much-needed foreign exchange for the country (Mihretu & Llobet, 2017). HIP was also constructed in just nine

(*continued*)

Box 8.3 (continued)

months, and its development is based not only on financial incentives, but also on institutional and practical coordination, and the genuine commitment of a government striving for manufacturing growth and industrialisation for Ethiopia (Hoque, 2017).

According to Dr Arkebe Oqubay, the former Ethiopian Prime Minister's Senior Adviser, many SEZs in Africa were "missing the 'basics' such as power, water and one-stop services, and were not aligned with national development strategy" (Fruman, 2015). In response to this, HIP was constructed with four important elements: expert housing units, a water treatment plant, the largest textile mill in Ethiopia (which is also a key part of the government's wider vertical integration plan) and factories, all of which are linked by an underground piping of 50 kilometres. The park's energy is derived from a mobile substation of 19 MW, which will later be substituted by direct supply from a 200 MW dedicated substation. To put this into perspective, the rest of the city is served by a power supply of just 75 MW (Hoque, 2017). The Ethiopian Investment Commission selects investors, assembles the strategy for industries within the park and is in close contact with the Prime Minister, which demonstrates the strong political will towards the programme at the highest level of government (Hoque, 2017). New companies entering the HIP are also supported by the Ethiopian Investment Commission through a one-stop service for institutional matters (visa, banking, work permits, etc.), which lowers set-up costs and accelerates decision-making (UNCTAD, 2020b). Beyond spurring positive economic externalities in terms of job creation, infrastructure and exports, the HIP follows strict conservation principles and is operating a facility of zero-liquid discharge (Hoque, 2017). In terms of labour, there are five million inhabitants within 50 kilometres of Hawassa, constituting an abundant labour supply.

From the investors' angle, foreign investment might be attracted to Ethiopia due to its export access to the United States and the European Union markets as a result of the AGOA and the Everything But Arms Agreement respectively. A total of 18 firms have already leased out all 52 of the park's units, including the US company PVH, which owns brands such as Tommy Hilfiger and Calvin Klein

(*continued*)

Box 8.3 (continued)
(Davison, 2017). PVH, discontent with increased production costs and weak institutions in Asia, considered five factors when deciding on a new production location: port accessibility, land accessibility, government stability, labour availability and energy cost. Long-term government commitment to the availability of these factors was also crucial (Mihretu & Llobet, 2017). While Ethiopia was mostly satisfied these conditions, the targeting of the textile industry by the government was the deciding factor for PVH (World Bank, 2017). A direct communication channel between senior government officials and PVH was also established, which increased trust and coordination between the two parties (Mihretu & Llobet, 2017).

The park, however, is facing challenges such as power failures, high transport costs between the park and Hawassa, high absenteeism and attrition of workers. Workers are thus moving to other factories once they have acquired sufficient skills. Similarly, managers are concerned at their inability to influence the staff selection process since only government job centres do the sourcing of workers (Hoque, 2017; Davison, 2017). However, the HIP programme is still in its infancy, and many are optimistic about the benefits such parks can bring for industrialisation in Ethiopia in the future (Davison, 2017; Hoque, 2017).

Source: UNCTAD (2020a, b)

The Hawassa Industrial Park and experience from China are important lessons which African governments must consider to successfully encourage investment in the SEZs. What is striking though is that, as part of its pragmatism, the Ethiopian government has strategically established industrial parks focusing on specific areas where the country has comparative advantage, taking advantage of the rising wages in Asia (UNCTAD, 2020a, b). Further, the country has set up robust institutions to facilitate investment such as PVH which have eventually given the park producers access to global markets (UNCTAD, 2020a, b).

Strategic Sector and Firm Targeting

In the Hawassa case, the strategic targeting of the textile industry also incentivised the company to locate there, as labour costs in their Asian operations were increasing (UNCTAD, 2020a, b) (see Box 8.3). While financial and infrastructure incentives are certainly important in fomenting investment in industrial parks, strategic sector targeting is also valuable.

Pursuit of Linkages and Spillovers

As argued by Farole (2011), static and dynamic economic outcomes and socio-economic outcomes can be used to measure spillovers to local economies. Static gains are generated in a short period of time and as such may include primary investments by SEZ-based firms, export generation, job creation, increase in government revenues and foreign exchange earnings (Zeng, 2016; Farole & Winkler, 2014).

In contrast, dynamic effects of SEZs have arisen from long-term structural and developmental legacies. These include economic and structural diversification, upgrading of local skills and technologies, improved local innovation capacity and increased openness (Farole, 2011). From a sustainable development perspective, the third type, the socio-economic consequences of SEZ policies, includes gender-related impacts, quality of employment and compensation or resettlement practices, and issues around land acquisition.

All these outcomes arise from interactions between SEZ firms, especially firms in surrounding areas and workers, backward and forward linkages, labour pooling, labour mobility between firms and knowledge spillovers (Frick et al., 2019). To this end, the stronger these interactions, the more spillovers are likely to be produced.

As discussed in Chap. 7, evidence shows that linkages and spillovers are a missing link in African SEZs although they are a critical force required to facilitate not only job creation but also skills upgrading, as technological spillovers from foreign firms, and to improve the skills of the local population (see Box 8.4).

Box 8.4 Nexus Between South Korean SEZs and Backward Linkages
South Korea's early EPZ regime (1970–1990) combined an enclave SEZ approach with a significant and effective backward linkage programme. From the 2000s, following the Asian Financial Crisis, EPZs were upgraded and a new breed of large open SEZs was introduced with a stronger sector approach as part of a comprehensive national industrial strategy modernisation.

Introduction (Timeline/Rationale/Challenge)

The objective of South Korea's EPZ regime was to acquire world-class technology, and upgrade the surrounding economy, while maintaining an import substitution (IS) and export only strategy for the rest of the economy. The EPZ regime was launched in 1970, with the Masan EPZ beginning operations in 1971. Domestic input to EPZ manufacturing operations increased steadily and quickly over the first decade, and by 1990, the surrounding economy had achieved the technological level of the EPZs. A new era of SEZs continued in South Korea after the Asian financial crisis. The upgraded EPZs and new Korea Free Economic Zones (KFEZs) took a more modern and nationwide approach. As part of a national industrial strategy, they had a greater sector focus (including sector-focused incentives), significantly upgraded administrative efficiency and greatly improved logistics and transportation.

Policies and Strategy

The design and growth of EPZs in South Korea was a priority national initiative, and it specifically targeted the upgrading of the local economy. In the 1970–1990 era of mercantilist global development, this technological learning approach could viably exist alongside a complementary import substitution policy. Key policies included the following:

- Backward linkage as local supplier policies were fundamental. In the first era (1970–1990), EPZs were seen as a technology-learning opportunity, and the backward linkage programme

(*continued*)

Box 8.4 (continued)

was fundamental. When the Masan Zone began operations in 1971, domestic firms supplied just 3.3% of materials and intermediate goods to firms in the zone. Four years later, they supplied 25% and, eventually, 44%. Consequently, domestic value added increased steadily from 28% in 1971 to 52% in 1979 (White, 2011). The government of Korea had specific policies to encourage backward linkages. For example, local companies supplying SEZ firms had preferential access to intermediate and raw materials.

- Most tax and duty incentives applied to the country as a whole and were not the defining characteristic of EPZs. Thus, (i) tax and duty rebates were provided to domestic firms supplying EPZ firms; (ii) there was a machinery fund for companies supplying EPZ firms; and (iii) proactive local authorities supported training and capacity-building initiatives.
- EPZ firms also benefited from significant land and rent subsidies. An enclave approach to EPZs (with an effective learning membrane) was complementary to the IS approach in the surrounding economy. SEZs/EPZs were also marginalised by the late 1980s.
- Following the Asian Financial Crisis (1997–1979), from around 2002, Korean SEZ policy moved from enclave FTZs to large multi-use SEZs. Manufacturing zones were upgraded with enhanced logistic capabilities, and new logistics-focused zones were established.
- KFEZs' regime was launched after 2002, reflecting a shift to open, multi-use zones (e.g. Incheon). Logistics capabilities were upgraded, administrative procedures significantly streamlined and sector strategies emphasised. There was a significant emphasis on logistics and transportation access.
- KFEZs have a more significant exemption regime, but are targeted towards particular sectors in line with industrial strategy.

Economic/Transformational

South Korea's EPZ programme was extremely successful, and was instrumental in stimulating nationwide economic transformation, especially over the 1970–1990 period. The FTZs (Masan in particular) fulfilled an important role over that period. Since then, and in

(continued)

Box 8.4 (continued)

general terms, FDI has been of less importance to Korea than to other countries. As of 2016, Korea's stock of inward FDI amounted to 13.2% of GDP, much lower than that of the United Kingdom (57%), the United States (31%) or Germany (31%) (Frederick & Lee, 2017).

Between 1973 and 1982, exports from Masan EPZ grew from US$145 million to US$601million, while imports grew from $91million to $281million. This indicates a significant increase in the value of domestic inputs and sales to the local market, and a rise in value added per worker from US$1450 to US$10,340 (Aaron, 2019). Employment at the Masan zone also rose from 21,000 in 1973 to 26,000 in 1982, and just under 40,000 at its peak in 1986 (Aaron, 2019). Employment also subsequently declined with the transition from labour-intensive to more capital-intensive industries. Most early investment was in textiles and clothing, but by 1993, 90% was in electronics and electrical industries, with R&D and high-tech investment growing steadily.

By 2010, the importance of zones for attracting FDI was significantly reduced. Over the period 2004–2014, only 7% of the firms (749 firms) and 21% (US$95 billion) of the total FDI inflows to Korea were through SEZs. Provincially, driven Foreign Investment Zones (FIZs) were the main hosts.

Takeaways, Lessons and the Future

Korea's EPZs have fulfilled a crucial role in the early decades of industrialisation (1970–1990s), generating significant exports with ever-increasing domestic value added. Korea actively encouraged domestic firm inputs to learn from foreign firms. Since 2000, Korea has adopted a much more open approach to zones focused around specific industries, R&D and so forth. Companies are encouraged to locate there for their knowledge and expertise, whether they are domestic or foreign.

Korea was also strategically and fundamentally involved in building skills and the capacity of the domestic private sector using investors. This involved strong policies, and financial and fiscal incentives. Backward linkages were very important, and the responsibility for that remained with the proactive integration of local and foreign firms through an effective industrial development strategy.

(continued)

Box 8.4 (continued)

The nature of incentives has also evolved over time towards a focus on innovation, skills building, appropriate logistical and industrial infrastructure, and the encouragement of carefully identified sectors. In a world where trade-focused incentives are more restricted, this sector and a public-goods focus have been particularly appropriate for countries seeking to exploit zones today.

Source: Aaron (2019)

8.4 Conclusion

As noted before, most African countries failed to use SEZs to attract high-tech investors into their economies, and thus failed to leapfrog into higher value-added activities and accelerate economic growth (UNCTAD, 2019, 2020). For example, the majority of the SEZs in Africa, just like early zones in Bangladesh, did not do very well. For Bangladesh, the zones started attracting significant investment after the authorities had allowed garment producers to invest (Farole & Akinci, 2011). In fact, the fastest-growing SEZs in developing countries appear to be those with lower technological components (Frick et al., 2019). This reflects the difficulties that countries face when aiming to transition from low to higher value-added industries. Ironically, countries such as China and South Korea and to some degree Ethiopia and Ghana witnessed significant success.

From the success cases, it emerges that critical success factors for SEZs which can be adopted by African countries should include the need to provide reliable infrastructure, building linkages and spillovers, mainstreaming SEZs into national development agendas, creating an enabling business environment and political will. In addition, what make SEZs successful has been shown to focus on policy considerations such as the need for strategic focus, experimentation, gradual approach, appropriate regulatory frameworks and governance structures as well as the value proposition for investors in the zone (UNCTAD, 2020a, b; Aaron, 2019).

This chapter further revealed that the performance of SEZs is dependent on external factors as well as factors that can be managed by governments and developers. External factors include high competition for internationally mobile investment and changes in the policy environment, such as shifting trade preferences. Manageable factors revolve around the strategic focus of zones, the regulatory and institutional framework and the infrastructure, and services and benefits provided to investors in zones. Moreover, factors such as poor site locations which require heavy capital expenditures or that are far from infrastructure hubs and poor utilities, weak governance structures or too much bureaucracy in zone management have been observed as major impediments for successful implementation of SEZs (UNCTAD, 2020a, b; Zeng, 2015, 2016; Tao et al., 2016).

Studies by UNCTAD (2019) and IPAs have shown that, apart from factors directly related to SEZs' location, design and management, contextual considerations are also critical for SEZs' success (UNCTAD, 2019). The IPAs argued that proximity to large markets is an important driver for zone performance (Frick et al., 2019), and that traditional advantages attracting FDI to the broader economy such as a pool of adequately skilled and relatively low-cost labour, remained key determinants of zone success. In addition, infrastructure support to investors and domestic presence of capable suppliers outside the zones were also top concerns, and more important than incentives, the cost of labour and/or zone specialisation was critical (UNCTAD, 2019; Frick et al., 2019).

References

Aaron, C. (2019). *Special Economic Zones: A Model for the Middle East and North Africa*. Konrad-Adenauer-Stiftung.

Akinci, G., & Crittle, J. (2008). *Special Economic Zones: Performance, Lessons Learned, and Implications for Zone Development*. Washington, DC: The World Bank.

Cling, J. P., & Letilly, G. (2001). *Export Processing Zones: A Threatened Instrument for Global Economy Insertion?* (Working Paper DT/2001/17). Paris: DIAL.

Davison, W. (2017, December 5). Park Life: Workers Struggle to Make Ends Meet at Ethiopia's $250m Industrial Zone. *The Guardian*. Available at: www.theguardian.com/global-development/2017/dec/05/ethiopia-industrial-park-government-investment-boost-economy-low-wages. Accessed 4 Oct 2019.

Du Plessis, R. (2016). *China's African Infrastructure Projects: A Tool in Reshaping Global Norms, South African Institute of International Affairs* (Policy Insights No. 35). Johannesburg: SAIIA.

Farole, T. (2011). *Special Economic Zones in Africa: Comparing Performance and Learning from Global Experience*. World Bank.

Farole, T., & Akinci, G. (Eds). (2011). *Special Economic Zones: Progress, Emerging Challenges, and Future Directions*. World Bank Group. Available at: https://openknowledge.worldbank.org/bitstream/handle/10986/2341/638440PUB0Exto00Box0361527B0PUBLIC0.pdf

Farole, T., & Winkler, D. (2014). *Making Foreign Direct Investment Work for Sub-Saharan Africa: Local Spill-Overs and Competitiveness in Global Value Chains*. Directions in Development, Trade. World Bank.

Frederick, S., & Lee, J. (2017). An Introduction to Korea's Economy. *In Korea in Global Value Chains: Pathways for Industrial Transformation*. Available at: https://gvcc.duke.edu/wp-content/uploads/2017-09-27_CH2-Introduction-to-Koreas-Economy.pdf

Frick, S. A., Rodríguez-Pose, A., & Wong, M. D. (2019). Toward Economically Dynamic Special Economic Zones in Emerging Countries. *Economic Geography, 95*(1), 30–64. https://doi.org/10.1080/00130095.2018.1467732

Fruman, C. (2015, August 27). *How to Make Zones Work Better in Africa*? World Bank Private Sector Development Blog. Available at: https://blogs.worldbank.org/psd/how-make-zones-work-better-africa. Accessed 4 Oct 2019.

Hoque, S. (2017, August 24). *Ethiopia's Economic Transformation and Job Creation: The Role of Hawassa Industrial Park*. SET ODI. Available at: https://set.odi.org/sonia-hoque-odi-ethiopias-economic-transformation-job-creation-role-hawassa-industrial-park/. Accessed 4 Oct 2019.

Mihretu, M., & Llobet, G. (2017). *Looking Beyond the Horizon: A Case Study of PVH's Commitment to Ethiopia's Hawassa Industrial Park*. World Bank. Available at: http://documents.worldbank.org/. Accessed 4 Oct.

Moberg, L. (2015). The Political Economy of Special Economic Zones. *Journal of Institutions, 11*(1), 167–190.

Saleman, Y., & Jordan, L. (2014). *The Implementation of Industrial Parks: Some Lessons Learned in India* (World Bank Policy Research Working Paper 6799). Available at http://documents.worldbank.org. Accessed 10 Nov 2020.

Tao, Y., Yuan, Y., & Li, M. (2016). Chinese Special Economic Zones: Lessons for Africa. *Africa Economic Brief, 7*(6), 1–11.

UNCTAD. (2019). *World Investment Report: Special Economic Zones*. United Nations.

UNCTAD. (2015). *Recent Trends in IIAs and ISDS. IIA Issues Note No. 1*. Geneva: UNCTAD.

UNCTAD. (2020a). *World Investment Report: International Production Beyond the Pandemic*. United Nations.

UNCTAD. (2020b). *Building and Utilising Productive Capacities in Africa and LDCs*. United Nations.

White, J. (2011). Fostering Innovation in Developing Economies through SEZs. In T. Farole & G. Akinci (Eds.), *Special Economic Zones: Progress, Emerging Challenges, and Future Directions* (pp. 183–206). Washington, DC: World Bank Group. Available at: https://openknowledge.worldbank. org/bitstream/handle/10986/2341/638440PUB0Exto00Box0361527B0PUBLIC0.pdf

World Bank Data. (2017). [Online]. [Accessed 24 Jan 2018]. Available at: https://data.worldbank.org/. Accessed 4 Oct 2019.

Xing, H., & Zhang, X. (2013). *The Logic of Adaptive Sequential Experimentation in Policy Design* (IFPRI Discussion Paper 1273). Washington, DC: International Food Policy Research Institute.

Zeng, D. Z. (2012a). *SEZs in Africa: Putting the Cart in Front of Horse?* World Bank.

Zeng, D. Z. (2012b). *An Overview of Six Economic Zones in Nigeria: Challenges and Opportunities* (World Bank Policy Note). World Bank.

Zeng, D. Z. (2015). *Global Experiences with Special Economic Zones – With a Focus on China and Africa*. World Bank.

Zeng, D. Z. (2016). Global Experiences of Special Economic Zones with Focus on China and Africa: Policy Insights. *Journal of International Commerce, Economics and Policy, 7*(3), 1–27.

Zhang, X. (2017). *Building Effective Clusters and Industrial Parks*. Industrialize Africa: Abidjan, AfDB.

CHAPTER 9

Special Economic Zones: Showcasing Success and Failures

9.1 Introduction

This chapter builds on the previous chapter on critical success factors of SEZs, and presents a three-pillared analytical framework as the magic behind successful SEZs. The core argument advanced here is that countries that adopt a well-structured approach towards SEZs that they can align with the broader development strategy execute and evaluate effectively, and change over time may be more successful in achieving SEZ-led economic transformation than others. This chapter shows evidence on countries which had strategic bureaucratic competencies in making the right choices, and setting clear strategic directions; strategic bureaucratic learning to dynamically and interactively engage in adjusting the strategies when needed; and strategic bureaucratic strengths to implement the strategies effectively. In addition, together with these elements, the chapter shows how effective political leadership with a strong development focus energised and motivated bureaucracies in successful implementation of SEZs.

Similarly, using grounded evidence on not-so-successful countries across the globe within this framework, the chapter raises some pertinent insights about SEZ-led development strategy that emerge from the analysis.

G. Mugano, *Special Economic Zones*,
https://doi.org/10.1007/978-3-030-82311-5_9

9.2 Special Economic Zones and Economic Transformation

The world economy and new industrial paths for developing countries have been revolutionised by the proliferation of GVCs (Aggarwal, 2019). Most developing countries, instead of building up industrial capacities from scratch, have joined existing supply chains and upgraded along them (Baldwin, 2013). To this end, using various tools, many developing countries are competing to attract GVC-linked investments. In this regard, SEZs are increasingly being used as one of the most powerful tools to promote GVC-linked investment (Aggarwal, 2019).

The unprecedented increase in the number of SEZs shows that SEZs have been trusted by policymakers as an effective tool for attracting investments to foster industrial transformation and sustain economic growth (Aggarwal, 2019). Specifically, as discussed in Chap. 1, there are 5400 zones in operation across 147 countries in the world (UNCTAD, 2019). SEZs are physically demarcated areas where host countries build efficient infrastructure, and relax rules and regulations and offer substantial fiscal and non-fiscal incentives in order to attract GVC activities which are highly responsive to business environments and costs (Aggarwal, 2019). Conventional wisdom shows that by facilitating the host country's insertion into GVCs, SEZs can promote trade and attract FDI inflows as well as technology transfers, which in turn generate spillover effects and catalyse the process of economic transformation in the wider economy.

Contrary to this, evidence shows that a handful of countries have managed to leverage SEZs to achieve far-reaching economic transformation (Aggarwal, 2012a). Although most countries have successfully attracted FDI into the SEZs, and eventually increased production, job creation and export growth, evidence shows that SEZs have had limited impact on the development process in the wider economy (Frick et al., 2018; FIAS, 2008). Ironically, in most other countries, SEZs have completely failed to attract investment and promote economic activity (Aggarwal, 2019; Farole, 2011).

This paradox in the performance of SEZs in attracting FDI and its subsequent impact on the wider economy raise critical questions as to why development outcomes of SEZs are so varied. The growing literature on critical success factors of SEZs, discussed in Chap. 8, focuses mainly on best practices to follow in developing SEZs to make them attractive for foreign investors. Although there are concerns about the wider economic impact of SEZs, evidence shows that general policy prescriptions such as lowering transaction barriers between SEZ and non-SEZ firms, and upgrading technical and human skills in the wider economy are usually in place; still the link between SEZs and national development strategies is missing (Aggarwal, 2019). As argued by Aggarwal, SEZs are designed as an enclave and thus are separated from the rest of the economy with little or no connection with the overall development strategy.

In order to stimulate wider economic impacts of SEZs, this chapter thus argues for the institutionalisation of the zones into policy and planning. Specially, the SEZs' legislative and policy framework must be an integral and sustainable part of the broader development strategy of a country. However, for avoidance of doubt, institutionalisation of SEZs means that SEZs must be able to respond to the dynamic realities of the economy as opposed to just entrenching SEZ practices (Aggarwal, 2019).

Accordingly, this chapter draws on literature by Aggarwal (2019) on a cohesive, comprehensive and integrated three-pillared analytical framework for linking SEZs with broader development planning, which is termed "integrated institutional framework [IIF] of SEZs".

The three pillars of the IIF are:

- First, a well-structured strategic approach to SEZs which is well grounded in a broader holistic economic development strategy.
- Second, strategic dynamism in the approach towards SEZs which is well informed by continuous changes in economic conditions to adapt the current SEZ strategies to new development challenges as well as opportunities.
- Third, effective implementation of these strategies.

The central argument is that countries which succeeded in using SEZs to have wider economic impact have adopted a well-structured strategic approach towards SEZs which they effectively executed, and continuously evaluated and changed over time (Aggarwal, 2019). This requires strategic bureaucratic learning to dynamically and interactively engage in adjusting the strategies when needed, bureaucratic competencies to make the right choices and set clear strategic directions and strategic bureaucratic strengths along with strong political support to implement the strategy effectively (Aggarwal, 2019). These elements in turn are contingent upon leadership that can energise bureaucracies to achieve the broader development goals to earn creditability, visibility and resources and political will with a strong development focus (Ellison, 1995). However, this feat can be performed only by a handful countries in the world (Aggarwal, 2019). This explains the paradox of the success of SEZs in economic transformation. In order to show that the performance of SEZs varies directly with these factors, this chapter draws on the experience of major SEZ users in the world. It concludes by raising some pertinent concerns about SEZ-led development strategy that emerge from the analysis.

The rest of the chapter discusses critical elements of each of the three pillars and revisits, within this framework, the experience of successful, not-so-successful and least successful countries across the globe. Success is defined by the extent to which SEZs could be leveraged for economic transformation in the wider economy.

9.3 The Integrated Institutional Framework of Special Economic Zones: Three Pillars

The three pillars discussed here are (i) linking SEZs with the economic development strategy; (ii) strategic dynamism in the approach towards SEZs; and (iii) effective implementation of these strategies.

Aligning Special Economic Zones with National Development Strategy

Evidence has shown that, if properly crafted, if well-designed, SEZs can be used as an effective tool for achieving broader economic goals (Aggarwal, 2019; UNCTAD, 2019; Zeng, 2015a). Precisely, SEZs are effective in promoting trade and FDI, regional integration or international relations, industrial growth and diversification, urbanisation and spatial rejuvenation and border development (Aggarwal, 2019). This requires a well-articulated strategic approach since this does not happen automatically. According to Aggarwal (2019), a strategic approach defines what policymakers anticipate to achieve with SEZs and the respective methodological approach.

In order to align SEZs with broader development strategy, the first pillar of the framework advocates for the need to undertake a strategic approach in the design of SEZs. Alignment between the SEZ programmes with broader strategies of industrialisation helps in ensuring long-term political support and resource commitments to zone development. More importantly, the synergies between a national development strategy and strategic approach to SEZs create a mutually reinforcing and self-supporting system wherein the benefits of zones flow backward, forward and vertically, expanding capacity and improving the competitiveness of the wider economy (Aggarwal, 2019). This requires a high level of bureaucratic expertise and rigour in assessing the synergies and possible trade-offs among different set strategic direction for SEZs and policy options at different levels so as to develop mutually reinforcing policies for achieving national goals and objectives (Aggarwal, 2019). In this regard, governments must have clear answers to three questions: What is the rationale for setting up SEZs? What objectives should be assigned to SEZs and how can they be achieved? How can SEZs be aligned with the broader development strategy?

Understanding the Rationale of Special Economic Zones
Although SEZs are an important instrument to foster economic development, they are not a panacea for all development ills of an economy. The nature of investment-binding constraints determines whether SEZs are required. SEZs are indeed an effective vehicle which can be used to address basically the inefficient regulatory institutions that can change quickly but are not necessarily changed because of socio-political compulsions, and investment-binding constraints (Aggarwal, 2019). If investment is constrained by structural factors such as exchange rate spikes, inflation, factor endowments, socio-political instability, lack of human skills or physical and geographical factors, SEZs and their respective incentives will be futile in attracting investments. What this means is that the significance of SEZs is context-specific and as such governments must have a clear comprehension of investment-binding institutions and the importance of SEZs in addressing them.

Aligning Special Economic Zones with National Development Strategies
Complementary, reinforcing or central are three broad approaches to aligning the SEZs with development strategy:

- *Complementary (or enclave) approach*: in a tariff-distorted economy, SEZs are used to counter the anti-export bias created by a protectionist development strategy. In such an establishment, SEZs are used to promote an accelerated economic growth process by allowing duty-free imports of the machinery and technology necessary for growth sectors, exports and foreign exchange earnings (Aggarwal,

2019). In a different situation, in order to ensure technology transfers and other related benefits, a country may establish SEZs to promote FDI inflows within SEZ localities, particularly in a country that follows highly restrictive policies for FDI to protect domestic industries from competition (Aggarwal, 2019). Likewise, SEZs are used as test laboratories for reforms in a wider economy by non-capitalist economies (Zeng, 2016). The role of SEZs in all these cases is to complement the national development strategy by overcoming FDI issues. Hence, as argued by Farole (2011), in order for the SEZs to be effective in addressing the binding constraints to economic development, SEZs, offering basic industrial infrastructure, streamlined administrative procedures, investor-friendly customs procedures, cheap labour and a wide variety of fiscal and non- fiscal concessions, must be developed as enclaves of liberal trade and FDI policy in strategic locations near airports, seaports and highways.

In addition, SEZs can complement the development goals such as promotion of capital-intensive or high-tech industrialisation with specific focus on job creation, promotion of linkages between large businesses and SMEs and/or to counter unbalanced regional development in the wider economy (Aggarwal, 2019). In doing so, the SEZ design, infrastructure, facilities and incentives must be contextualised within the national goals.

- *National strategy reinforcing approach:* SEZs can play a more active role of reinforcing the development strategy as opposed to the traditional view of complementing it. For example, in a globalised regime, by driving FDI, exports and technology flows, SEZs may underpin export-oriented industrialisation (Aggarwal, 2019). This approach requires governments to provide SEZs with a highly favourable business climate which is combined with intense marketing aimed at attracting FDI into SEZs. As argued by Aggarwal (2019), by focusing only on making SEZs attractive and doing nothing else, governments may adopt an enclave approach towards SEZs. Alternatively, in order to catalyse FDI spillovers in the wider economy through promotion of linkages with the rest of the economy, governments may develop action plans which will be used to achieve this goal. This means, transaction costs between SEZs and outside firms must be lowered so as to incentivise them to undertake business transactions. Alternatively, governments may take a more proactive approach which would require them to design SEZs strategically to attract

FDI into industries which are defined as priority industries in the broader development strategy (Aggarwal, 2019). Evidence has shown that entry into GVCs helps countries to access global pool of skills, new technologies, markets, capital and learning opportunities through technology spillovers in the target industries (Aggarwal, 2019). Ironically, economies face new challenges such as technology gaps, patchy supply chains and insufficient scale as they transition from one stage of development to another, and target new industries (Aggarwal, 2019). SEZs have thus been used by governments as policy laboratories to expose firms to global product standards and reduce learning costs (Aggarwal, 2019). Hence, SEZs are traditionally used as incubators of economic and industrial policies for catalysing growth and economic development in the wider economies (Aggarwal, 2019). In addition, SEZs are also used to reinforce development strategies for promoting small businesses (in Taiwan Province of China) or large businesses (in India); or balanced regional development (Republic of Korea) or regional cooperation (Mali, Burkina Faso, Côte d'Ivoire or Brunei, Indonesia, Malaysia, the Philippines).

- *Development-centred approach:* As observed in China, based on the notion that externalities created by SEZs can drive economic growth, the third alternative is to place SEZs at the centre of the development strategy (Aggarwal, 2019). Conventional wisdom states that aligning investment with the rest of the economy, together with FDI attracted by SEZs, will help in building domestic capacities in SEZ industries (Aggarwal, 2019). In this case, Aggarwal (2019) argued that governments must focus on developing domestic production capabilities in SEZ industries instead of picking winners and building domestic capabilities in them. Subsequently, governments must proactively fund networks of researchers, start-ups, established firms and consortia to ensure advancements in all segments of the production processes to build domestic capabilities along the value chains, and develop policies, agencies and institutions (Aggarwal, 2019; Milberg et al., 2014).
- *Setting SEZ objectives with a commensurate action plan:* in order to stir wider economic impact of SEZs, a set of objectives must be developed with a clear appreciation of how each of the objectives may contribute to the overall strategic role proposed for the SEZs (Aggarwal, 2019). However, if the strategic goals and objectives are

not accompanied by a well-designed action plan, they will remain aspirational statements with no grounding in reality.

Strategic Dynamism

The economic realities are not static but dynamic. For example, as development takes place, new challenges and opportunities emerge and domestic conditions change. Concurrently, new agents of change may appear which will result in the shifts in power, perceptions, interests and the subsequent positioning of the existing actors, and instant demand for new institutions which must adapt to new realities (Aggarwal, 2019). This change in institutional dynamics presents a completely new set of goals which demands new ways for dealing with institutional challenges. Policymakers must always therefore endeavour to respond to the dynamic realities of the economy and its challenges within the SEZs.

In this regard, strategic learning must continuously inform the strategic approach towards SEZs. This requires policymakers to assign new roles, preferential packages and roles to SEZs, and continuously upgrade the existing ones in order to respond to the dynamic realities of the economy. In addition, this process can be scientifically supported by monitoring and evaluation (M&E) mechanisms which must be embedded within the SEZ policy. Because M&E involves regular collection of data; tracking of results; systematic and objective periodic assessment of the SEZ policy including its objectives; and design, implementation, outcomes and impacts, it therefore provides government officials and stakeholders with the means to learn by doing, which will provide the basis for responding to dynamic realities of the economy (Aggarwal, 2019).

Strategic Implementation

The success of SEZs is underpinned by efficient execution of the strategic approach. It is thus linked positively with bureaucratic strengths, which in turn draw on the technical skills, government commitment and political will to support the SEZs, as well as managerial and social skill sets (Aggarwal, 2019).

First, it is important to note that SEZ policy is implemented through the collective efforts of various stakeholders, which include government ministries and their respective departments, as well as the private sector, which in a number of cases may have conflicting agendas, concerns and incentives (Matland, 1995). In order to foster effective implementation of SEZs, there is need to enforce effective vertical coordination between layers of government, and horizontal coordination across government departments and public support (Matland, 1995). In India, for example, failures of SEZs were mainly a result of conflicts between interest groups (Aggarwal, 2019). Interestingly, empirical evidence has shown that where top authorities regulate SEZs directly as in Bangladesh, Morocco, the United Arab Emirates and Jordan, and where the state has assumed a strong development role as in China and the Republic of Korea and Taiwan, SEZs are successfully implemented (Aggarwal, 2019).

Second, the ability of SEZs to attract investments such as the FDI determines the success of the SEZs (Aggarwal, 2019). Literature also shows that this ability depends on offsite, onsite, social and technological infrastructure; regulatory facilitation; marketing efforts and services provided to SEZ tenants, and all of these have financial implications (Aggarwal, 2019; Zeng, 2015; Farole, 2011). It therefore means that effective implementation of SEZs may require massive financial resources for their development, management, operations and promotion. This could also be the reason SEZs across the globe have been developed by the private sector as they still required significant public resources for offsite development and administration (Aggarwal, 2019).

Third, public sector responsibilities in the SEZs are not eliminated by private participation in SEZ development. Rather, administrative capabilities within host governments will ensure adequate facilitation, regulation, implementation and conflict resolution between and among the players; hence both private and public players are required to work symbiotically (FIAS, 2008).

Fourth, sound macroeconomic management is essential to create an environment in which trade and investment can grow exponentially for the successful implementation of SEZs (Aggarwal, 2019). This requires a number of support policies aimed at trade and investment which include regional and multilateral trade agreements, bilateral agreements on FDI and multilateral investment guarantee agencies; fiscal, regulation of monetary and exchange rate policies; efficient legal systems; physical property rights and intellectual property rights (Aggarwal, 2019).

Finally, well-designed strategies for risk and cost management are required for effective implementation of SEZs. Market risks and SEZ-related risks are the two types of risks attached to SEZs (Aggarwal, 2019). SEZ-specific risks include non-compliance, money laundering and fraud, and changes in the government attitude towards SEZs. Market risks arise from political upheavals, business cycles and macroeconomic mismanagement. In addition, the literature shows that socio-economic and environmental costs also affect the implementation of SEZs. This therefore calls for rigour, pragmatism and special skills in the design and implementation of the action plans which mainstream various risks which may affect SEZs.

The three-pillared framework presented earlier provides a comprehensive set of conditions for leveraging SEZs for economic transformation. Central to this framework is the argument that it is particularly important that the government should adopt a highly structured approach to developing, implementing and reviewing SEZ policies and strategies. To achieve phenomenal development outcomes using SEZs, the three pillars must continuously reinforce each other.

9.4 The Integrated Institutional Framework and the Global Experience

Relative to the IIF discussed earlier, this section revisits the SEZ experiences of major SEZ-user countries across the globe. In this regard, this section discusses three groups of countries: most successful, not-so-successful, and least successful or unsuccessful. The term "success", in this chapter, represents the extent to which countries successfully leveraged on SEZs to foster economic transformation in the wider economy (Aggarwal, 2019).

Most Successful Countries

The Republic of Korea, China and Taiwan Province of China, by far, have been the most successful economies in leveraging SEZs to achieve far-reaching economic transformation. Over the years, these countries have experienced an unmatched level of sustained economic growth in economic history (Aggarwal, 2019). These countries have used SEZs as a key element of their fully structured development strategies. Because of their unique national development strategies and social, national and institutional contexts, these economies used different policy approaches to SEZs which they constantly reviewed and effectively implemented to achieve phenomenal success in transforming their respective economies (Aggarwal, 2019).

The strategic approach: the Republic of Korea, in the 1960s, focused on import-substitution in heavy industries (fertilisers, cements, steel, machinery and oil refining) in the wider economy (Aggarwal, 2019). The Republic of Korea also created SEZs of the enclave variety (officially called "manufacturing-oriented free trade zones") in order to counter the anti-export bias of the regime and attract FDI in export-oriented light industries (Aggarwal, 2019). This strategy was anticipated to generate foreign currency required for its import substitution programme, to absorb the vast educated workforce, to promote exports, to provide access to new technologies and to promote competitiveness in the light manufacturing without posing any competition to domestic companies (Aggarwal, 2019).

The Taiwan Province of China, in contrast, adopted the "development strategy reinforcing approach" towards SEZs based on EPZs (Aggarwal, 2019). As part of its development strategy and leveraging on EPZs, to upgrade them technologically in their early states of their development, the SEZs placed major focus on SMEs in the light consumer sector and leveraged EPZs to upgrade them technologically at an early stage of their development (Aggarwal, 2019). The government also adopted both pro-active and reactive policy approaches aimed at encouraging linkages between EPZ firms and non-EPZ firms to spur wide economic impact (Wang, 1990).

With regard to the reactive policy, the government reduced barriers of transactions between the EPZ firms and non-EPZ firms in order to encourage subcontracting and local sourcing. Following this, a thousand Taiwanese firms were subcontracted by EPZ firms in 1988 with a value of US$392 million (Wang, 1990).

Regarding the proactive approach, the government supported small businesses in the wider economy through the use of targeted subsidies, import protection, credit and incentives packages in order to help small businesses to build their productive capacities to participate in these transactions, (Evans, 1995; Wade, 1990; Amsden, 1989). By giving them access to a global pool of new technologies, skills, capital and markets, integration with GVCs strengthened the technological competitiveness of SMEs (Aggarwal, 2019). Once integrated with GVCs, these enterprises moved from the assembly of imported inputs to increased local production and sourcing as original equipment manufacturers (OEMs), to original design manufacturing (ODMs) and finally to sell their own branded merchandise (OBMs) (Aggarwal, 2019).

Unlike the Republic of Korea and Taiwan Province of China, China traversed a distinctly different trajectory. China adopted an "SEZ-centred development approach" and placed SEZs at the centre of its cluster-based industrialisation strategy. It laid the foundation for a distinct model of SEZs with an institutional structure that provided considerable economic incentives and leeway to local authorities, large city-like size and openness. These provided ideal conditions for cluster development. SEZs in China were also turned into engines of remarkable growth due to its proximity to Hong Kong (China), extremely low wages, its disciplined labour, its strategic location, its reforms in land policy and massive investment in offsite infrastructure (Zeng, 2016).

Dynamism: as these countries developed, they refocused their SEZs. For example, SEZs in the Republic of Korea, which hosted large conglomerates that were at the centre of the growth process, were marginalised by the late 1980s (Aggarwal, 2019). After the East Asian crisis, Korea leveraged its SEZs to initiate the process of restructuring the economy by giving priority to the development of the logistics industry, which later positioned itself as a logistics hub in the region (Aggarwal, 2019). In this regard, the Republic of Korea set up new logistics-oriented FTZs and upgraded its manufacturing zones with logistics facilities (Aggarwal, 2012b). Both types of zones, between 2008 and 2010, generated US$14.6 billion of exports and US$8.3 billion of imports as well as employing 13,676 people (WTO, 2012). However, SEZs were placed at the centre of balanced regional development and economic transformation in 2002, which resulted in the country transitioning from the enclave-type FTZs to large open SEZs (Aggarwal, 2019). This was buttressed by the establishment of the "free economic zones" (FEZs) programme, which was part of the country's strategy to attract foreign investment, especially in ultra-high-tech and R&D services. FEZs are world-class cities equipped with cutting-edge infrastructure and services, and they are at the centre of the ambitious goals of the development strategy. As of 2014, FEZs in the Republic of Korea hosted 4467 companies with FDI of US$16 billion (Aggarwal, 2019). Because the base of the economy was broadened, FEZs contributed significantly to the resilience of the Korean economy to crises (SaKong & Koh, 2010).

The Taiwan Province of China, like the Republic of Korea, also changed its SEZ strategy over time. However, while the Republic of Korea continuously upgraded the role assigned to SEZs in its development process, the Taiwan Province of China continued to follow the strategy of reinforcing the development strategy through SEZs. That way, the country upgraded its EPZs as incubators of new industries, which resulted in the country's industrial structure experiencing several transformations during the process of development (Aggarwal, 2019). EPZs were upgraded to attract capital-intensive activities in the late 1970s, to align with economic restructuring in the rest of the economy, to high-tech industries in the late 1980s and to the logistics industry in the 1990s. It was therefore possible for SEZ enterprises to establish linkages with domestic producers and further augment their capabilities because the country had domestic capabilities (Aggarwal, 2019). This helped in developing a two-way relationship between EPZ and non-EPZ firms. EPZ investors have thus become important customers for Taiwanese companies outside the zones.

For this reason, domestic inputs which were shipped into the Kaohsiung zone were equivalent to 48% of the zones' total export value in 20,015 (Crook, 2016). EPZs still enjoy immunity from institutional rigidities in the labour market and the FDI regime despite the fact that the administrative regime has been simplified in the wider economy (Aggarwal, 2019). To date, the Taiwan Province of China has ten EPZs and six logistics-oriented FTZs which are clustered together to form two growth poles, in Kaohsiung and in Taichung, which are also reinforced by science parks and industrial parks of various types to act as the force driving their dynamism (Aggarwal, 2019).

Encouraged by the initial success of SEZs, China aggressively established several smaller zones near existing zones, clusters and industrially developed locations so as to generate synergies between them and promote a critical amount of economic activity (Aggarwal, 2019). This way, a myriad of industrial clusters were established to complement SEZs. Like with external economies and complementarities, synergies were created between the SEZs and regional economies using appropriate policy packages and tax incentives (Aggarwal, 2019). Agglomeration economies generated in the process turned the zones into industrial hubs of unprecedented magnitude. For example, by 2007, in 300 of the 326 municipalities, there were 1346 SEZs (Wang, 2013). By locating smaller SEZs within the larger ones to augment them further so that the benefits could also flow within the SEZs, the SEZ sector was also expanded vertically. Strategically, the government played a catalytic role by promoting a network of R&D facilities in higher education institutions and creating conditions for private entrepreneurship to thrive. Further entrants and investment by both foreign and domestic investors were facilitated by clustering of industries (Wang, 2013).

China successfully transformed its SEZs into growth poles (see Chap. 10). For example, in 2015, SEZs led to the establishment of 11 city clusters and industrial clusters of unprecedented size, which accounted for two-thirds of economic output and one-third of the population (Bertaud, 2016). According to the official statistics, the Yangtze economic area alone accounted for 46% of total exports in 2014 (GOC, 2015). With time, China developed strategies with a strong spatial focus to address increasing economic disparities at the regional level within China (Aggarwal, 2019). China also took a strategic approach to use SEZs as the centrepiece of balanced regional development strategies. Thus, the country has since 2020 established about 135 additional economic and technological development zones, of which 77 SEZs were located in inner areas (Aggarwal, 2019). In order to provide a wide range of support in their development under the dynamic support network programme, SEZs were paired with successful SEZs in the East.

Furthermore, in collaboration with Myanmar, Vietnam and the Lao People's Democratic Republic, China initiated the development of border areas by setting up economic zones in these areas in the 1990s (Aggarwal, 2019). In recent years, especially after its ascendance into the WTO in early 2000, the country witnessed synergies between its increasing economic diplomacy and development strategy. In this regard, China is using SEZs as a critical tool of the new strategy (Aggarwal, 2019) (see Chap. 10). As part of the economic diplomacy, through its "going out", China encouraged its Chinese companies to promote the establishment of overseas industrial and trade zones in mid-2000 (Aggarwal, 2019). Thus, as observed by the Ministry of Commerce in 2017, Chinese enterprises established 75 economic cooperation zones in 24 countries, with 3412 enterprises operating in them, and creating 209,000 jobs in the local regions. As SEZs are emerging along the Belt and Road Initiative of China, this number is likely to increase. This evidence clearly demonstrates that China has become a role model for the world in leveraging SEZs to drive economic growth.

Implementation: undoubtedly it is always a challenge to implement an evolutionary strategic approach. However, international experience has shown that, developing economies could exercise their powers for effective implementation of their development strategies and planning by maintaining a strong state in charge of development (Aggarwal, 2019).

Strong political backing, as observed in the Republic of Korea and China, has been critical in ensuring efficient coordination between government ministries, departments and various layers of government with very limited resistance from the public (Aggarwal, 2019). On the economic front, all the three economies offered investors a highly lucrative and comprehensive package of streamlined administrative control, preferential fees for land or facility use, generous tax incentives, reduced duties on imports, free or low-rent standard factories, depreciation allowances, flexibility in hiring and firing workers, good infrastructure, low wage rates and cheap land in order to generate a critical mass of activity within the SEZs (Aggarwal, 2019). In China, in order to ensure effective implementation of SEZs, the government took a devolution approach where administrations were given the powers of provincial government to develop their own regulations for their jurisdiction, facilitate reduction of administrative fees, approve procedures and enhance the service function of government organs (Aggarwal, 2019). In addition, all the three countries had invested in human capital, improved and strengthened the quality of institutions and adopted sound macroeconomic policies (Aggarwal, 2019). They also instituted a number of export-promotion policies such as elimination of quantitative restrictions and tariffs, undervaluation of their foreign exchange rates and regional cooperation agreements. As was always the case, the success of SEZs in these three countries was further supported by political and social stability. Tactically, significant amounts of money were injected into infrastructure development both in the zones and territories outside the SEZs (Aggarwal, 2019).

From these discourses, the lessons we can draw from these three countries are that using the SEZ strategy, a well-structured development model is a prerequisite to achieve phenomenal industrial transformation. What is apparent is that the role of the government is not reduced by the SEZs. In fact, it means an extended development role of government which calls for strong bureaucratic competencies and political will focused on the competitiveness of the economy and continuous strengthening of its capacity.

Not So Successful Countries

Several countries in South Asia, South-East Asia, Latin America, and Central and East Europe have succeeded in leveraging on SEZs to bring about economic transformation. However, such transformation is basically driven by successful SEZ localities. The success of these localities in strengthening the productive capacity in the wider economy is elusive (Aggarwal, 2019). Countries which fall in this category include Indonesia, Cambodia, Malaysia, Thailand, the Philippines and Vietnam in South-East Asia; India, Bangladesh and Sri Lanka in South Asia; Costa Rica, Guatemala, El Salvador, Honduras and Nicaragua in Central America; Jamaica, the Dominican Republic and Panama in the Caribbean Region; Mexico in North America; Poland in Central and East Europe; Jordan, Egypt, Tunisia, Morocco and the United Arab Emirates in the Middle East and North Africa; and Mauritius in Sub-Saharan Africa. SEZs became instrumental in the emergence and growth of the automobile industry (in Mexico, Morocco, Poland, Thailand and Tunisia); electronics processing (in Costa Rica, Indonesia, Malaysia and the Philippines); textile, apparel and other light industries (in Bangladesh, Mauritius, Sri Lanka, Vietnam as well as countries in the Middle East and North Africa, and Central American and Caribbean countries), and the information technology industry (in Ghana, India and the Philippines) (Aggarwal, 2019). SEZs also accounted for a sizeable share of exports, FDI and in some cases even employment in these countries.

In 2010, the electronics sector in Malaysia contributed 27% of the country's manufacturing output, 49% of exports and 32.5% of overall employment (Rasiah et al., 2015). Conversely in the Philippines, SEZs accounted for 2% of employment and 73% of exports in 2011. In Bangladesh, eight small traditional EPZs accounted for 20% of the total exports in 2016–2017, and employed 283,620 workers. In Thailand automotive exports constituted 19% of total manufactured goods exports and 16% of total merchandise exports in 2014 (Warr & Kohpaiboon, 2017). Between 2014 and 2015, SEZ exports accounted for 58% of total exports for the Dominican Republic (World Bank, 2016) and this share was 80% in the early 2000s (World Bank, 2016). Over 2800 Maquiladora companies operating in Mexico also accounted for over 55% of Mexico's exports, and 15% of manufacturing employment.

In the United Arab Emirates, FZ trade accounted for a third of the country's 80% of non-oil exports and non-oil economy (OECD, 2018). The Tanger Med Zones in Morocco accounted for approximately 25% of national exports in 2016 (COMCEC, 2017).

Evidence has also shown that although SEZs in these countries have contributed to the production and export structures mainly by successfully integrating them into GVCs, their contribution in building productive capacities with the rest of the economy has remained marginal (see

OECD, 2017; KPMG, 2014) for Central and East Europe (Hausmann et al., 2017; Frick et al., 2018 and Heron, 2004), for Latin America (Manasan, 2013), for the Philippines (Dassel et al., 2013), for the Middle East and North Africa (Rasiah et al., 2015) and for Malaysia (Karunaratne & Abayasekara, 2013) for Sri Lanka.

The zones fuelled economic growth in Caribbean and Central American countries during the 1990s and the early 2000s. In the 1990s, primary goods accounted for more than half of total exports in goods, and by 2006 their share had fallen to one-third. But the expiry of the MFA led to unprecedented rates of bankruptcy, capital flight and job loss in the face of strong competition in the textile and apparel industry from Asia (World Bank, 2016). Thus, Mauritius, which is normally viewed as a successful case, underwent a similar experience. More so, South-East Asia, which had seen phenomenal growth in exports and built impressive production capabilities in SEZs in relatively high-skill sectors, could not manage to leap to high-income status. Most production at the high end was dominated by foreign multinationals, while low-end activities were performed by local companies. These then began to raise questions on the viability of these SEZ models regarding the missing solutions to the puzzle.

Lack of Integration Between Development Planning and SEZs

The majority of these countries established SEZs as "industrial infrastructure" mainly to attract FDI with a specific emphasis on the manufacturing sector so as to create jobs, exports and foreign exchange but did not align the SEZs with broader development agendas. The majority of the early adopting economies were endowed with natural advantages in exporting, largely related to their geography and factor endowment (Aggarwal, 2019). To this end, by keeping the cost of business low, they effectively leveraged on their SEZs to strengthen their natural advantages and built impressive production capabilities (Aggarwal, 2019).

Malaysia, which is one of the most developed among developing countries, registered 93.23% (close to US$6 billion) of the electronics sector investment originating mainly from Germany, Japan and the United States (Rasiah et al., 2015). Likewise, upgrading and spillovers were limited in Penang due to the proactive approach of the regional government that integrated its SEZ development plans with the regional development plan.

Although Bangladesh succeeded in becoming the second largest exporter of apparel, even after more than 50 years of SEZ experience, the country still focused on the volume-based segment of the industry. In addition, the country continued to import knitting, spinning, dyeing, weaving and other machinery worth billions of foreign currency. Because of the absence of any strategic planning, there were no automatic spill-overs and SEZs remained enclaves of FDI and trade.

Lack of Dynamism in SEZ Approach

Countries encouraged by the performance of SEZs were continuously expanding the number of SEZs with little dynamism in their approach. Evidence shows that countries that had more innovative features aimed at attracting FDI, and the underlying objective was to create these zones in newer sectors and areas. Thus the number of zones continued to increase unrelated to the development process outside the economy. In the absence of dynamism in the zones, mature economies were now competing with emerging low-cost destinations to maintain their competitive advantages in low-end activities. Evidence suggests that in the Malaysia EPZ, firms had successfully lobbied to keep the market open for migrant workers (Rasiah et al., 2015; Somo, 2013; Henderson & Phillips, 2007) to keep it artificially attractive to low-value operations. Similar patterns were also observed in Latin America. The number of industrial parks in the Dominican Republic, which stood at 60 in 2014, had grown to 74 over the past five years. Furthermore, most Latin American countries have had plans to expand their SEZs over the next few years (Mitchell, 2017). Many of these countries were resorting to competitive currency devaluations to continue to attract multinational corporations. There has thus been an intensification of regional competition to attract FDI in the zones. In Central and East Europe, Poland initially established SEZs for a period of 20. Since then, it has extended the programme continuously to keep its SEZs alive. Recently, a new law had extended the SEZ benefits to all of Poland's surface area. Other major economies in the region have adopted similar measures to attract FDI. However, the development impacts on the wider economy have been marginal.

Implementation

As observed in China, Taiwan Province of China and the Republic of Korea, effective implementation is the key factor that explains why these countries succeeded with SEZs. On the contrary, a host of other forgone factors also explain the effective implementation of SEZs in these countries. Such factors include political stability, political support, successful management of macro policies, pro-trade exchange rates and trade policies, successful promotion of SEZs and participation in regional trading agreements (Aggarwal, 2019). These countries are essentially weak developmental states which have failed to make hard decisions necessary to upgrade the wider economy. Following this, they are trapped in the low end of GVCs, and continue to compete with lesser developed countries in this segment (Aggarwal, 2019).

Least Successful Countries

Countries in Central Asia and Sub-Saharan Africa are relative latecomers to economic zones. In Africa, Liberia, Kenya and Mauritius took the lead to set up SEZs in the 1970s. Ironically, amongst the three countries from Africa, only Mauritius succeeded whilst the other two countries SEZs remained dormant. Africa witnessed a mushrooming of SEZs in the post-1990 period and yet 43 of the 54 countries have passed SEZ legislation.

Central Asian economies on the other hand embraced the policy in the post-2000 period. To date, all the five countries in the Central Asian economies have SEZ regimes in place. However, empirical evidence shows that SEZs in these regions have failed even in attracting investment (Aggarwal, 2019; Asian Development Bank (ADB), 2018a, b).

According to Aggarwal (2019), structural factors which are prevalent in most developing countries are some factors that have impeded investment. In addition, the majority of these economies are endowed with natural resources which together with heavy foreign aid inflows have created a "resource curse"-like situation. Additionally, due to relatively high foreign exchange rates and high wages, these countries lose competitiveness in tradable sectors, other than the primary sector. Moreover, many countries in these regions are landlocked, a condition that adds to the costs of logistics and trade. SEZs are typically seen as compensating for an overall lack of competitiveness by offering extended tax holidays, subsidised land, utilities and direct financial incentives to individual investors to attract investment. However, evidence has suggested that the incentive package cannot compensate for lack of competitiveness (Aggarwal, 2019; ADB, 2018a, b). Investor flight from SEZs in Latin American and African countries on the expiry of the MFA is also a case in point.

Interestingly, Egypt, Jordan, Morocco, Tunisia and the United Arab Emirates have all managed to generate substantial gains from their SEZs. Even Sub-Saharan countries such as Ethiopia, Ghana and Kenya have shown dynamism in their SEZs. These countries have managed to overcome structural impediments. However, bureaucratic failures to appropriately address the multiple challenges of SEZ establishment have remained some of the major constraints to effectively implement SEZs. Other factors which were also noted as limiting the performance of SEZs and poor investment climate within and outside SEZs have included weak industrial, transport and communication infrastructure; excessive regulation; poor planning and management; unsuitable locations; low-productivity labour supplies; and rent seeking and a lack of an industrial culture (ADB, 2018a, b; Zeng, 2012; Farole, 2011). These are clear manifestations of bureaucratic failures, lack of technical skills, poor economic management skills, poor social and political climate and lack of motivations. At the root of these lies the predatory nature of these states. Many of these countries are resource-rich and have autocratic governments that exercise unconstrained political authority through "extensive networks of personal patronage that include inefficient bureaucracies staffed with officials selected for their political loyalty rather than for their technical qualifications" (Reno, 2015). The fact that many of these countries are high on the fragility index due to ethnic violence, political instability and rampant corruption bears testament to the predatory nature of the state. SEZs in these countries may thus be a tool for enhancing the political power and wealth through patronage, rather than to bring about economic transformation.

9.5 Conclusion

This chapter has been built on the previous chapter on critical success factors of SEZs and has sought to present a three-pillared analytical framework as the magic behind successful SEZs. The core argument advanced here was that countries that adopt a well-structured approach towards SEZs that can be aligned with the broader development strategy, execute them effectively, and continuously evaluate and change over time, are more successful in achieving SEZ-led economic transformation. This chapter has also shown that South Korea, China and Taiwan have successful SEZs because they had ideal strategic bureaucratic competencies in making the right choices and setting clear strategic directions; had strategic bureaucratic learning to dynamically and interactively engage in adjusting their strategies when needed; and had strategic bureaucratic strengths to implement the strategy effectively. In addition, the chapter has also shown how effective political leadership with a strong development focus energised bureaucracies in successful implementation of SEZs.

Similarly, using grounded evidence on not-so-successful countries from Latin America, Africa, Eastern and Central Europe and least successful countries across the globe, mainly from Africa and Central Asia, this chapter raised some pertinent insights about SEZ-led development strategy that emerge from the analysis. Moreover, to stimulate wider economic impacts, this chapter has argued for institutionalisation of the zones into policy and planning. Specially, the SEZs legislative and policy framework must be an integral and sustainable part of the broader development strategy of a country. For avoidance of doubt, institutionalisation of SEZs means that SEZs must be able to respond to the dynamic realities of the economy as opposed to just entrenching SEZ practices (Aggarwal, 2019).

To this end, this chapter also drew on literature by Aggarwal (2019) on cohesive, comprehensive and integrated three-pillared analytical framework for linking SEZs with broader development planning called IIF.

The following are the three pillars of the IIF :

A well-structured strategic approach to SEZs which is well grounded in a broader holistic economic development strategy; strategic dynamism in the approach towards SEZs which is well informed by continuous changes in economic conditions to adapt the current SEZ strategies to new development challenges and opportunities, and lastly effective implementation of these strategies.

The central argument was that countries which succeeded in using SEZs to have wider economic impact have adopted a well-structured strategic approach towards SEZs which they effectively executed and continuously evaluated and monitored (Aggarwal, 2019). This requires strategic bureaucratic learning to dynamically and interactively engage in adjusting the strategies when needed; bureaucratic competencies to make the right choices and set clear strategic directions; and strategic bureaucratic strengths along with strong political support to implement the strategy effectively (Aggarwal, 2019). These elements in turn were seen to be contingent upon leadership that can energise bureaucracies to achieve the broader development goals and earn creditability, visibility, resources and political will for positive economic transformation (Ellison, 1995). However, this feat can be performed by only a handful countries in the world, mainly China, South Korea and Taiwan (Aggarwal, 2019).

References

ADB. (2018a). *Strategic Framework for Special Economic Zones and Industrial Zones in Kazakhstan*. Asian Development Bank.

ADB. (2018b). *Strategic Framework for Free Economic Zones and Industrial Parks in the Kyrgyz Republic*. Asian Development Bank.

Aggarwal, A. (2012a). *Social and Economic Impact of SEZs in India*. OUP Catalogue, Oxford University Press.

Aggarwal, A. (2012b). SEZ-Led Growth in Taiwan, Korea, and India: Implementing a Successful Strategy. *Asian Survey, 52*(5), 872–899.

Aggarwal, A. (2019). SEZs and Economic Transformation: Towards a Developmental Approach. *Transnational Corporations, 26*(2), 27–48.

Amsden, A. (1989). *Asia's Next Giant: South Korea and Late Industrialization*. Oxford University Press.

Baldwin, R. (2013). Global Supply Chains: Why They Emerged, Why They Matter, and Where They Are Going. In K. E. Deborah & L. Patrick (Eds.), *Global Value Chains in a Changing World*. Fung Global Institute, Nanyang Technological University, and World Trade Organization Secretariat.

Bertaud, A. (2016, December 14). The new Chinese City Clusters: Would the Current Urban Transport Technology Be Able to Serve These Very Large Urban Labour Markets? *World Resources Institute*. http://www.wri.org/sites/default/les/new-Chinese-city-clusters.pdf

COMCEC. (2017). *Special Economic Zones in the OIC Region: Learning from Experience*. Report Submitted to the COMCEC Coordination Office.

Crook, S. (2016, December 19). Taiwan's Export Processing Zones: Forward-Looking at 50. *Taiwan Business Topics*.

Dassel, K., Eckermann, K., & Barclay, S. (2013). Economic Security and Competitiveness: Using Special Economic Zones to Drive Job Creation in MENA. *Monitor Deloitte*. https://www2.deloitte.com/content/dam/Deloitte/us/Documents/strategy/us-consulting-economicsecurity.pdf

Ellison, B. A. (1995). A Conceptual Framework for Analysing Bureaucratic Politics and Autonomy. *The American Review of Public Administration, 25*(2), 161–182.

Evans, P. (1995). *Embedded Autonomy: States and Industrial Transformation*. Princeton University Press.

Farole, T. (2011). *Special Economic Zones in Africa: Comparing Performance and Learning from Global Experiences*. World Bank Publications.

FIAS. (2008). *Special Economic Zones: Performance, Lessons Learned and Implications for Zone Development*. Report of Facility for Investment Climate Advisory Services, the Multi- Donor Service Managed by the International Finance Corporation. Unpublished. World Bank Publications.

Frick, S. A., Rodríguez-Pose, A., & Wong, M. D. (2018). Towards Economically Dynamic Special Economic Zones in Emerging Countries. *Journal of Economic Geography, 95*(1), 30–64.

GOC. (2015). China Statistical Yearbook, 2015. http://www.stats.gov.cn/tjsj/ndsj/2015/indexeh.htm

Hausmann, R., Obach, J., & Santos, M. A. (2017). *Special Economic Zones in Panama: Technology Spill-Overs from a Labour Market Perspective* (Working Paper). Harvard University Centre for International Development.

Henderson, J., & Phillips, R. (2007). Unintended Consequences: Social Policy, State Institutions and the "Stalling" of the Malaysian Industrialization Project. *Economy and Society, 36*(1), 78–102.

Heron, T. (2004). *The New Political Economy of United States-Caribbean Relations: The Apparel Industry and the Politics of NAFTA Parity*. Routledge.

Karunaratne, C., & Abayasekara, A. (2013). *Impact of EPZs on Poverty Reduction and Trade Facilitation in Sri Lanka* (ARTNeT Working Paper Series No. 134). ESCAP.

KPMG. (2014). *Twenty Years of Special Economic Zones in Poland: A Guide to SEZs*. https://www.paih.gov.pl/les/?id_plik=24349

Manasan, R. G. (2013). *Export Processing Zones, Special Economic Zones: Do We Really Need to Have More of Them?* (Policy Notes). Philippine Institute for Development Studies.

Matland, R. E. (1995). Synthesizing the Implementation Literature: The Ambiguity-Con ICT Model of Policy Implementation. *Journal of Public Administration Research and Theory, 5*(2), 145–174.

Milberg, W., Jiang, X., & Geref, G. (2014). Industrial Policy in the Era of Vertically Specialized Industrialization. In J. Salazar-Xirinachs & R. Kozul-Wright (Eds.), *Transforming Economies: Making Industrial Policy Work for Growth, Jobs and Development*. UNCTAD and ILO.

Mitchell, J. (2017, February 16). Latin America Braced for SEZ Surge. *FDI Magazine*. Financial Times Publication.

OECD. (2017). *Tracking Special Economic Zones in the Western Balkans: Objectives, Features and Key Challenges*. Organisation for Economic Co-operation and Development.

OECD. (2018). *Trends in Trade and Investment Policies in the MENA Region: Background Note*. http://www.oecd.org/mena/competitiveness/WGTI2018-Trends-Trade-Investment-Policies-MENA-Nasser-Saidi.pdf. Accessed 10 Aug 2019.

Rasiah, R., Crinis, V., & Lee, H. (2015). Industrialization and Labour in Malaysia. *Journal of the Asia Pacific Economy, 20*(1), 77–99.

Reno, W. (2015). Predatory States and State Transformation. In S. Leibfried, E. Huber, M. Lange, J. D. Levy, & J. D. Stephens (Eds.), *The Oxford Handbook of Transformations of the State*. Oxford University Press.

SaKong, I., & Koh, Y. (Eds.). (2010). *The Korean Economy: Six Decades of Growth and Development*. Korea Development Institute.

SOMO. (2013). *Outsourcing Labour: Migrant Labour Rights in Malaysia's Electronics Industry*. Somo Centre for Research on Multinational Corporations.

UNCTAD. (2019). *World Investment Report 2019: Special Economic Zones*. United Nations.

Wade, R. (1990). *Governing the Market: Economic Theory and the Role of Government in Taiwan's Industrialization*. Princeton University Press.

Wang, K. S. (1990). Linkage Effects in Taiwan EPZs. In R. L. Bolin (Ed.), *Linking the Export Processing Zone to Local Industry*. Flagstaff Institute.

Wang, J. (2013). The Economic Impact of Special Economic Zones: Evidence from Chinese Municipalities. *Journal of Development Economics, 101*(C), 133–147.

Warr, P., & Kohpaiboon, A. (2017). *Thailand's Automotive Manufacturing Corridor* (ADB Economics Working Paper Series 519). Asian Development Bank.

World Bank. (2016). *Special Economic Zones in the Dominican Republic: Policy Considerations for a More Competitive and Inclusive Sector*. World Bank.

WTO. (2012). *Trade Policy Review, South Korea*. WTO.

Zeng, D. Z. (2012). *SEZs in Africa: Putting the Cart in Front of Horse?* (Blog). Washington, DC: World Bank.

Zeng, D. Z. (2015). *Global Experiences with Special Economic Zones: Focus on China and Africa* (World Bank Policy Research Working Paper 7240). Washington, DC: World Bank.

Zeng, D. Z. (2016). Global Experiences of Special Economic Zones with Focus on China and Africa: Policy Insights. *Journal of International Commerce, Economics and Policy, 7*(3), 1650018.

PART V

What Can Africa Learn from China and Other Asian Countries About Special Economic Zones

CHAPTER 10

Chinese Experiences on Special Economic Zones

10.1 Introduction

China is regarded as one of the most successful countries in terms of leveraging on SEZs to achieve comprehensive economic transformations. The secret behind China's success was the methodological approaches used in the establishment of the SEZs. In this regard, China used a gradual approach where the country started with four zones at the initial stage to experiment with market-oriented economic reforms, which involve laws, regulations, taxation, land, labour, finance, customs, immigration and so on (Zeng, 2010, 2015a, b). After being successful, the zone programme and relevant reforms were sequentially and gradually rolled out throughout the country in more diversified forms, and some of the zones were designed with more sophisticated agendas, such as the high-tech industrial parks (Zeng, 2010).

Together with the numerous industrial clusters, the SEZs have contributed significantly to national GDP, employment, exports, and attraction of FDIs. It was estimated that in recent years, SEZs at national level accounted for about 22% of national GDP, 46% of FDI and 60% of exports, and had generated in excess of 30 million jobs (UNCTAD, 2019; Zeng, 2015a, b). SEZs have also played important roles in bringing new technologies to China, and in adopting modern management practices (UNCTAD, 2019). While most lessons in China are positive, such as gradualism with a pragmatic and experimental approach; reform-oriented mindset; strong

G. Mugano, *Special Economic Zones*,
https://doi.org/10.1007/978-3-030-82311-5_10

commitment and active facilitation of the state; opening up to FDIs; sound infrastructure; effective marketing and investment promotion; and continuous technology learning and upgrading (Zeng, 2015a, b), there have also been some adverse lessons for the latecomers such as the "mushroom approach" at the local levels and high-level overlaps of various zones with vicious competitions at the later stage; environmental degradation; and limited urban–industry integration, with some exceptions such as the Suzhou Industrial Park.

This chapter therefore presents a detailed analysis of the Chinese SEZs' methodological approach as well as various forms of SEZs, their successes and their failures as learning points for developing countries.

10.2 Overview of Special Economic Zones in China

Special economic zones were part of the special policies reforms and flexible measures which were undertaken by the Chinese government from July 1979 (Yeung et al., 2009). In August 1980, China initially designated SEZs in Shenzhen, Zhuhai and Shantou in Guangdong Province (Yeung et al., 2009). In October 1980, additional SEZs were established in Xiamen in Fujian Province.

All the four SEZs were similar since they enjoyed special financial, investment, trade privileges and comprised large areas within which the objective was to facilitate comprehensive economic development. To shield the SEZs from political interference and risks, they were deliberately located far from the centre of political power in Beijing (Zeng, 2012a, b).

The coastal areas of Guangdong and Fujian, which had a long history of being a gateway to the rest of the world as well as Hong Kong, Macao and Taiwan, hosted the four SEZs (UNDP, 2015). Shenzhen was chosen because of its strategic nature since its location was across a narrow river from Hong Kong; the principal area from which China could learn capitalist modes of economic growth and modern management technologies (Yeung et al., 2009).

The impact of the SEZs was immediate. For example, in 1981, 59.8% of total FDI in China was accounted for the four zones, with Shenzhen contributing to a significant share of 50.6% (Wong, 1987). Although the share of FDI in the four declined in the next three years, these zones still accounted for 26% of China's total FDI (UNCTAD, 2019; Zeng, 2018).

In 1985, the four zones realised FDI amounting to US$1.17 billion, which was 20% of the total FDI recorded by China (Wong, 1987).

The zones witnessed phenomenal growths rates which were higher than the national average annual GDP of 10% between 1980 and 1984. Precisely, Shenzhen grew at an unprecedented rate of 58% per year, followed by Zhuhai (32%), Xiamen (13%) and Shantou (9%). By 1986, Shenzhen had already developed basic markets in labour, capital, land, technology, communication and other areas of production (Yeung et al., 2009).

The early success of the SEZs noted here was the result of the right combination of factors in the production in these zones and favourable policies.

Building on this success, China agreed to extend the reforms beyond the four initial zones. In this regard, in 1984, the government established different types of SEZs which were dubbed economic and technological development zones (ETDZs), or rather known as China's national industrial parks. The distinct difference between the ETDZs and the SEZs is one of scale. Naturally, an SEZ is both comprehensive and occupies a much larger area (sometimes an entire city or province) whilst the ETDZ normally occupies a small area, for example, along a coastal area (Zeng, 2016).

Following the expansion agenda of SEZs, China established 14 TDZs in the coastal cities between 1984 and 1985, and in the subsequent years more ETDZs were created in the cities along the Yangtze River Delta, the Pearl River Delta and the Min Delta in Fujian (Zeng, 2012a, b, 2016). In addition, the province of Hainan was designated as the fifth SEZ, while Shanghai and Tianjin were respectively granted SEZ status in 1989 and 2006.

In 1992, the Chinese government established 35 additional ETDZs (Farole, 2011). Through the establishment of these ETDZs, China aimed to extend the ETDZs from the coastline to inland regions and to focus less on fundamental industries and more on technology-intensive industries. By December 2008, 54 state-level ETDZs were established. The number of ETDZs increased to 69 by April 2010 which were distributed among Yangtze River Delta (18), Pearl River Delta (10), central region (15), Bohai Bay region (11), north-east region (2) and western region (13) (Farole, 2011).

Over and above the SEZs and ETDZs, China established more specialised SEZs, which included FTZs, high-tech industrial development zones (HIDZs) and EPZs.

High-Tech Industrial Development Zones

The main objective of the HIDZs is to use the technological capacity and resources of research institutes, universities and large and medium enterprises to expedite the commercialisation of R&D, and to develop new and high-tech products (World Bank, 2010). The first HIDZ was established in 1988 in Zhongguancun (Beijing) and as of 2012 there were 54 state-level HIDZs in China of which 29 were in inland regions while 25 were in the coastal region (Tao et al., 2016).

Like ETDZs, the HIDZs made a significant contribution in promoting China's high-tech industries (China Knowledge Online, 2009). Furthermore, in 2006, the five top performers in terms of value-added were Beijing Zhongguancun, Shanghai Zhangjiang, Nanjing, Wuxi and Shenzhen (Brautigam & Xiaoyang, 2011).

Free Trade Zones

FTZs were established as part of the Chinese experiments with free trade before China's accession to the WTO (Yuan et al., 2010). The main thrust of the FTZs was three -pronged, which is foreign trade, export processing and logistics and bonded warehousing. In 1990, China established the first state-level FTZ in Shanghai called the Waigaoqiao FTZ (Zeng, 2012a, b).

The Chinese government established 15 FTZs in its 13 coastal cities (Farole, 2011). However, the uniqueness of the FTZs and their respective advantages faded away after the country acceded to the WTO. In order to maintain competitive advantages of the FTZs, China linked the FTZs with nearby ports by 2004. In this way, by adding scope on the functions of FTZs, particularly by strengthening their roles in warehousing and logistical function in foreign trade, FTZs became more relevant and effective in promoting investments in China (China Knowledge Online, 2009).

These FTZs were viewed as enclaves within China. Interestingly, they functioned outside China's customs regulations even though they were physically inside China's border. As part of fiscal incentives, China granted tax refunds on exports, concessionary VAT and exemption on duty for companies in the FTZs (Zeng, 2012b).

Export-Processing Zones

EPZs were created to promote the establishment of export-oriented industries and enhance foreign exchange earnings. Although EPZs were identical to FTZs, they were exclusively established for the purpose of managing export processing. This way, companies involved in export trading and processing have preferred FTZs, while manufacturing enterprises which export most of its products, and all of it in some cases, have preferred EPZs because they have more location advantages (ProLogis, 2008).

In this regard, the first EPZ was established in Kunshan in 2000. To date, China has established 61 EPZs, 17 of which are located inland while 44 are located in the coastal region (Zeng, 2012a, b; Yuan et al., 2010).

10.3 Contributions of Special Economic Zones to China's Development

The SEZs remained an effective vehicle for the transformation and success of the Chinese economy. The most interesting aspect of the SEZs was that they were used to successfully test the market economy and new institutions, and hence became "role models" for the rest of the country (Tao et al., 2016; Zeng, 2012, 2016; Brautigam & Xiaoyang, 2011).

SEZs have also made significant contribution towards the country's GDP, exports, employment and attraction of foreign investment and new technologies, as well as adoption of modern management practices among others.

Contribution to Gross Domestic Product

With respect to GDP, in 2006, for example, the five initial SEZs accounted for 5% of China's total GDP (Tao et al., 2016; Zeng, 2012a, b, 2016; Brautigam & Xiaoyang, 2011; Yuan et al., 2010 and others). Likewise, in 2006, 54 national ETDZs accounted for 5% of total GDP (Zeng, 2012a, b, 2016; Brautigam & Xiaoyang, 2011; Farole, 2011). In 2006, the 54 state-level ETDZs, 53 state-level HIDZs and 15 FTZs accounted for a combined 11.1% of China's total GDP (Tao et al., 2016; Zeng, 2012a, b, 2016; Yuan et al., 2010).

However, when all forms of SEZs were combined, that is, SEZs including the seven comprehensive SEZs, ETDZs, HIDZs and FTZs, they accounted for approximately 18.5% of China's total GDP in 2006 (Tao et al., 2016; Farole, 2011).

Contribution to Foreign Investment

The SEZs have acted as a major platform for attracting foreign investment. For example, in 2007, US$7.3 billion of FDI was realised in five initial SEZs (Zeng, 2012a, b). Shanghai Pudong and Tianjin Binhai combined attracted US$7.2 billion while the ETDZs attracted about US$17.3 billion and the FTZs raked in US$2.6 billion (Zeng, 2012a; Zhong et al., 2009).

In summary, based on the available data, of the US$74 billion attracted by China in 2007, the SEZs combined (EPZs, FTZs, SEZs and ETDZs) contributed to about 46% of the total FDI (Zeng, 2012a, b, 2018; UNCTAD, 2019).

Contribution to Employment

One of the objectives of the SEZs is to create employment. Rightly so, SEZs in China significantly contributed to job creation. For example, by 2006, the initial five SEZs contributed a cumulative figure of approximately 15 million jobs, that is, 2% of national employment (Zeng, 2012a, b). Likewise, in 2007–2008, Shanghai Pudon area contributed about 1.47 million jobs (Shanghai Pudong Government, 2008), 17% of the total employment of the municipality of Shanghai. In the same vein, in 2007, Tianjin Binhai SEZ created 0.33 million jobs, which is 5.4% of the total Tianjin municipality employment (Zeng, 2012b).

In addition, in 2007, 54 ETDZs and 54 HIDZs created total employment of about 5.35 million and 6.5 million, respectively (MOST, 2009). Cumulatively, the seven SEZs, ETDZs and HIDZs accounted for about 4% of total national employment in China (770 million). However, Zeng (2012a, b) argued that this figure is conservative, and if all the SEZs in many subnationals were included, the total employment could be above 10% (Zeng, 2016).

Contribution to High Technology

As anticipated, the SEZs in China contributed significantly to the establishment of new technology and high-tech firms. For example, in 2007, the 54 HIDZs hosted approximately 50% of the national high-tech firms and science and technology incubators (Zeng, 2012a, b; Zhong et al., 2009). As a result of this, SEZs contributed to over 50,000 invention patents of which more than 70% were registered by domestic firms (Zhong et al., 2009). The SEZs also hosted 1.2 million people working on R&D, that is 18.5% of employees in HIDZs, and accounted for 33% of the national high-tech output (Tao et al., 2016; Qian, 2008).

Consistently, for over 15 years since their formation, HIDZs accounted for 50% of China's high-tech gross industrial output and one-third of China's high-tech exports (Zeng, 2015a, b). Likewise, the ETDZs, on their own contributed to 33% of China's high-tech industrial output and exports (Zeng, 2012a, b, 2016; Yeung et al., 2009).

To date, because of the impact of the SEZs (ETDZs and HIDZs), a number of Chinese-patented products have a large share of the international market, for example, ZTE, Huawei and Great Wall computers (Yeung et al., 2009).

10.4 Major Factors for Success and Lessons Learned

Many factors contributed to the success of China's SEZs, and in every case, the situations and factors might be different. However, their success draws on some common key elements and points to some common lessons.

Strong Commitment to Reform and Pragmatism from Top Leadership

The reforms process which was initiated by Deng around 1978 got endorsement from the top leadership of the country notwithstanding the uncertainty around the reforms (Zeng, 2012a, b, 2016; Farole, 2011; Yuan et al., 2010 and others). To be specific, at the inception of the reforms, political and ideological wars were prevalent, but China decisively abandoned such debates and embraced a practical path to development. This sentiment is vividly captured in Deng's famous saying:

> *No matter if it is a white cat or a black cat, as long as it can catch mice, it is a good cat.*

Most importantly, the Chinese government was very pragmatic in its approach as it used both experiments on and a gradual approach to the reforms process. This gave an opportunity to the government to learn and correct the shortcomings of the reforms as it scaled up the reform agenda. As part of its pragmatism, China contextualised the SEZs model to its own unique situation and circumstances as opposed to simply copying ready-made models (Farole, 2011).

Preferential Policies and Institutional Autonomy

In order to attract investors into the zones, China promulgated several preferential policies including provision of cheap land, easy repatriation of profits and capital investments, tax breaks, rapid customs clearance, duty exemptions on imports of raw materials as well as intermediate goods going into production of export-destined products, export tax exemption and a limited licence to sell on the domestic market, among others (Enright et al., 2005). Moreover, attractive policies such as provision of research funds, subsidies for children's education and housing were put in place to attract skilled labour and the overseas diaspora (Chen & de'Medici, 2009).

In addition, the government granted the SEZs (particularly the comprehensive SEZs and ETDZs) greater economic and political autonomy. In this regard, the country has legislative framework which empowers its municipalities to develop municipal laws in line with national laws and regulations, including local tax rates and structures, and to govern and administer these zones (UNCTAD, 2019; Zeng, 2018). This discretion allowed various provinces more freedom in pursuing the new policies and the development measures deemed necessary to vitalise the economy. For example, SEZs were used as a vehicle to establish a labour market. In this regard, firms operating inside the zones were allowed to enter into enforceable labour contracts with specific term limits and provisions that they could dismiss underperforming employees, and also had flexibility to wages in line with market dynamics (ProLogis, 2008). These factors were critical to attracting the right talent.

Strong Support and Proactive Participation of Governments

In order to create an open and conducive legal and policy environment for SEZs, central government decentralised its power (Zeng, 2015a, b). Combined with this, local governments made extra efforts to establish a sound and conducive business environment for investors. In this regard, the local authorities put in place not only an efficient regulatory and administrative regime but also sound and good infrastructure such as water, roads, gas, electricity, sewerage, telephone and ports, which at the initial stages were funded by the government (UNDP, 2015).

Over and above basic infrastructure, local governments provided various business services to a number of the SEZs, particularly to the ETDZs and HIDZs, which included legal, accounting, marketing, business planning, import–export assistance, management consulting and skills training. For example, in Suzhou Technology Park, the government offered seed money, laboratories, information services, technology-trading rooms, product-testing centres and other benefits to start-ups (Zeng, 2001, 2012a, b).

In response to changing market conditions, changing business needs and the development stage of the SEZs, the governments made timely adjustments to relevant regulations and policies in order to guarantee the initial attractiveness of the zones and their relevance to the economic development of the country (Farole, 2011). For instance, after recording impressive success, the government placed more emphasis on the need to create a level playing field for both domestic and foreign enterprises towards the production of technology-intensive or high-value-added products. For this reason, in 2007, China established a common effective tax rate of 25% for both domestic and foreign companies (Chen & de'Medici, 2009).

Land Reforms

Prior to the introduction of reforms and SEZs, in particular, the government had total ownership of all land in China. However, as part of the support mechanism for the SEZs, land reforms which started from Shenzhen have significantly contributed to the SEZs (Chen & de'Medici, 2009). The land reforms, which were started in November 1981 after the Guangdong government passed the Provisional Regulations of Land Control in the Shenzhen SEZ, allowed investors to apply to the SEZ authorities for land use certificate, which has a lifespan of 20–50 years depending on the type of activity and the sector (World Bank, 2010). The land use certificate had quoted standard land use fees within the SEZ which are at concessionary rates. Provincial governments used the fees to finance initial infrastructure and real estate development. By 1987, all coastal SEZs were allowing foreign investors to lease land from governments.

Foreign Direct Investment and the Chinese Diaspora

The Chinese diaspora and FDI contributed to the success of the SEZs through a number of ways which included attracting capital investment, technologies and management skills; generating learning and spillovers; and ultimately building local manufacturing capacity (Zeng, 2016; Tao et al., 2016). Coincidentally, at a time when Hong Kong, Macao and Taiwan were starting to upgrade their industrial structure and transfer out their labour-intensive manufacturing sectors, China was beginning its reform agenda and the SEZs were its flagship project (Zeng, 2016; Tao et al., 2016).

Favourable policies such as generous fiscal incentives, cheap labour and good infrastructure in the SEZs attracted FDI into the zones from the diaspora. Given the language, culture and location advantages, diaspora investments were dominant in the beginning stage, particularly for the early SEZs (UNCTAD, 2019).

Technology Learning, Innovation, Upgrading and Strong Links with the Domestic Economy

One of the key strengths of the SEZs, in particular the HIDZs and ETDZs, is that they have a high concentration of very skilled people, including many R&D personnel. To this end, they have become centres of knowledge and technology generation, diffusion, adaptation and innovation (Wong & Chu, 1984). In line with conventional wisdom, which states that FDI should provide a good opportunity for technology learning and transfer, this was the case with China. However, what was striking is that China recognised that the nexus between FDI and technological transfer is not automatic or guaranteed but requires that governments strongly emphasis on technology learning and innovation, and on technology-intensive industries.

For example, the Shenzhen government established an intellectual property office and promulgated various policies and regulations that protect intellectual property rights. In addition, in order to promote technology such as R&D spending, software and integrated circuits, and attract technology talents and capital investments, the Shenzhen government implemented a number of preferential tax policies and fiscal incentives (Chen & de'Medici, 2009). Similarly, in the Tianjin Economic-Technological Development Area, China placed great emphasis on technological innovation. For example, within the zone, the government built major technology innovation platforms, such as R&D centres, innovation parks and industrialisation bases (Farole, 2011).

In addition, the policy matrix of China fostered SEZs, through supply chains or value chains, to closely link to local businesses and industrial clusters. This linkage did not only help to stimulate synergistic learning and boost industrial competitiveness but also enhanced economies of scale and business efficiency (Chen & de'Medici, 2009).

Innovative Cultures

The composition of people in the SEZs, in addition to institutional flexibility, helped nurture innovation and entrepreneurship. The SEZs were open to all qualified workers and were attractive to a large number of immigrants from across the country and overseas (Farole, 2011). As expected, such a strongly motivated migrant community mix generated an innovative and entrepreneurial culture. For instance, in Shenzhen, migrants accounted for 83% of the total population. Among its permanent citizens, 21% were under 16 while 62% are between the ages of 17 and 44 (Asian Development Bank, 2007).

Such a young and innovative culture made Shenzhen one of the most dynamic SEZs in ChinaS. As a result, Shenzhen was the first city in China to privatise part of its state-owned enterprises through stock-sharing plans, establish a centre to monitor currency exchange rates, allow the entry of foreign banks and establish a stock exchange in 1990 (Asian Development Bank, 2007).

Clear Objectives, Benchmarks and Intense Competition

SEZs in China were established in a sequential and gradual manner. As initially highlighted, the country started with four SEZs, and built and drew lessons from, and refined, the SEZs until they reached a stage where the government could launch more SEZs rapidly (Farole, 2011; Chen & de'Medici, 2009).

Besides this is the fact that China hosts the largest number of SEZs, that is, 50% of world SEZs, all with clear goals and targets such as GDP, exports, growth, employment, FDI and revenues (Chen & de'Medici, 2009).

Peculiarly, the thousands of SEZs in China are highly competitive among themselves. In this regard, each SEZ endeavours to distinguish itself in quality of infrastructure, service and appearance to attract new enterprises and achieve certain set development goals (UNCTAD, 2019). This kind of competition, which is unique, has helped in making the SEZs more competitive and efficient.

Location Advantages

The majority of the SEZs in China are located near major cities or in the coastal region with a tradition of foreign trading or history of business, and are therefore easily linked to the international market (Zeng, 2012b). The SEZs are also linked to major infrastructures such as airports, ports and railways. For example, SEZs in the Min Delta (close to Taiwan, China) and the Pearl River Delta regions have location advantage.

On the other hand, Hong Kong, in particular, provided China with capital, access to international markets, logistical support, technology, management know-how and management skills (Farole, 2011). Likewise, the Pearl River Delta region has provided the SEZs with land, labour and natural resources. It can thus be argued that these local advantages have enabled the Greater Pearl River Delta region to emerge relatively quickly as one of the world's major manufacturing bases (Enright et al., 2005).

10.5 Conclusion

This chapter has explored the SEZs programmes undertaken by China which resulted in the country being regarded as one of the most successful in terms of leveraging the SEZs to achieve comprehensive economic transformations. The secret behind China's success was the methodological approaches used in the establishment of the SEZs. In this regard, China used a gradual approach where the country started with four zones at the initial stage to experiment with market-oriented economic reforms which involved laws, regulations, taxation, land, labour, finance, customs and immigration (Zeng, 2010, 2015a, b). After being successful, the zone programme and relevant reforms were sequentially and gradually rolled out throughout the country in more diversified forms, and some of the zones were designed with more sophisticated agendas, such as the high-tech industrial parks (Zeng, 2010).

Together with the numerous industrial clusters, the SEZs have contributed significantly to national GDP, employment, exports and attraction of FDI. It was estimated that in recent years, SEZs at national level accounted for about 22% of national GDP, 46% of FDI and 60% of exports, and had generated in excess of 30 million jobs (UNCTAD, 2019; Zeng, 2015a, b). The SEZs have also played important roles in bringing new technologies to China and in adopting modern management practices (UNCTAD, 2019). While most lessons in China are positive, such as gradualism with a pragmatic experimental approach, reform-oriented mindset, strong commitment and active facilitation of the state, opening up to FDIs, sound infrastructure, effective marketing and investment promotion, and continuous technology learning and upgrading (Zeng, 2015a, b), there are also some adverse lessons for the latecomers to avoid, such as the "mushroom approach" at the local levels and high-level overlaps of various zones with vicious competitions at a later stage, environmental degradation and limited urban–industry integration, with some exceptions such as the Suzhou Industrial Park. Thus far, the Chinese experience has enormously provided us with important lessons for developing countries wanting to use SEZs for similar purposes.

References

Asian Development Bank. (2007). *Special Economic Zones and Competitiveness: A Case Study of Shenzhen, China*. PRM (Pakistan Resident Mission) Policy Note, Islamabad.

Brautigam, D., & Xiaoyang, T. (2011). African Shenzhen: China's Special Economic Zones in Africa. *Modern African Studies, 49*(1), 27–54.

Chen, X., & de'Medici, T. (2009). *The "Instant City" Coming of Age: China's Shenzhen Special Economic Zone in Thirty Years* (Working Paper No. 2). Centre for Urban and Global Studies at Trinity College.

China Knowledge Online. (2009). *China Special Report: Industrial Parks—China's Vehicles for Manufacturing*. http://www.chinaknowledge.com

Enright, M. J., Scott, E. E., & Chang, K.-m. (2005). *Regional Powerhouse: The Greater Pearl River Delta and the Rise of China*. John Wiley & Sons (Asia).

Farole, T. (2011). *Special Economic Zones in Africa: Comparing Performance and Learning from Global Experience*. World Bank.

MOST (Ministry of Science and Technology). (2009). *China Torch Statistical Yearbook 2009*. China Statistics Press.

ProLogis. (2008). China's Special Economic Zones and National Industrial Parks—Door Openers to Economic Reform. *ProLogis Research Bulletin* (Spring).

Qian, J. (2008, December). *National High-Tech Industry Development Zones.* Presentation to the EU Science and Technology Counsellors Meeting, Beijing.

Tao, Y., Yuan, Y., & Li, M. (2016). Chinese Special Economic Zones: Lessons for Africa. *Africa Economic Brief, 7*(6), 1–11.

UNCTAD. (2019). *World Investment Report: Special Economic Zones.* United Nations.

UNDP. (2015). *Comparative Study on Special Economic Zones in Africa and China.* UNDP.

Wong, K. (1987). China's Special Economic Zone Experiment: An Appraisal. *Geografiska Annaler Series B. Human Geography, 69*(1), 27–40.

Wong, K., & Chu, D. K. (1984). Export Processing Zones and Special Economic Zones as Generators of Economic Development: The Asian Experience. *Geografiska Annaler, 66*(1), 1–16.

World Bank. (2010). *Chinese Investments in Special Economic Zones in Africa: Progress, Challenges, and Lessons Learned.* World Bank.

Yeung, Y., Lee, J., & Kee, G. (2009). China's Special Economic Zones at 30. *Eurasian Geography and Economics, 50*(2), 222–240.

Yuan, Y., et al. (2010). *China's First Economic Zone: The Case of Shenzhen –Building Engines for Growth and Competitiveness in China.* World Bank.

Zeng, D. Z. (2001). *"Suzhou Technology Park." Research Note for WBI Development Series* (China and the Knowledge Economy: Seizing the 21st Century). World Bank.

Zeng, D. Z. (2010). *Building Engines for Growth and Competitiveness in China: Experience with Special Economic Zones and Industrial Clusters.* World Bank.

Zeng, D. Z. (2012a). *SEZs in Africa: Putting the Cart in Front of Horse?* World Bank.

Zeng, D. Z. (2012b). *An Overview of Six Economic Zones in Nigeria: Challenges and Opportunities* (World Bank Policy Note). World Bank.

Zeng, D. Z. (2015a). *Global Experiences with Special Economic Zones – With a Focus on China and Africa.* World Bank.

Zeng, D. Z. (2015b). *Global Experiences with Special Economic Zones: Focus on China and Africa* (World Bank Policy Research Working Paper 7240). World Bank.

Zeng, D. Z. (2016). Global Experiences of Special Economic Zones with Focus on China and Africa: Policy Insights. *Journal of International Commerce, Economics and Policy, 7*(3), 1–27.

Zeng, D. Z. (2018). *Special Economic Zones: Lessons from the Global Experience.* World Bank.

Zhong, J., et al. (Eds.). (2009). *Annual Report on the Development of China's Special Economic Zones.* Beijing: Social Sciences Academy Press.

PART VI

Conclusions and Way Forward

CHAPTER 11

Towards a New Generation of Special Economic Zones

11.1 Introduction

Analysis in this book has shown that SEZs are ubiquitous although the majority of them have performed dismally. Evidence presented in Chap. 1 shows that SEZs are used by more than 140 economies around the world of which 70% are developing countries and transition economies (UNCTAD, 2019). In recent years, countries have also used SEZs as part of their industrial policies, thereby resulting in the surge of SEZs (UNCTAD, 2018, 2019). As noted by UNCTAD (2019), more than 500 SEZs are in the pipeline, thus reflecting countries' desire to seek relatively low-cost shortcuts to economic development and integration into international production networks in response to increasing competition for internationally mobile investment.

Countries' approach to zone development varies along several dimensions such as the predominance of a few large zones, multiple free points or combined schemes, the number and physical dimensions of zones, the design of zones as stand-alone industrial sites or integrated townships, the level of zone specialisation and the degree of international cooperation (UNCTAD, 2019; Aggarwal, 2019; Frick et al., 2018; Zeng, 2016; Farole, 2011 and others). Many new types of zones are being developed that focus on industries such as high-tech, financial services, tourism and environmental performance.

G. Mugano, *Special Economic Zones*,
https://doi.org/10.1007/978-3-030-82311-5_11

However, despite the heterogeneity in countries' approach to zones, the basic value proposition of SEZs, especially the regulatory advantages and fiscal incentives offered by zones have remained similar across zone programmes (UNCTAD, 2019; Aggarwal, 2019; Frick et al., 2018) . In particular, zones overall offer regulatory facilitation and streamlined administrative procedures and customs duties as well as tax relief (UNCTAD, 2019; Tao et al., 2016).

Similarly, as outlined in previous chapters, the majority of developing and transition economies have offered similar policy and institutional framework for their respective SEZs (UNCTAD, 2019; FIAS, 2008). Interestingly, most countries adopted a dedicated law that sets out the framework enabling the development of SEZs and the investment conditions within zones (UNCTAD, 2019). Again, quite consistent in most countries is the fact that actual zone operating conditions are determined by lower levels of government and zone-level decrees, management companies and developers, which are largely private operators (Zeng, 2016). National policy frameworks beyond direct legislation on SEZs which include trade and investment policies significantly influence the attractiveness of zones (Aggarwal, 2012a, b, 2019; UNCTAD, 2019; Tao et al., 2016).

Although there is little evidence regarding the impact of SEZs on investment, export and employment generation in the zones, anecdotal evidence suggests that a limited number of large and high-performing zones, mostly in Asia, account for a sizeable share of SEZs' economic activity worldwide (UNCTAD, 2019; Aggarwal, 2019). There are also numerous countries which have zones that languished for long periods after their initial creation. In Asia, however, countries such as South Korea, Taiwan and China have had their SEZs positively contributing towards economic growth (Aggarwal, 2012a, b, 2019; UNCTAD, 2019; Tao et al., 2016; Cheesman, 2012; Chen & de'Medici, 2009 and other scholars).

Previous chapters identified critical success factors for SEZs such as government commitment, gradual specialisation and evolution along the SEZ development ladder, use of SEZ clusters and provision of sound infrastructure, business and investment facilitation and good location as key to the success of SEZs (UNCTAD, 2019; Tao et al., 2016).

Although past experiences on the performance of SEZs and their remarkable impact on China, South Korea and Taiwan economies provide important lessons for African economies, the context has totally changed to the extent that African policymakers cannot cut and paste some of these strategies. Modern-day SEZs have to respond to new challenges which include the need to mainstream the fourth industrial revolution (4IR) and sustainable development goals (SDGs) (UNCTAD, 2019). It is against this background that African economies, as they draw lessons from successful economies, have a need to move towards a new generation of SEZs. This requires absorbing lessons learned on the design, operations and impact management of zones as economies respond to modern challenges.

11.2 Lessons Learned from Special Economic Zones Experience

Building on evidence provided in the previous chapters, lessons learned from SEZs experience can be synthesised in a number of lessons learned about the design of SEZ programmes, the operation of SEZs and the optimisation of the development impact of SEZs (UNCTAD, 2019; Aggarwal, 2019) (see Table 11.1).

Special Economic Zone Programme Design

Dynamic integration of SEZs in the country's long-term development strategy is critical in the design of SEZ programmes (UNCTAD, 2019; Aggarwal, 2019). Contrary to the current policy framework on SEZs in most African economies, SEZs cannot be guided by a static policy tool but rather a dynamic one (UNCTAD, 2019). This is particularly true considering the findings from this study which show that different stages of development require different forms of SEZs (Aggarwal, 2019). Thus, as countries develop, it is important to constantly evaluate the extent to which SEZs are fit for purpose and to adapt zone programmes to evolving development objectives and contexts. This means that, from the onset, SEZs must have built-in flexibility which will allow governments to adjust the SEZ policy in line with the changing environment and developmental goals while taking into account international trade and investment commitments (Aggarwal, 2019; UNCTAD, 2019; Tao et al., 2016).

UNCTAD (2019) has argued that, using sustained sources of competitiveness, SEZ programmes should aim to complement existing competitive advantages and build dynamic capabilities. International experience

Table 11.1 Lessons learned from Special Economic Zone experience

Areas	Lessons Learned
Programme Design	• Integrate SEZs dynamically in development strategy • Complement existing competitive advantages • Take into account the national investment climate and governance capabilities • Design zones to be self-financing
Operations	• Get the basics right: business facilitation, infrastructure, labour pool • Promote clusters and linkages • Ensure strong institutions and good governance • Coordinated investment promotion
Development Impact	• Set clear goals and performance metrics for economic and ESG contributions • Conducteffectivemonitoringandevaluation,withconsequencemanagement • Maximize synergies between institutions and levels of government

Source: UNCTAD (2019)

has also shown that designing and building zones that require skills, industrial and technological infrastructure which are not readily available in the economy are likely to lead to zone failures which can be extremely expensive in terms of time and capital (UNCTAD, 2019; Aggarwal, 2019; Baldwin, 2013). In order to harness the success of the SEZs and their competitiveness, countries must endeavour to modify but not nullify traditional locational determinants of investment which enter natural resources, strategic geographies and/or the workforce (UNCTAD, 2019). By building dynamic capabilities through industrial upgrading in resource value chains, improving connectivity of strategic geographies and developing skills of the workforce, countries can establish long-term sustainability of these sources of competitiveness (Baldwin, 2013).

As noted in the previous chapters, countries such as China, South Korea and Taiwan, which successfully used SEZs to foster economic transformation, established SEZ policies which were closely entwined with the national economy, investment climate and governance capacities of relevant national and local authorities (Aggarwal, 2012a, b, 2019; UNCTAD, 2019; Tao et al., 2016, among others).

As submitted by UNCTAD (2019: 197), the following lessons are drawn for African economies:

> *SEZs are not an end in themselves; they need to provide an impulse to the industrial development of the economy and yield benefits beyond their confined geographical area. Conversely, the successful development of SEZs depends on the parallel development of the surrounding economy. Just as SEZs should not be developed as isolated economic enclaves, SEZ policies should not be developed in*

isolation from the economy's broader policy framework. In other words, SEZ policies should be coherent with trade and investment policies, and with business and fiscal regulatory frameworks beyond the zones. Finally, effective zone governance by, and coordination between national and local authorities, developers and operating entities is key to gaining – and maintaining – investors' trust in the zone and is a precondition for zone success.

Finally, when designing zones, SEZ programmes should be designed to ensure cost recovery. Thus, aligning objectives with development of long-term dynamic capabilities, industrial upgrading, skills and technology dissemination, without taking into account financial viability of the zones, may undermine long-term sustainability of SEZs (UNCTAD, 2019). This is particularly so because long-term economic development contributions of the zones are uncertain and difficult to predict. In situations where immediate economic contributions of SEZs which include fiscal contributions, rents and services fees are insufficient to cover zone costs, their fiscal impact will be increasingly difficult to justify to the ecosystem of stakeholders around them (Aggarwal, 2019). And, in programmes that allow existing domestic firms to convert to zone status, thereby eroding the tax base without significant investment in new productive capacity, the risk of negative fiscal impacts is higher (UNCTAD, 2019).

Special Economic Zone Operations

Attractive business environments which include an adequately skilled labour force, good infrastructure and efficient services are the major drivers of the performance of SEZs (Aggarwal, 2012a, b, 2019; UNCTAD, 2019; Tao et al., 2016 and others). Contrary to excessive provision of fiscal incentives and subsidies with a view to attract investors to African economies, evidence has shown that SEZs can be developed successfully without excessive reliance on incentives (Aggarwal, 2012a, b, 2019; UNCTAD, 2019, among other scholars).

In contrast, complex procedures, weak governance and insufficient infrastructure and services have been singled out as primary reasons for the failure of many programmes (UNCTAD, 2019; Farole, 2011). Effective zone development has often relied on pragmatically resolving mundane problems ranging from slow connection of businesses to utilities to a lack of public transport links for workers living outside the zone. Most importantly, zone contexts, objectives and investor profiles must inform priority services offered to the zones as opposed to a cut-and-paste approach from successful zones. For example, SEZs with extensive warehousing and logistics operations require effective security services and as such provision of such services can be a key competitive advantage (UNCTAD, 2019).

In order to further enhance the attractiveness of SEZs for investors, through promotion of clusters and linkages with the local economy, as evidenced in China and South Korea, synergies and economies of scale have been used effectively to lure investors into the zones (Aggarwal, 2019). In this regard, vertically specialised zones provide greater scope for synergies while multi-activity zones are effective in promoting cost-sharing arrangements for facilities such as warehousing, transportation and shared services (Zeng, 2016). Smart co-location strategies, within large multi-activity zones, can bring industries with greater scope for collaboration physically closer to each other (Zeng, 2016). Evidence has also shown that matchmaking programmes and training initiatives for local SMEs outside the zone may stimulate linkages that are important not only for SEZs' broader economic impact but also for their long-term prospects (UNCTAD, 2019).

As part of the operations modalities for successful SEZs, international experience has shown that well-designed legal and regulatory frameworks, institutions and good governance are vital (Aggarwal, 2012a, b, 2019; UNCTAD, 2019; Tao et al., 2016; Cheesman, 2012). In order to foster effective implementation of SEZ policy, the enabling legal infrastructure of the SEZ, especially the national SEZ laws, should be sufficiently stable to ensure consistency, transparency and predictability (UNCTAD, 2019). In addition, SEZ operating procedures should be practical and responsive to the needs of investors. Similarly, the legal infrastructure should set out institutional arrangements, SEZ investment rules, fiscal incentives and tax administration, licensing and regulation of business activities, customs control and trade facilitation, and dispute settlement mechanisms (Bertaud, 2016; Zeng, 2016). Most importantly, competencies of the SEZ authority responsible for the enforcement of the legal framework are crucial for the success of the SEZ programme (Aggarwal, 2019). Finally, rule of law and good governance which include effective anti-corruption procedures are also very crucial.

In order to foster an effective approach to potential investors, coordinated promotion efforts between SEZ authorities, developers and IPAs are equally important (UNCTAD, 2019). Although the institutional set-up and the role of IPAs vary between countries, in a number of cases, IPAs do not distinguish their activities for SEZs from their other investment promotion efforts. As suggested by UNCTAD (2019), in order to integrate SEZs more seamlessly into national investment promotion strategies, a joint effort could lead to targeted initiatives for SEZs since it has the advantage of promoting more effective linkages with investment facilitation efforts in the rest of the economy. In addition, clearly defined roles must be assigned by separating responsibilities for approval processes, promotion efforts, granting of incentives and monitoring of adherence to zone policies (UNCTAD, 2019).

Optimising Development Impact

In order to maximise the positive development impact of SEZs, policymakers must establish clear goals for SEZ performance with economic contributions, labour rights, social and environmental standards (Aggarwal, 2019; Farole, 2011). Although most SEZ programmes are established with broad objectives for investment, export and employment contributions, granular targets for aspects such as capital expenditures, skill levels, training and local content are required to maximise long-term contributions to productive capacity and industrial development, as well as technology and skills (UNCTAD, 2019; Tao et al., 2016; Cheesman, 2012; Chen & de'Medici, 2009). Moreover, to design incentives schemes and active clustering support, investment promotion, facilitation, matchmaking and linkages programmes such as targets are also needed (UNCTAD, 2019; Tao et al., 2016; Cheesman, 2012).

Similarly, to enhance effective development and implementation of monitoring and evaluation mechanisms, clear goals are needed. These goals should be centred on the SEZ sustainable development impact assessment (or "profit and loss statement") presented in previous chapters. Beyond setting goals, policymakers must pay attention to the monitoring process, scope and modalities for corrective action when required (UNCTAD, 2019).

Finally, coherence of different policy areas, as outlined earlier, and synergy creation between different parts of government at national and subnational levels are key to achieving success (Aggarwal, 2019). Effective coordination, as part of good governance, is also required in circumstances where multiple ministries and agencies are involved in the regulation of SEZs (Aggarwal, 2019; ADB, 2018; Farole, 2011).

Systemic and Strategic Considerations

In a classic demonstration of the need for pragmatism in dealing with SEZs, over and above the practical lessons learned about SEZ design, operation and impact optimisation, current trends in the development of SEZs point to a number of systemic and strategic considerations or notes of caution which African policymakers must take into account.

First, technocrats have concerns about a "race to the bottom"—with low taxation and relaxation of regulations and standards applicable to (predominantly international) investors as countries seek to capitalise on the proliferation of SEZs around the world which are largely driven by competitive pressures in a tightened market for internationally mobile investment in an industrial capacity (UNCTAD, 2019). Developmental economists and various development partners have also built global consensus on the need to use sustainable development as a mechanism to address this kind of market failure (Aggarwal, 2019; UNCTAD, 2019). This is particularly important for African countries with traditional disadvantages such as desperation for investment for industrialisation, thereby easily falling prey to implementing SEZ programmes that traditionally include the full spectrum of investment promotion levers which do not take into account the developmental aspect (Zeng, 2018).

In addition, international experience has shown that, in some developing countries such as Ethiopia, zones that attract a very large proportion of manufacturing investment can turn into enclaves of internationally mobile economic activity (Zeng, 2018). In large integrated zones that include townships or residential areas, this situation has raised concerns for the level playing field relative to domestic firms and the local labour force. In situations like these, policymakers need to carefully deal with these risks since they present policy trade-off as the zones may increase incomes of part of the population while negatively affecting certain groups of the population such as those depending on the informal sector (Farole, 2011). In dealing with this situation, policymakers from poor countries, in particular, must weigh the outcomes against the need to mobilise investment and use SEZs as a stepping stone towards broader development, with zones potentially acting as gateways to GVCs and creating spillovers, crowding-in and demonstration effects (UNCTAD, 2020).

For African countries, in view of the fact that most SEZs have failed, as argued by UNCTAD (2019), there is a need for African policymakers to question more generally the need to combine all investment promotion levers in SEZs. Individual levers are often sufficient under certain circumstances and for certain types of investment. Rather than using confirmed areas to spur investments, a number of common development or investment constraints can be addressed by alternative policy options applied throughout the economy (UNCTAD, 2019). Common industrial parks (without special regimes) can also be an appropriate policy option if the key constraint to industrial development is limited access to land or inadequate infrastructure (UNCTAD, 2019).

Likewise, if attracting investment in specific economic activities is a key objective, targeted incentives that leave investors to decide on the most advantageous location in the country may be as effective as zones (UNCTAD, 2019). Through alternative regulatory options, such as bonded warehouse programmes or duty drawback schemes, facilitation of customs procedures for trade-dependent activities can be offered. In successful countries such as China and South Korea, individual constraints on development or investment attraction have rarely justified the creation of SEZ programmes (UNCTAD, 2019; Tao et al., 2016; Cheesman, 2012; Chen & de'Medici, 2009). As in the case of low-income countries, SEZs can be the preferred option when multiple constraints apply and when alternatives are not feasible or too difficult to implement (UNCTAD, 2019).

11.3 A Forward-Looking Perspective

The challenges which come with the sustainable development imperative, the new industrial revolution, the digital economy and changing patterns of international production and GVCs has called for the need for strategic reorientation, reform and repackaging of SEZ programmes. An overview of possible policy responses to these challenges which are lessons for Africa is presented in Table 11.2.

MNEs' strategic decisions and operations are driven by the sustainable development agenda, which should be reflected in the value proposition that SEZs and IPAs market to investors (UNCTAD, 2019). Shared services related to sustainability, such as common waste management installations, health and safety services, and renewable energy sources will become increasingly important and can be considered in SEZs policy. SEZs that market their environmental performance (ecozones), as noted by UNCTAD (2016), are already emerging and the enforcement and active promotion of high environmental, social and governance (ESG) standards will increasingly become a feature of SEZs (see Box 11.1).

Table 11.2 Policy responses to emerging challenges

Policies/ standards	*Sustainable development imperative*	*New industrial revolution and the digital economy*	*Changing patterns of international production*
Strategic orientation	• Integrate sustainable development indicators in SEZ programme design • Explore new SEZ models focused on incubating business activities that promote sustainable development	• Modernise SEZ service provision by integrating digital technologies • Promote investment in business activities of digital firms • Partner with global platform providers to enhance SEZ competitiveness	• Focus specialised SEZs on services and manufacturing activities in line with global industrial restructuring • Link SEZ development to regional integration, including through new international cooperation models
Regulatory reform	• Establish, monitor and enforce ESG performance indicators for SEZ investors • Promote global standards in SEZs	• Consider the interaction between the policy framework for SEZs and the national regulatory regime for the digital economy	• Adapt facilitation and regulations to new forms of investment (non-equity modes of international production) • Anticipate shifts in international rules and trade preferences, and regional integration efforts
Repackaging of the value proposition	• Provide supporting services and training programmes in ESG factors • Reorient incentive schemes towards sustainable development contributions	• Provide adequate digital infrastructure within zones • Facilitate digital start-ups through focused clustering and linkages programmes • Adjust HRD programmes to include digital skills	• Incentivise upgrading and diversify exports • Strengthen entrepreneurshippolicies and mobile dynamic local entrepreneurs to catalyse FDI in SEZs • Provide on demand or shared manufacturing, design or testing spaces or services

Source: UNCTAD (2019)

Box 11.1 Using Special Economic Zones to Promote the Green Growth

SEZs play a pivotal role in Ethiopia's industrial development strategy and its Climate-Resilient Green Economy strategy, which entails the mitigation of both excessive emissions and unsustainable use of natural resources. The country has announced plans to build 30 industrial parks by 2025 to boost manufacturing output from 5% to 20% of GDP. Five public industrial parks are already in operation, and six more are under construction. Government outlays so far amount to approximately $1.3 billion. Private investors are also being encouraged to develop parks, either independently or through PPPs. Currently, three private parks are operational, benefiting from similar incentives as the publicly owned sites. The flagship Hawassa Eco-Industrial park is being developed as a model of the Climate-Resilient Green Growth strategy. The park is focused on the textile and apparel industry and houses a number of global manufacturers, including American luxury conglomerate PVH Corporation, which owns brands such as Tommy Hilfiger and Calvin Klein. The government has installed a state-of-the-art zero-liquid-discharge common-effluent treatment plant, which enables the cleaning and recycling of 90% of the water in the park and minimises its impact on surrounding soil salinity, groundwater and river bodies. In addition, the zone is served entirely by renewable hydropower and has energy-efficient appliances such as LED lights installed in premises. In 2018, only the second complete year of its operation, the Hawassa Industrial Park reported exports of a little under $50 million (of the total exports from industrial parks of $100 million), a number which is set to grow in the coming years. This is significant considering that total exports from Ethiopia are less than $ 1.3 billion, and the contribution of the country's consumer goods to total exports has historically been low (12.5% in 2016).

Ethiopia's experience illustrates the potential value of environmentally sustainable zones to international investors. During the design of Hawassa Park, the government invited potential investors to provide input for design and construction so that the park met the latest international standards. Many of its innovative elements, particularly those related to environmental and safety standards, were inputs provided by PVH, the largest manufacturing foreign investor in Ethiopia to date (World Bank, 2017).

Source: UNCTAD (2019)

Although fiscal incentives were traditionally used to attract investments with a view to create jobs and increase export, new evidence shows that they can be used to promote a range of social and environmental indicators and have the potential to become a key tool for driving SEZs' ESG performance and sustainable development impact (Aggarwal, 2019; UNCTAD, 2020). In this regard, policymakers may consider new SEZ models which evolve around promotion of investment focusing on sustainable development contributions. For example, countries may specialise in zones that focus on innovative products that offer low-cost solutions to social and environmental problems in low-income countries or manufacturing activities in renewable energy (Zeng, 2018).

Regarding the 4IR, countries have seen the adoption of advanced robotics, digital technologies, 3-D printing, big data and the internet of things changing the landscape of manufacturing industries (UNCTAD, 2019). Going forward, undoubtedly, the 4IR comes with a declining importance of labour costs as a locational determinant for investments, which will have fundamental implications for SEZs.

In order to remain relevant, potentially through partnerships with platform providers, SEZ development programmes will need to adapt their value propositions to include access to high levels of data connectivity, skilled resources and relevant technology service providers commensurate with the demands of the 4IR (UNCTAD, 2020). For example, digital service provision by SEZ operators through mechanisms such as online single windows for administrative procedures will become an increasingly important signal to potential investors (UNCTAD, 2020). At the strategic level, developing countries may need to scout for new opportunities by targeting digital firms and orienting their strategic strengths in logistics facilitation towards the distribution activities of e-commerce firms (UNCTAD, 2019). Alternatively, SEZs could follow the incubator model and promote clustering and linkages with local digital start-ups within and outside their confines, thereby transforming SEZs into Digital Innovation Hubs. From a regulatory and institutional framework, in order to pursue such opportunities and see new SEZ models succeed, national digital policies such as those on privacy legislation, data storage and security will also become an area to integrate with the SEZ regulatory and institutional framework (UNCTAD, 2019).

Regarding changing patterns of international production and GVCs, taking the traditional production methods may become obsolete as overseas operations shift towards intangible and asset-light forms

(UNCTAD, 2020). This trend is likely to result in increasing numbers of zones specialising in smaller-scale manufacturing (e.g. digital twins) on the one hand, and in services on the other (UNCTAD, 2020). Since both developments can potentially lead to higher technology and intellectual property content in SEZ production, in order to foster contributions to industrial upgrading and skills development, the SEZ policy and respective incentives need to be recalibrated (UNCTAD, 2019).

Changing patterns in international production which are characterised by constant shifts of MNEs to GVCs as a response to changes in preferential market access or new trade barriers may undermine the competitiveness of SEZs (UNCTAD, 2019). Furthermore, due to the push for the development of regional zones, cross-border zones and other forms of international cooperation zones are being fostered by the trends towards more regional rather than multilateral economic cooperation. This then will make local SEZs and their respective infrastructures irrelevant in African economies.

11.4 Sustainable Development Goals Model Zones

The SDG model zone is modelled around the 2030 SDGs. The SDG model zone, according to UNCTAD (2019), would be built around three key elements, that is (i) a strategic focus on attracting investment in activities which promote SDGs, (ii) the highest levels of ESG standards and compliance and (iii) the nexus between linkages and spillovers and inclusive growth (see Table 11.3).

By setting benchmarks and acting as catalysts for improvements across all zones through innovation and experimentation with new approaches, SDG model zones could adopt the highest international standards in establishing new models of SEZs. For example, as argued by UNCTAD (2019), SDG model zones could be designed for zero emissions and minimum waste. In addition, and beyond the traditional targets of SEZs, the SDG model zones endeavour to achieve (and publish results on) a gender-equality benchmark or the measurement of zone contributions to public revenues. Furthermore, other considerations can be adopted by policy-makers into the SDG model zones in line with the suggestions of UNCTAD (2019) as the following:

Table 11.3 Policy options for SDG Special Economic Zone model

Policy options	*Policy objectives*	*Focus*	*Promotion/facilitation*
Strategic reorientation	• Catalyse SDG implementation • Incubate pro-SDG business activities	• Sustainable agriculture, food security and nutrition • Basic infrastructure, utilities, water and sanitation services • Health care and essential medicines • Renewable energy and climate change mitigation • Education	• Target SDG sectors and incubate SDG activities • Reorient incentive schemes towards SDG contributions • Prepare a pipeline of SDG projects • Facilitate impact investment and social entrepreneurs • Cooperate with development partners
Regulatory reform	• Establish, monitor and enforce ESG performance indicators for SEZ investors • Promote global standards in SEZs	• Consider the interaction between the policy framework for SEZs and the national regulatory regime for the digital economy	• Adapt facilitation and regulations to new forms of investment (non-equity modes of international production) • Anticipate shifts in international rules and trade preferences, and regional integration efforts
Repackaging of the value proposition	• Provide supporting services and training programmes in ESG factors • Reorient incentive schemes towards sustainable development contributions	• Provide adequate digital infrastructure within zones • Facilitate digital start-ups through focused clustering and linkages programmes • Adjust HRD programmes to include digital skills	• Incentivise upgrading and diversify exports • Strengthen entrepreneurshippolicies and mobilise dynamic local entrepreneurs to catalyse FDI in SEZs • Provide on demand or shared manufacturing, design or testing spaces or services

Source: UNCTAD (2019)

(a) In order to facilitate improvements, implement best practices and obtain third-party certifications, SDG model zones could provide services to control and support the ESG performance of firms operating in the zone. Such services could include training, financial support and inspection services on health and safety standards.
(b) Likewise, with respect to environmental performance, services ranging from consultancy to identification of recycling opportunities and implementation of solutions for the reduction of waste, emissions and energy use may also be provided in the SDG model zones.
(c) SDG model zones could also offer facilities with benefits for the broader community which include waste management plants with additional capacity or other utilities with benefits beyond the zone (e.g. water treatment) or renewable energy installations that not only serve the zone but also feed the grid (or supply outside the zone). In addition, they could also offer amenities that would benefit the broader community such as healthcare and education facilities, residential areas and social housing, recreational areas and other services (e.g. fire services).
(d) SDG model zones would also explicitly operate under the highest standards of governance. In this regard, in generating new ideas for initiatives that would benefit the local community, within the broader economy or the environment, they are expected to involve a broad range of stakeholders. For example, by instituting anti-discrimination rules, providing childcare infrastructure and protection, promoting women entrepreneurship and providing training, they may facilitate women's employment in the zones (UNCTAD, 2014). Such zones could be developed by involving specific investor groups with a stake in sustainable development, ensuring continuous monitoring of, and reporting on, ESG performance (e.g. through gender equality audits). Companies operating in the zone could also voluntarily sign up to customised codes of conduct, making the SDG model zone a partnership between authorities, zone developers and zone investors. Alternatively, access to SEZ benefits could be subject to initial and continuing certification of ESG performance.

11.5 Conclusion

As a build up to the evidence presented in previous chapters on the dismal performance in most zones across the globe, this chapter has argued for a new generation of SEZs which takes into account new challenges associated with modern SEZs.

In particular, this chapter has argued that although past experiences on the performance of SEZs and their remarkable impact on China, South Korea and Taiwan economies have provided important lessons for African economies, the context has totally changed to the extent that African policymakers cannot just cut and paste strategies from these successful countries. Modern-day SEZs have to truthfully respond to new challenges which include the need to mainstream the 4IR, the sustainable development imperative and SDGs (UNCTAD, 2019). To this end, African economies, as they draw lessons from other successful economies, need to move towards a new generation of SEZs. This requires analysing, synthesising and adopting the lessons learned on the design, operations and impact management of zones as economies respond to emerging challenges.

References

ADB. (2018). *Strategic Framework for Special Economic Zones and Industrial Zones in Kazakhstan*. Asian Development Bank.

Aggarwal, A. (2012a). *Social and economic impact of SEZs in India*. OUP Catalogue. New Delhi: Oxford University Press.

Aggarwal, A. (2012b). SEZ-Led Growth in Taiwan, Korea, and India: Implementing a Successful Strategy. *Asian Survey, 52*(5), 872–899.

Aggarwal, A. (2019). SEZs and Economic Transformation: Towards a Developmental Approach. *Transnational Corporations, 26*(2), 27–48.

Baldwin, R. (2013). Global Supply Chains: Why They Emerged, Why They Matter, and Where They Are Going. In K. E. Deborah & L. Patrick (Eds.), *Global Value Chains in a Changing World*. Fung Global Institute, Nanyang Technological University, and World Trade Organization Secretariat.

Bertaud, A. (2016, December 14). *The New Chinese City Clusters: Would the Current Urban Transport Technology Be Able to Serve These Very Large Urban Labour Markets*? World Resources Institute. http://www.wri.org/sites/default/les/new-Chinese-city-clusters.pdf

Cheesman, A. (2012). *Special Economic Zones and Development: Geography and Linkages in the Indian EOU Scheme* (Working Paper No. 145). Development Planning Unit, The Bartlett, University College London.

Chen, X., & de'Medici, T. (2009). *The "Instant City" Coming of Age: China's Shenzhen Special Economic Zone in Thirty Years* (Working Paper No. 2). Centre for Urban and Global Studies at Trinity College.

Farole, T. (2011). *Special Economic Zones in Africa: Comparing Performance and Learning from Global Experiences.* World Bank Publications.

FIAS. (2008). *Special Economic Zones: Performance, Lessons Learned and Implications for Zone Development.* Report of Facility for Investment Climate Advisory Services, the Multi- Donor Service Managed by the International Finance Corporation. Unpublished. World Bank Publications.

Frick, S. A., Rodríguez-Pose, A., & Wong, M. D. (2018). Towards Economically Dynamic Special Economic Zones in Emerging Countries. *Journal of Economic Geography, 95*(1), 30–64.

Tao, Y., Yuan, Y., & Li, M. (2016). Chinese Special Economic Zones: Lessons for Africa. *Africa Economic Brief, 7*(6), 1–11.

UNCTAD. (2014). *World Investment Report 2014.* United Nations.

UNCTAD. (2016). *World Investment Report 2016.* United Nations.

UNCTAD. (2018). *World Investment Report 2018.* United Nations.

UNCTAD. (2019). *World Investment Report 2019: Special Economic Zones.* United Nations.

UNCTAD. (2020). *Building and Utilising Productive Capacities in Africa and LDCs.* United Nations.

World Bank. (2017). *Special Economic Zones: An Operational Review of Their Impacts.* Washington, DC. World Bank.

Zeng, D. Z. (2016). Global Experiences of Special Economic Zones with Focus on China and Africa: Policy Insights. *Journal of International Commerce, Economics and Policy, 7*(3), 1650018.

Zeng, D. Z. (2018). *Special Economic Zones: Lessons from the Global Experience.* World Bank.

Index

G. Mugano, *Special Economic Zones*,
https://doi.org/10.1007/978-3-030-82311-5